C. Wright Mills and the Endir

Palgrave Macmillan books by the same author

ANTI-CATHOLICISM IN NORTHERN IRELAND 1600–1998 (*with Gareth Higgins*, 1998)

CAN SOUTH AFRICA SURVIVE? (*editor*, 1989)

POLICE, PUBLIC ORDER AND THE STATE (*with Adrian Guelke, Ian Hume, Edward Moxon-Browne and Rick Wilford*, 1988 and 1996)

RESTRUCTURING SOUTH AFRICA (*editor*, 1994)

Other books by the same author

A-Z OF SOCIAL RESEARCH (*co-editor with Robert Miller*)

AFTER SOWETO: An Unfinished Journey (1986)

BLACK AND BLUE: Policing in South Africa (1994)

CRIME IN IRELAND 1945–95 (*with Bill Lockhart and Paula Rodgers*, 1997)

ETHNOGRAPHY (2000)

INSIDE THE RUC (*with Kathleen Magee*, 1991)

MOSLEY'S MEN (1984)

THE ROYAL IRISH CONSTABULARY: An Oral History (1990)

C. Wright Mills and the Ending of Violence

John D. Brewer
Professor of Sociology
Queen's University Belfast

© John D. Brewer 2003

All rights reserved. No reproduction, copy or transmission of this publication may be made without written permission.

No paragraph of this publication may be reproduced, copied or transmitted save with written permission or in accordance with the provisions of the Copyright, Designs and Patents Act 1988, or under the terms of any licence permitting limited copying issued by the Copyright Licensing Agency, 90 Tottenham Court Road, London W1T 4LP.

Any person who does any unauthorised act in relation to this publication may be liable to criminal prosecution and civil claims for damages.

The author has asserted his right to be identified as the author of this work in accordance with the Copyright, Designs and Patents Act 1988.

Published by
PALGRAVE MACMILLAN
Houndmills, Basingstoke, Hampshire RG21 6XS and
175 Fifth Avenue, New York, N. Y. 10010
Companies and representatives throughout the world

PALGRAVE MACMILLAN is the global academic imprint of the Palgrave Macmillan division of St. Martin's Press, LLC and of Palgrave Macmillan Ltd. Macmillan® is a registered trademark in the United States, United Kingdom and other countries. Palgrave is a registered trademark in the European Union and other countries.

ISBN-13: 978–0–333–80180–2
ISBN-10: 0–333–80180–6

This book is printed on paper suitable for recycling and made from fully managed and sustained forest sources.

A catalogue record for this book is available from the British Library.

Library of Congress Catalog Card Number: 2003048276

Printed and bound in Great Britain by
Antony Rowe Ltd, Chippenham and Eastbourne

In memory of
my mother, Eileen Margaret 1929–2002
and my aunt, Mary Josephine 1911–2002

Contents

Preface and Acknowledgements ix

Introduction: Conflict, Violence and Peace 1

1 C. Wright Mills and the Sociological Imagination 17

2 The Historical Specificity of the Peace Process 45

3 Individual Biographical Experiences and Peace 71

4 The Intersection of Politics and the Social Structure 109

Conclusion: The Sociological Imagination
and the Peace Process 151

Bibliography 179

Index 191

Preface and Acknowledgements

This book argues that it is possible to develop a sociological framework to explain the emergence and progress of the peace process in Northern Ireland and South Africa, two ethnically structured societies that, when put in the long perspective of history, began at roughly the same time to dismantle centuries-old division and conflict. One of the best North American-based writers on Irish affairs, Padraig O'Malley (2001: 279), in commenting on these two societies, doubted that comparisons could be usefully drawn between their peace processes because, as he eloquently phrased it: 'each beats to the rhythms of its own contradictory impulses, distortions of reality, warped perceptions and insatiable demands for revenge that are the legacy one generation bequeaths the next.' I argue to the contrary and suggest that the discipline of sociology lacks something if it does not at least try; it evacuates its proper terrain when ceding public issues to analysis by other social sciences. In attempting a sociological analysis I use a framework drawn from Charles Wright Mills's account of the 'sociological imagination', which I believe can be used to hold the two processes together and explain the emergence, progress and oscillating fortunes of the peace process in both countries. Despite the manifold differences there are between the two societies and the obvious variation in the details and events in their peace processes, I argue that there is equivalence between the two processes in the way that they can be understood sociologically.

Mills's framework is normally condensed to describe an approach that combines individuals and society in a dynamic relationship capable of explaining all social life. This is very oversimplified and involves a misreading of his famous book *The Sociological Imagination*. In truth the sociological imagination is distinguished by the view that the discipline must demonstrate the intersection between individual biographical experience, history, social structural changes, and developments and events in the political process. Sociology can all too readily be divorced from politics, and the 'sociological imagination' needs to hold together real human experience, the social structure and events in the political process. It is a similar failing to separate sociology and history. Therefore, while focusing on the ending of violence in Northern Ireland and South Africa, this volume simultaneously addresses itself to clarifying Mills's depiction of sociology.

The book is not intended as an exhaustive history of the negotiations that led to the settlements in both countries, or of each country's political conflicts and history. Nor is the book a review of the various political models that shaped their respective constitutional reforms or an analysis of political events in the post-settlement period. The literature on all these topics is voluminous and while some of this is well worth repeating, this is not the place. Only a few of the references to this vast literature by political scientists and historians will be cited. What the book offers instead is an interpretative history – what the Scottish Enlightenment in the eighteenth century used to call a conjectural history – of the peace process in both societies based on a particular kind of sociology. In using the term 'conjectural history' the intention is not to aggrandise my arguments by equating them with the wonderful treatises by Scots such as Adam Ferguson, John Millar or Adam Smith, which in majestic broad sweeps took in the history of society in its various stages. My purpose in deliberately using this term is twofold. It was precisely through writing conjectural histories that the Scots arrived at a kind of proto-sociology and thus it seems fitting to apply this term when attempting to write a sociology of the South African and Northern Irish peace processes. Above all, the kind of sociology that was envisaged by Charles Wright Mills was, in my view, exemplified two centuries before in the work of the Scots, particularly Adam Ferguson and John Millar. This was a kind of sociology that took in topics including human nature (what we now call agency), the social structure and politics, all couched within a historical perspective. This study uses the peace process in South Africa and North Ireland to champion a particular way of doing sociology. If you like, the book makes a rescue attempt. It seeks to save analyses of the peace process from the dominance of political science perspectives by using Mills's conception of sociology's imagination. Thus, a particular kind of sociology is used to see if it illuminates our understanding of the peace process, while these events are used to throw light on the utility of Mills's approach to sociology.

The book is based on an idea I first developed in a conference paper in 1999 entitled 'A prolegomenon towards a sociology of the peace process in Northern Ireland and South Africa'. The paper was delivered at the conference on 'South Africa: Transition to Transformation', held in Dublin, 4–5 March 1999, and was organised by the South African Embassy in the Irish Republic. A word of thanks is owed to the then Ambassador, Pierre Dietrichsen, for bringing our group of scholars together. My colleagues on that occasion included Jack Spence, Adrian Guelke, Sandy Johnston, Jesmond Blumenfeld, Mark Shaw, Kanya Adam, Heather Deegan, Roger Boulter and Charles Villa-Vicencio. I am grateful for their comments on the original paper, especially those of Jack Spence. I am particularly in debt to Palgrave Macmillan, and especially Tim Farmiloe, who have patiently waited for this manuscript since 1999 while the demands of administration kept me from writing. My tenure as Head of the School of Sociology and Social Policy at Queen's University of Belfast came to an end in July 2002 after nine long years and I am grateful to the University for awarding me a sabbatical which at last allowed me the opportunity to complete the manuscript. I absolve the following colleagues, who kindly read some or all of the manuscript, from any responsibility for its remaining faults: John Eldridge, Anthony Marx and David McCrone. I am also grateful for years of long discussion with Steve Bruce about this project and Northern Ireland generally. Above all, I am grateful to the Master and Fellows of Corpus Christi College, Cambridge for awarding me a Visiting Fellowship in Michaelmas 2002–2003, from where I have written most of the manuscript.

Finally, I offer a word of love and thanks to my children, Bronwen and Gwyn, who in the course of various acknowledgements have grown from beautiful toddlers to wonderful adults. This book is for them, and their Nan and Great Aunt Mary, with much love and fond memory.

Cambridge, December 2002

Introduction: Conflict, Violence and Peace

This book is deliberately written as a prolegomenon. This is a word that has intrigued me since I first came across it as an undergraduate. Peter Blau used it in reference to his thoughts towards a sociological theory of bureaucracy. This is the second occasion I have used it in reference to my own work. The first was as a postgraduate, writing a sociological account of fascist membership. There is something of the same hesitancy bred by anxiety in this second usage. It is a very functional word, for it is a caveat, useful for suggesting that the ideas described by it need qualification and are best seen as tentative and preliminary, a kind of work-in-progress statement which is none the less perhaps the author's best effort. That this book is a prolegomenon is only in part because of my own deficiencies, for it also reflects the subject matter. The book is a sketch towards understanding, sociologically, peace processes that have yet to come to full fruition, meaning that we are in the middle of profound change not at the end. As W.G. Runciman (1999: 155) wrote in his introduction to sociology, sociologists (and others) best understand the course of historical events only with hindsight. Mature reflection after the fact is not yet possible in this case, leaving imperfect attempts to understand events as they unfold. Nor is there any certainty that the end product of the process will be 'peace' as people ideally and perfectly perceive it, although there are none the less still profound changes in each society that need to be explained sociologically. Not least of these is the near-complete ending of indiscriminate terrorism. If the communal violence is not entirely over, as du Toit (2001) and Sisk (1994) emphasise with respect to South Africa and as the streets of

Belfast witness four years after the negotiated settlement known as the Good Friday Agreement was supposed to bring an end to conflict, communal violence is no longer what it was.

It is worth emphasising this point so that what is meant by the ending of violence as a sociological issue is fully understood and to avoid being accused of belittling subsequent acts of violence that have caused people suffering. Hayes and McAllister (2001a: 901) make the point that there is a naïve assumption that where violence is a consequence of problematic politics, once a permanent settlement is reached violence is thought irrevocably and swiftly to disappear. However, rarely is there a complete cessation of all forms of violence and the ending of violence in most post-violence societies is only relative. As MacGinty and Wilford write (2002: 5), peace processes are universally fragile affairs, rarely prospering over the long term without active public support. Peace agreements are never final and often go through several iterations: the Guatemalan peace accord was rewritten nine times, the Middle Eastern agreement has failed so far no matter the number of times it has been finessed. (The INCORE website has details of most of the world's peace agreements and their iterations, see INCORE, 2000.) Wallensteen and Sollenberg (2000) estimate that of 110 armed conflicts between 1989 and 1990, only 21 were ended by peace agreements and only a minority of those agreements survived. The negotiated peace settlements in Northern Ireland and South Africa may have stopped large-scale, indiscriminate use of violent force and terror, but other forms of violence continue on a much reduced scale, such as so-called structural violence in the form of unemployment and economic inequality (notably Latin America), criminal violence (notably South Africa) and street violence by groups of youths (Northern Ireland). However, the violence that remains is much lower in intensity, is different in form from terrorism, and played by rules that try to ensure it is controlled enough to avoid destabilising political gains and the overall peace process. Thus, while peace processes never eliminate all forms of violence, there is none the less a transformation in communal violence that needs to be explained sociologically, which the discipline so far has failed to do.

Sociology has not been productive to this point in understanding the peace processes. No sociological theory was successful in predicting the changes in Northern Ireland and South Africa, although to be fair to sociology, as Runciman (1999: 12–13 *passim*) reminds us, the

Introduction: Conflict, Violence and Peace 3

discipline is not a predictive science, a principle established firmly by Karl Popper. However, neither has the discipline tried to explain the events. This partly reflects the inadequacies of specific sociological theories but also what Dixon (1973: 118) calls the pretentiousness of sociology's theoretical ambitions. Sociology is often quite bad at developing theory. Sociology's theories only parody scientific theorising and often distort history and events. Although this runs against much sociological theorising, we should, according to Dixon (1973: 120), trim the sails of our theoretical pretensions to the winds of contingent possibility. We should opt for clarity, plausibility and historical and empirical accuracy in sociological explanations rather than aggrandise our efforts with the prefix 'theory'.

It would be foolish thus to claim too much for a sociology of the peace process in Northern Ireland and South Africa, making what follows truly a prolegomenon; it is certainly not ennobled by being called a 'theory'. Instead the book attempts to sketch a sociological framework by which we can conceptualise together the peace processes in both countries, as well as explain why the changes in each society represented by the so-called peace process have occurred at this particular historical juncture and are so problematic to significant sections of the community. The social phenomenon to be explained, therefore, is why the peace process has emerged now after many failed attempts in the past, as well as the progress of the process and its subsequent travails. Its sub-text is why the Northern Irish peace process is not as successful as South Africa's. The framework is not mine but draws on Charles Wright Mills's formulation of what he calls the 'sociological imagination' (2000 [1959]). This is a view of the sociological enterprise that is worth revisiting because its fruits were left under-developed as a result of Mills's death within three years of his initial explication, and it captures all that is necessary in order to explain sociologically the peace process in the two societies.

It is necessary at this early stage to clarify what it meant by this framework. Runciman has given a wonderful description of the critics' caricature of Mills. He 'was the sort of sociologist whose critics are apt to dismiss him as an up-market journalist who doesn't have a theory at all beyond a generalized hostility to the established institutions of his own society' (1999: 59). Runciman seems to suggest Mills's contribution is chiefly debunking naked emperors: Mills's 'attack on Parsons ... should be copied out every morning by any sociologist who thinks that a platitude is less of a platitude if it's dressed up in more and longer words' (1999: 59). But while not developing a theory as such, his perspective on the *nature* of sociology has become one of the motifs of the discipline and it is this perspective that is operationalised here.

The phrase 'sociological imagination' is bandied about almost constantly, and Mills is remembered above all as its progenitor. In many cases the term is simply a bumper sticker of approval to describe the particular way sociologists represent the relationship between individuals and the wider society. There are competing terms – Berger's 'sociological consciousness' and Bauman's 'sociological sixth-sense' and 'sociological way of thinking' – but it is Mills's term that has entered the popular lexicon. There are good reasons for this. It has come to represent in summary form the defining idea that marks sociology as distinct, namely the exploration of the intersection between individuals and society. As such it was recognised as an early account of the agency–structure debate and has maintained its popularity as this debate takes over much of sociological theorising since. This exemplifies the often slipshod use of the term, for as we shall see in Chapter 1, Mills meant something significantly more by the term. To the more discerning, the phrase is popular for other reasons. It is seen as the defining characteristic of Mills's whole approach to sociology and the phrase is commonly employed as the emblem of this style. Two characteristics define Mills's approach to sociology, one conceptual, the other discursive. Conceptually, sociology is a radical debunking of the hidden structures of power that threaten human freedom and social justice, while discursively, it should use language that simultaneously demystifies the social world and empowers ordinary people to act within it. The 'sociological imagination' has thus come to represent a view of the discipline that sees sociology as about engagement with public issues in order to bring about social arrangements that help people realise social virtues, coupled with the avoidance of a conceptual vocabulary that simply obscures and obsfucates. One would not get Mills employing the kind of prose Bauman once used to describe the modern condition to a popular audience, a state, he said, of 'liquid modernity', which is 'the continuation of disembedding coupled with the dis-continuation of re-embedding' (see Bauman, 2002: 2). This is the professional type Runciman ridicules as platitude merchants (1999: 57 *passim*), who impose impenetrable language on simple ideas. Rather, the sociological imagination is about making the complex simple and is championed by those sociologists who want to dialogue with ordinary people not confuse them.

In employing the sociological imagination to render simple the complex process by which communal violence ended in Northern Ireland and South Africa, this volume rides two horses at once or, put another way, is Janus-faced. At one level it is about the ending of large-scale communal violence in two ethnically structured societies that are often held in comparison. Readers who are interested in Northern Ireland or South Africa or in peace processes *per se* may wish to have no truck with sociology, even less with Charles Wright Mills. He died, afterall, in 1962 – another member of the Dead Sociologists Society, and, perhaps, less well known than most members of that illustrious group. Indeed, the book might be considered past its time now, since the story of Northern Ireland's and South Africa's emergence out of violence has been told before. There are at least two books comparing the ending of violence in these two societies (Knox and Quirk, 2000; Weiss, 2000) and many articles that draw parallels between their peace settlements (for a selection see Guelke, 1991, 1994, 1996a; Arthur, 1995; McGarry, 1998; O'Malley, 2001). What stamps this book is that it uses the peace process in Northern Ireland and South Africa as a case study to exemplify a particular kind of sociology. At the other level, therefore, it illustrates a way of doing sociology, and the focus on Northern Ireland and South Africa is merely instrumental. Readers with a sociology background may want more on Mills himself and thus find the book's substantive focus on the ending of violence wearisome; perhaps even not the most relevant exemplar of Charles Wright Mills's work (for an attempt to show the contemporary relevance of Mills's sociological imagination to the topical issue of globalisation, see Langman, 2000). The book therefore risks its author falling off both saddles.

On the other hand, hopefully Millsian specialists will realise this is an opportunity to practise what he preached about sociology's engagement with public affairs. Sociology began as a discipline with the social and public concerns of its founders – this is true of the Scots, who wanted to understand the changes around them as Scotland became a commercial society, as well as the nineteenth-century giants of the discipline such as Max Weber, Herbert Spencer, Emile Durkheim and Karl Marx. It is only very recently that this present generation's leading figures, like Giddens and his arguments about the 'third way' or Bourdieu's engagement with the topical issues of modern French society, have urged that we return to playing a public role. The ending of violence in two societies otherwise notorious for conflict is a public issue that the discipline of sociology ought to try to explain. This case thus has the potential to show the fertility of Mills's understanding of the nature of sociology and its particular 'imagination' or way of thinking, while simultaneously offering comment on an important issue of public affairs. The account of Northern Ireland and South Africa's transition into post-violence societies is an issue of supreme public importance to people living in those places as well as to people in similar societies who are just beginning the process of negotiating an end to violence. While post-violence societies never eliminate all forms of violence immediately, the transformation of communal violence in these societies none the less offers a test case for the utility of Mills's account of the sociological imagination.

When Mills first outlined the sociological imagination in 1959, he was challenging three pretensions in sociology, general theorising, abstract empiricism and social administration, which divorced themselves from the important public issues in modern society, thereby evacuating the discipline from its proper terrain. He argued that sociology should be concerned with a subject matter that is historically specified, by which he meant located in time and space, referring to real events, people and processes. What is more, in its approach sociology needed to show the intersection and connection between four dimensions, the social structure, individual personal biography, history and the political process (and not just the first two). It will be argued in this study that it is possible to explain the peace process in Northern Ireland and South Africa in this historically specified period only by holding together these dimensions in one framework. The peace process in these two countries thus acts as a useful illustration of the sociological imagination at work in public affairs.

Northern Irish–South African links

Northern Ireland and South Africa are societies normally considered in comparison, a tendency reinforced today by their concurrent peace processes. The journal *Southern Africa–Irish Studies* celebrates the relationship between the two countries. The links go much further back than Ireland's championing of the anti-apartheid movement in 1964, although the Irish Republic did become perhaps the leading European anti-apartheid nation and a large funder of development aid. Irish missionaries have been an integral part of the relationship, and today they comprise the largest group of missionaries in South Africa. The links are conceptual as well as historical. The models that political scientists fondly develop of types of political system have seen the two societies compared, for example, as consociational systems (for example, McGarry and O'Leary, 1995; Lijphart, 1996; O'Leary and McGarry, 1996; O'Leary, 2001; cf. Taylor, 2001; also see Horowitz, 1991). Sociologists tend to have favoured the concept of 'divided society' to facilitate many comparisons between the two, along with other similar societies, notably Israel. Divided societies are those social formations that have a characteristic social structure (hence the attraction of this notion to sociology). What distinguishes this kind of social structure is that it is split by a single social cleavage, such as 'race', religion or nationality. These tend to be absolute criteria permitting no ambiguity and subsuming all other possible lines of differentiation in a zero-sum conflict. Conflict adheres around this cleavage and tends to pull the society apart as people's whole identity becomes defined by this boundary and groups work selfishly to their own best interest. Ironically, the whole point of the 'divided society' idea was to suggest that division was immutable – in some hands also justifiable – because of the absolutist nature of the social rifts. The divisions were seen as almost impregnable and it was only in 1990 that the search for peace in the two societies was described as elusive (see Giliomee, 1990). Northern Ireland and South Africa have also been coupled in terms of their conservative Protestant politics (Akenson, 1992; Bruce, 1998), policing models (Brewer, 1991a) and history of fraternal relations (Guelke, 2000). More recently, their respective peace processes have seen the two countries compared in terms of their human rights legislation (Bell, 2000) and the direction of their peace negotiations and political events, both by academics (Arthur, 1995; Guelke, 1996a; McGarry, 1998) and journalists (Weiss, 2000). Comparisons have also been drawn between their respective patterns of violence and terrorism (Johnston, 1997) and, most interestingly of all, in terms of Jean Paul Lederach's model of peace-building (Knox and Quirk, 2000; also see Lederach, 1995, 1997).

It is a comparison loaded with political effect. Partisans the world over make parallels with other conflicts in order to draw attention to their own. Sinn Féin and the ANC, for example, have drawn parallels between themselves as anti-colonialist movements, and many supporters have suggested that there is equivalence between the position of Northern Irish Catholics and Black South Africans. Outsiders have made the same link. The MacBride principles used by the government in the United States to regulate investment in Northern Ireland as a way of registering support for the position of Irish Catholics, were modelled on the Sullivan principles governing trade between the US and South Africa which were used to signal support for Black South Africans (McGarry, 2001: 12). Addressing this theme, however, O'Malley (2001: 282–3) argues there is no similarity in the level of disparity or suffering experienced by Catholics compared to Black South Africans, and to suggest so trivialises the scale of apartheid's injustices. Above all, he distinguishes the moral difference between the IRA's armed struggle and the ANC's in terms of the widespread support possessed by the latter, which made its conflict almost like a just war, whereas the IRA 'at best represented a minority (physical force hardliners) of a minority (republicans) of a minority (nationalists) in Northern Ireland and were even more unrepresentative of the South's political proclivities' (2001: 283). Political and demographic calculations might revise this as an opinion of Sinn Féin, but the point is well made that comparisons between conflicts are often more complex than partisans suggest (comparisons have also be made between Northern Irish Catholics and Black Americans, see Dooley, 1998). None the less, the linkages are clear. Some of Belfast's best murals celebrate what Republicans consider to be IRA–ANC solidarity (on the sociology of murals, see Rolston, 1995), a view endorsed by Nelson Mandela. Guelke (1996a: 145) shows that this link was beneficial in the IRA's decision to abandon the armed struggle, and its acts of decommissioning have been made palatable by the encouragement and assistance of ANC figures like 'Mac' Maharaj and Cyril Ramaphosa (McGarry, 2001: 13).

Afrikaner Nationalists and Northern Irish Unionists made the opposite connection as dominant political and ethnic groups who saw themselves subject to violent opposition and threat from minorities (see Follis, 1996). McGarry (2001: 11) makes the point that Unionists have been less adroit in the analogies they have drawn, with them ending up expressing sympathy for pariahs like the White regime in Rhodesia and Serbia. Israeli flags now adorn Loyalist areas because Palestinians are Israel's Catholics. The Afrikaner connection is longer established but equally unfortunate. Unionist Party governments in Stormont felt empathy with the National Party, rooted in their demographic fear of the tyranny of simple majority rule, and militant Loyalists were in dialogue with the apartheid regime in the 1980s over arms sales (Guelke, 1996a: 143–4). This fraternity was cemented by their shared cultural background as Calvinists and conservative evangelicalism, with the belief jointly held that God had scripted their land possession and political dominance, giving the same theological edge to *realpolitik* in the two countries.

These sorts of comparisons were regularly drawn in order to speak to local circumstances in one or other place. Often the political intent behind the comparison was malign. As we have seen, Republicans in the North compared the position of Catholics with the Black majority under apartheid, despite the clear differences in the level of disparity and inequality experienced, and the National Party incredulously held up Northern Ireland as an evil spectre that awaited South Africa unless Black political opposition was stamped out aggressively. The lesson intended by the comparison was once all about armed struggle; now it is about peace processes. Their respective peace processes have enabled more benign comparisons to be drawn, with South Africa being suggested as the model for Northern Ireland when its developments lagged behind South Africa's; the spirit and example of South Africa often infuses the sluggish momentum in the Northern Irish peace process. A striking feature of South Africa's settlement was its do-it-yourself character. No brokers and third parties were involved – there were no George Mitchells or Oslo meetings – and the South Africans are justifiably proud that they initiated and managed their own conflict resolution (Weiss, 2000: 13). Ironically, then, they try assiduously to broker other conflicts. The South Africans have hosted various *indaba* (Zulu for peace meetings or meeting of minds) between themselves and representatives of the conflict in Northern Ireland (O'Malley, 2001: 284–99, reviews one held in De Hoop in May 1997). Israeli and Palestinian peace activists visited Northern Ireland in 2002 for much the same purpose. The traffic of South African politicians, negotiators and peace-builders to Northern Ireland has been busy offering themselves as midwives of peace; and it transpired that it was always thus. Justice Richard Feetham, the Chair of the Irish Boundary Commission settling the cartography of partition of the island in 1924, had been a South African MP and later returned there to be Vice Chancellor of Witwatersrand University. Jan Smuts, himself having fought the British over national sovereignty during the Boer War, felt the relevance of the contrast when he warned once that South Africa's conflict could make it another Ireland, and he offered to act as intermediary between the British government and Irish Republicans during the War of Independence in 1921 (Guelke, 2000: 139–41). Then, as now, the parallels between the two societies made such linkages obvious. It is worth briefly discussing the reasons for this.

Conflict, violence and peace

For a very long time, the two societies had in common a rigid social structure with a single line of social cleavage based on ethnicity and national identity rather than social class, which in South Africa's case was socially marked by 'race' and in Northern Ireland by religion. While 'race' and 'religion' are different social markers – race is phenotypical not cultural, is more deterministic and less avoidable (Brewer, 1992: 355–8) – they are functional equivalents in structuring stratification along ethno-national lines. The coincidence of ethnicity with national identity in both places ensured that ethnic mobilisation was seen as a form of national struggle over sovereignty and survival. What further underpinned the national identities of the respective dominant ethnic group in Northern Ireland and South Africa was their sense that they were God's people, possessed of a territory as a national homeland bequeathed by divine will (see Wallis and Bruce, 1986; Akenson, 1992; Bruce, 1998). Land, sovereignty and Scripture were a powerful mix historically in the two societies, which continues to the present day. It is this fusion of ethnicity with communal and national identity that reduces the importance of any difference between 'race' and religion as the social boundary markers used in the two places, reinforcing the value of a comparison between the two countries (for an opposite view, see Dickie-Clarke, 1976).

In both societies the ethno-national cleavage had long historical roots in European colonial expansion. This cleavage was reinforced over the centuries by a system of constant causes and by social processes that led the patterns of differentiation to reproduce themselves. Patterns of differentiation thus remained static, ensuring that the social structure in each case became solidified across time around one cleavage, represented by racial segregation and apartheid in South Africa and Protestant ascendancy in Ireland (and later Ulster, more commonly known as Northern Ireland). The social structures had embedded in them patterns of differentiation that gave a historical legacy of sustained and prolonged conflict, often violent, which became one of the defining features of the two societies. The conflict was also increasingly zero-sum, and, especially in Northern Ireland, a binary sum at that, in which social groups solidified and polarised into two antagonistic 'sides', defining their interests and identity in opposition to each other. (For sociological accounts of Northern Irish history which stress this, see Ruane and Todd, 1996; Brewer, 1998; in South Africa's case, see Moleah, 1993.) Patterns of social exclusion and stratification in both societies took on similar forms because the lines of social cleavage reproduced an unequal share of socio-economic and political resources between the dominant and subordinate groups. Thus, Northern Ireland and South Africa became synonymous as societies in which economic wealth and social and cultural capital coincided with ethno-national identity, and in which, politically, the settlers and their descendants had democracy, as the West understood it, and the 'natives' and their descendants something less (although how much less differed in the two places).

As Lewis Coser (1964) argued, in flexible social structures with a diversity and plurality of social cleavages, conflicts are multiple and cross-cut each other, preventing conflict emerging solely around one axis of differentiation. The multiple group affiliations of people make them participate in various group conflicts, so that their whole identity is not enshrined in any one. For example, people may be 'Black' or 'Catholic' but also 'female', 'environmental campaigners', 'working-class', or whatever, supplying different cross-cutting issues in which they engage, ensuring that their identity is not wholly wrapped up in one overarching conflict which subsumes everything they consider themselves to be as a person. Coser thus formulated the proposition that segmental participation in a multiplicity of conflicts was a balancing mechanism within the social structure (this idea was taken up by Nordlinger, 1972). However, in rigid social structures, patterns of cleavage coalesce around one axis, simultaneously narrowing and focusing social conflict, so that people participate in fewer groups, but this group membership assumes and envelops more of the individual's total identity (the absence of cross-cutting cleavages in Northern Ireland was noted long ago; see Budge and O'Leary, 1973). To be 'Protestant' or 'White', for example, may define one's total identity, so not only does this ethnic bloc interest define the position taken on all other issues, every issue is reduced to the simple matter of whether or not ethnic bloc interests are served by it. Furthermore, when the source of differentiation and conflict is the axis of national identity and is thus perceived to be about ethnic group survival, the conflict tends to subsume all others, making it difficult to settle housing, education, health and other social problems while the national issue remains unresolved. As Frank Wright once remarked: 'to describe the conflict as national is to say that it has become a conflict about everything because particular issues become difficult to isolate' (1987: 163). And when the social cleavage is binary or can be presented as binary – Protestant versus Catholic, 'Irish' or 'British', 'Black' versus 'White' – the tendency is increased for the conflict to become zero-sum. Zero-sum conflicts are those that permit no sense of mutual interest and common good. Every gain one group makes is a victory over the other; every loss one group suffers means the other group has stolen a march at their expense. In zero-sum cases, conflict is simultaneously narrowed and broadened at the same time. It is narrowed because everything becomes reduced to the simple issue of 'us' and 'them', 'their' interests and 'ours', but also broadened because everything is rendered in terms of this simple divide. This kind of conflict accurately represented the situation in both Northern Ireland and South Africa for a very long time and in 1990 Giliomee (1990: 299) confidently predicted more of the same for decades to come.

Social scientists who are foolishly persuaded to make predictions can become prisoners of events (see Runciman's discussion of analyses of the fall of Soviet communism, 1999: 16). By the beginning of the 1990s, a peace process began in South Africa, with Northern Ireland catching up by the end of the decade. The process is changing long-established patterns of differentiation, conflict and violence.Leaving aside the subjective assessment of whether or not the process is capable of delivering peace in either society as ordinary people perfectly perceive it, and could properly be described as a 'peace process' at all, a process of sorts has begun reflecting objective and observable social changes, the emergence and course of which at this specific time needs to be explained sociologically. This explanation does not imply that the outcome of the process will be 'peace' as this is subjectively understood by everyone, but it needs to account for the objective social changes which are represented by, and encapsulated in, the so-called 'peace process'.

However, subjective notions about the meaning of 'peace' cannot be entirely dismissed. An important distinction needs to be drawn between peace as it is understood in the sense of the cessation of communal violence, and peace in terms of broader social, political and economic restructuring and the introduction of equality and justice. The wish for the violence to stop is natural enough. Where conflicts are zero-sum they can be terminated only with the extermination of one of the contenders, giving total victory for one and total defeat for the other. Alternatively, both groups can be annihilated in what Albert Camus, referring to his native Algeria, called the 'fatal embrace': two crazed peoples, unable to live side by side, can be locked, unwittingly, in a fatal embrace, opting to die together fighting each other rather than unite. Mandela made reference to this when he and other South Africans met Northern Irish politicians in May 1997. Drawing out the lessons of South Africa's case he said:

> Whenever things threatened to fall apart during our negotiations we would stand back and remind ourselves that if negotiations broke down the outcome would be a bloodbath of unimaginable proportions, and after that bloodbath we would have to sit down again and negotiate with each other. The thought always sobered us up, and we persisted, despite many set backs. (quoted in O'Malley, 2001: 276)

No rational actor could consciously prefer the 'fatal embrace'. Recognition of its implications ensures that even in zero-sum conflicts, most people have a wish for the violence to end. However, this is different from a will to make peace. 'Peace' requires the readiness to accept a second-best solution that is mutually advantageous; the cessation of violence involves only a wish for the killing to stop. The desire for an end to violence may encourage the will to make peace, but it need not. 'Peace' requires that the two parties to the zero-sum conflict redefine the nature of the conflict in non-zero-sum terms. As Coser (1964: 349) argued, parties to zero-sum conflicts need to agree norms for the termination of conflict, although his argument was circular, for the conditions he laid down for this were themselves only possible with a redrawing of the conflict itself. The termination of zero-sum conflict required, Coser argued, that the parties make a realistic assessment of their relative power position and strength, that they be prepared to stop short of full victory for their objectives, perhaps because their aims cannot be achieved or only at too high a price, that they come to see common interests and mutual dependencies, and that they see termination as neither total defeat nor total victory for either group but as a mutual advantage. In this way, the conflict will disappear or at least become institutionalised in various 'safety-valve' mechanisms, whereby cross-group forums, organisations, institutions, bodies and processes replace the gun, bomb and riot as the expression of conflict.

Using Coser's ideas, 'peace' can be defined as: *the reconciliation of group conflicts by either removing the grounds for future conflict or institutionalising conflict so that in future it occurs in ways that do not destabilise society*. The former tends to involve ordinary people in grassroots peacemaking activity, the goal of which is the reconciliation of differences in local settings and thus the removal of the source of conflict, the latter involves top-level negotiated settlements. In a study of grassroots peacemaking in Northern Ireland (see Brewer, Bishop and Higgins, 2001), it was shown that peacemaking at this level can be categorised into various types, with a distinction being made between what was called 'active' and 'passive' peacemaking. Passive peacemaking involves commitment to peace as an ideal without practising it. Peace is after all socially desirable to the point that it equals apple pie as a virtue unchallenged. Passive peacemaking not only involves ritualised expressions of its social desirability, but also trenchant denunciations of violence and atrocity. Active peacemaking lives out the commitment to peace as a practice. It is broader than attempts at intervention to stop the violence, important as this is. Active peacemaking in Northern Ireland also involves, amongst other things, engagement with the terms of the conflict to redefine it in non-sectarian and non-zero-sum terms, efforts to reintroduce and restore justice and equality and attempts to solve the problems of Northern Ireland's transition to a post-violence society. At the grassroots level, this reflects in several different kinds of activity, such as ecumenism (which involves the breaking down of barriers and stereotypes and developing contact in a religious context), conflict mediation and resolution, cross-community activities and initiatives, participation in formal peace groups and initiatives, attempts at wrestling with the issue of anti-sectarianism and dealing with the social, political and human problems involved in the transition beyond violence. In contrast, top-level peacemaking tends to focus on negotiated settlements that involve the implementation of good governance, found in such things as new voting systems, new elected assemblies, constitution-building, a bill of rights, and so on, the goal of which is to engage in institutional reform to enable divisive issues to be pursued democratically. A 'peace process' comprises the methods for achieving both sets of goals at the grassroots and the top level.

The questions begged by this definition are why a peace process emerges at a particular, historically specified period, and how it is able to transform a zero-sum conflict by removing its rationale or institutionalising it in socially manageable and acceptable ways. It is the contention of this study that sociology supplies answers to both questions – or at least, sociology understood in a particular way – in that the 'sociological imagination', as outlined by Charles Wright Mills, suggests a framework for understanding how the peace process emerged and currently works in Northern Ireland and South Africa. This involves, for example, consideration variously of how history impacts on the process both to enable and constrain it, the ways in which what Mills calls the personal troubles of ordinary people caused by the violence get translated into public issues around either the cessation of violence or more broad peace issues, how the different individual biographical experiences of people intersect with the social structure to impact on support for, or opposition to, the peace process, as well as the ways in which social structural conditions and political events combine to affect the process, positively and negatively. Mills's portrayal of the sociological imagination helps us understand the emergence of the process, the form it took and the problems it encountered, but it does not predict an outcome to the process. Only theories predict; explanations alone cannot. But this explication does establish the sociological bases on which future termination of the conflict might be possible. First, it is worthwhile outlining what Mills meant by the sociological imagination.

1
C. Wright Mills and the Sociological Imagination

Introduction

To many of its critics, sociology is a strange subject. As an 'ology', to use the idea of a popular British television advertisement several years ago, it appears to have sufficient prestige and honour that the proudest of Jewish grandmothers can take pleasure when their grandchildren pass it at examination. It takes its place amongst a range of other 'ologies' that no one decries; no one criticises biology, psychology or pharmacology for merely existing. To some who think they know sociology better, it lacks substance, being too little like natural science subjects and too much like common sense. With respect to the latter, as I have argued elsewhere (2000a: 13–15), sociology is unique by having a subject matter ordinary people are interested in. Few people in the street talk about the orbits of the moons of Jupiter, or if they do they are not taken seriously, but hairstylists, taxi drivers, neighbours over garden fences and the like think they know about sociology's subject matter and are all too keen to explain why crime is rising, how unemployment is supposed to be affected by immigration, or why schools are thought to be failing. But if sociologists have a subject matter that interests people, it has to share that domain with habitual, common-sense knowledge of the same things. People live their daily lives in the fabric of the institutions, processes and structures that sociology studies and ordinary people develop a natural working knowledge of them. Workers *know* how to cope with boredom in a factory, lovers how to court, the religious how to behave in worship, or children in school. If in studying these things sociology comes up with findings that are contrary to common sense, the research is ridiculed as counter-intuitive (for one such criticism of my ethnographic work on crime in Belfast, see Dickson, 1995). In confirming common-sense notions we make ourselves superfluous, since people supposedly knew this already without the need for sociologists to tell them. But it is common sense that is the problem here, not sociology. Common-sense views of sociology are oblivious to the rigorous methods used to underscore its explanations compared to the lack of rigour hairstylists and taxi drivers use in developing their explanations of the same subject matter. Runciman (1999: 79, 131–5) makes a similar point in relation to sociology's obligation to avoid treating as unproblematic ordinary people's own accounts of their behaviour.

This is relevant to our present discussion in two ways. Ordinary people have their own explanations as to why the peace process emerged and progressed in the way it did in either South Africa or Northern Ireland or both, and the account proffered here will compete with common-sense ideas of the same things. The tendency to dismiss as counter-intuitive explanations of the peace process that do not conform to one's own common-sense understanding of it is reinforced when such explanations are prefixed by being called 'sociological'. Any account our discipline proffers is undermined by common-sense understandings of sociology itself. The prospects, therefore, of convincing anybody of sociology's contribution to understanding the peace process in either society are not good. But if one were to try – and Runciman's introduction to sociology urges practitioners to 'go for it' (1999: x) – the starting place is with an outline of the sociological imagination in order to disabuse people of any common-sense notion of what it means. Before we move to the case study therefore, it is necessary to begin with the subject of sociology.

Sociology rules OK?

Its founding generation in the nineteenth century considered sociology to have replaced philosophy as the mother of all disciplines. While in the eighteenth century discourse on moral philosophy once opened up discussion of several social science subjects, at least amongst the Scottish Enlightenment (Brewer, 1988), by the nineteenth century sociology had replaced it as the vocabulary to discuss human and public affairs. Discourse on sociology opened up debate about such things as human nature, motivations, feelings and attitudes, power, political processes, economic conditions and trends, historical events and circumstances, as well as contemporary social conditions, institutions and processes. Sociology in the nineteenth century ranged widely across topics now narrowly cordoned off as the domain of one discipline or the other. Sociology at that time was a way of thinking, to use Zygmunt Bauman's (1990) more recent terminology, which encapsulated history, psychology, politics and economics, amongst others. Some of the great sociological treatises of this generation – *Social Statics*, *The Elementary Forms of Religious Life*, *Economy and Society* or *The Protestant Ethic and the Spirit of Capitalism* – illustrate how broad the sociological imagination spread, and figures like Spencer, Durkheim and Weber were not narrow disciplinary people; Spencer after all wrote separate books about the principles of ethics, psychology, biology, education and sociology.

The professionalisation of the disciplines in the twentieth century, to which ironically Durkheim and Spencer contributed, reduced the sociological imagination along with the boundaries of the subject to be essentially about the intersection between individuals living in a society and the social structure that characterises that particular social formation. Sociology lost its concern with political power, the historical past and human nature, although it tended to keep alive a concern with economics through its focus on employment status as a key variable in the intersection between individuals and the social structure. Sociologists in subsequent generations have had to fight to reclaim some of the discipline's early concerns and have had long debates about, for example, the relationship between sociology and history, the nature of power, and the relationship between social structure and human agency, as human motivation, feelings, meanings and action came to be called. These debates gave identity to subdisciplines such as historical sociology and political sociology, which sought to recapture the proper domain of the discipline as a broad and encompassing discourse about human and public affairs.

Charles Wright Mills's book *The Sociological Imagination*, first published in 1959, was at the beginning of this trend to revisit the narrow professionalisation of sociology and his description of the sociological imagination sought to reclaim a territory that had been given over to the separate social sciences decades before. (This is now *de rigueur*. For example, Runciman's introduction to sociology, *The Social Animal*, published in 1999, now covers much of this terrain.) Both Howard S. Becker (1994) and Irving Horowitz (1985) stress Mills's resistance to the professionalisation of American sociology at this time. And both call him an intensely American sociologist as a result, in the sense that he objected to the retreat American sociology was making from the classic European tradition, exemplified by Marx and Weber, toward a technically competent but politically disengaged subject. (On the relationship between American and European sociological traditions in Mills's work, see Seidman, 1998: 173–82; for other general studies on Mills see: Press, 1978; Tilman, 1984; Eldridge, 1985.) Interestingly enough, the book appears to have been written largely while Mills was on a sabbatical in Europe (mostly the London School of Economics and Copenhagen), where intellectual traditions reflected this broad vision for sociology. It was written with voracious speed and energy; he states in one of his letters to a friend in America that he was writing up to 15 hours at a stretch (Mills and Mills, 2000: 236). His letters home contain phrases that he was 'very excited about it all' (Mills and Mills, 2000: 230); to Lewis Coser, a fellow sociologist, he wrote, 'it's really quite an exciting little thing' (Mills and Mills, 2000: 234). Two things excited him in particular. The first was his sense of fulfilling an obligation to the discipline. He wrote to Bill Miller, a close friend in America, on 5 February 1957: 'I think it's time I wrote something about my own kind of sociology and against the current dominant schools. I'm not in a hurry about it, but it's coming along' (Mills and Mills, 2000: 228). To Ralph Miliband he wrote about the need to write a 'little technical book' about his intellectual craft, although it was Miliband who recommended that the first three chapters of the draft on intellectual craftsmanship be removed from the main body of the text and put as an appendix, advice Mills followed (see Mills and Mills, 2000: 265). Perhaps the main reason for his delight was his realisation that the book would be iconoclastic. Indeed, he wrote to Miller urging him not to tell anyone about the draft he had just read: 'I want it to be just one big dandy surprise: as from a prophet who comes in from a desert' (Mills and Mills, 2000: 230).

The analogy is a revealing one and gives a clue to how Mills saw its contents. Prophetic is not an overstatement of the book. It was intended as no less than a thorough revision of the method and approach of the social sciences. Indeed, in a letter to Miliband in January 1958, Mills revealed that his original title for the book had been 'The Social Sciences' (Mills and Mills, 2000: 262). In a footnote in the book he explained how colleagues from other disciplines who read the manuscript in draft form suggested it could be retitled 'the political imagination' or the 'anthropological imagination' and so on (2000 [1959]: 19). He explained that the academic discipline of sociology was not what was being implied in his term, and elsewhere in the text he wrote about the essential unity of all the social sciences (2000 [1959]: 141) based on a concern with institutional orders – political, economic, religious, military – as a way of solving society's significant problems. It was called 'sociological', he explained in the footnote, because 'man's fate in our time' is the major of such problems and the key classical sociologists of the past, whom he valorised, had the same 'quality of mind' in approaching these topics. Elsewhere he made the point that the leading political scientists, psychologists or economists of his day – Galbraith, Dahl, Riesman, Almond and Truman – were sociologists in this broad sense (2000 [1959]: 139).

In re-establishing sociology as also about things like history, politics, public affairs and human nature, Mills simultaneously railed against sociologists who preferred to keep it narrow, and perhaps his book is most well known for his trenchant critique of sociology's main traditions at that point in time. It is necessary to outline his arguments about the encompassing nature of the sociological imagination in order to show later that the sociology of the peace process in Northern Ireland and South Africa justifiably incorporates history, politics, individual human agency as well as the social structure. This requires that we also outline his complaints against narrower notions of sociology's domain. First, however, it is necessary to learn something of the man behind these ideas, for his outlander status as a sociologist owes much to his upbringing in Texas and his immersion in its culture of self-reliance and dogged independence.

Charles Wright Mills

There is a tendency amongst sociologists to write bad biography by constantly locating a person's ideas in terms of their position in the social structure – this afterall is what the sociology of knowledge is all about – claiming that their ideas were the products of their social class, gender, 'race' or whatever else their location in the social structure made them. This tends to reverse the obsession of professional biography with early childhood experiences and psychoanalytic-sexual trauma. I do not want to engage in any such speculation, save to say that Mills was a fascinating man who led a very interesting life. Photographic images hint at such. He commuted to Columbia University in New York on a motor bike, and one photo has him looking much like Marlon Brando in the film *The Wild One*, the epitome of the rebel. Others catch him with slicked-back hair, deep eyes and strong features, much like an Irish poet or dramatist, lustful for love, life and its pleasures but a damn good storyteller as well, a Brendan Behan look-alike, imagery equally rebellious (for a picture gallery of Mills, see the family photo album in http://www.cwrightmills.org). One of his students recalls him riding to work on his BMW bike in plaid shirt, old jeans and working boots, with books in a duffel bag strapped across his chest (Wakefield, 2000: 6), clearly cocking a snook at the conservative professors in grey flannels and Cadillacs. For a big man – he was over six feet tall and 14 stone in weight – he had boundless energy and restlessness, which, along with his excesses in eating, drinking and working, contributed to the diagnosis of high blood pressure at a very young age, leading later to angina and heart disease. However, in later life, he wrote to leading sociologists like Coser and Miliband with an adolescent's pleasure about the weight he had lost, counting the pounds, and that he had stopped drinking. Indeed, his last letter to Miliband, written four days before his death, he announced his abstinence, sadly a little too late (see Mills and Mills, 2000: 339–40). It is an irony, true, perhaps for all for whom death comes early and as a surprise, that he wrote to Miliband in this letter that he would see him soon and he was not to worry, 'I am quite all right'.

Charles Wright Mills was born in Waco, Texas, in 1916 into a deeply religious Catholic family. He married four times, marrying and divorcing his first wife twice. Two daughters have recently brought out a valuable collection of his letters and correspondence (Mills and Mills, 2000). He retained love and affection for all his children all his life, as he did for his parents (he pre-deceased them both). In letters to his parents well into adult life he still referred to them as 'Momma and Papa' and would sign himself on times as 'little Charlie'. This did not stop him rejecting his conservative Texan upbringing, and in adolescence he became an atheist (he referred to himself as a 'pagan', although he had a Quaker funeral). Texas remained deep within him though. Texas was probably to blame for his attitude towards women. Becker (1994) refers to his 'undoubted machismo'. His letters reveal a surprising manner with women, at least to our generation. He was writing in a context before women's liberation but he was wont to make a few gratuitous comments in his letters on women's bodies – he referred to one well-known female writer as 'chronologically fifty; body: 30; face: lovely, early forty' (Mills and Mills, 2000: 64). He was voracious in those appetites as well; he had affairs with at least one of his research assistants (whom he later married). He worked in an institution which at that time was male only, and one student recalls him telling them to get their girlfriends round to cook for them (Wakefield, 2000: 8) so they did not have to live as bachelors. He also wrote a scathing review of de Beauvoir's *Second Sex* (published posthumously), suggesting that her arguments realised Colleridge's prophecy of androgynous people living in an androgynous world: distinctions of masculinity and femininity remained important to him. This was one form of inequality and injustice that Mills was not attuned to, although few others passed him by, and it only serves to show that he was a creature of his Texan culture.

Texas produced other contradictions in his life. While rejecting his upbringing, he never changed his Texan drawl, would often draw long and slow on his pipe thinking as if sitting on his stoop, he loved the television programme *Rawhide* (according to his daughter, Mills and Mills, 2000: xviii) and talked fondly in letters to Miliband about going hunting there with his father. He became famed amongst his students for his capacity to eat double dinners of Texan steak and beef. One likened his gargantuan stomach and voracious appetite to the quality of his mind, being huge in both (Wakefield, 2000: 10). At a deeper level, Mills showed himself to be a feisty Texan in his philosophy of self-help and individual autonomy. He was an outlander: he built his own motorbike, constructed his own homes, baked his own bread and exhorted his students to the value of self-sufficiency. In one of his letters to his parents he described himself as 'self-made' but expressed his philosophy of Texan independence much clearer in responding to a letter his parents wrote asking him and his young wife, then newly married, if they needed anything: 'My father asks, do we need anything? Does a man ever really need anything but that what is in him? No: there is nothing I need that can be given to me by others. In the end a man must go to bat alone' (Mills and Mills, 2000: 40; this point is also made by Gitlin, 2000: 230, who uses the same sources of correspondence). This is all the more paradoxical when it is understood that throughout his academic life, Mills had a devotion to helping others, not just his students – he was a brilliant teacher – but primarily the marginal, downtrodden and exploited poor. This was another of his contradictions. None the less, this outlander self-sufficiency enabled him to suffer the deep unpopularity of his convictions. As a supporter of Cuba in Cold War America he clearly was not dismayed by notoriety and boldly ignored FBI interest in his activities. His letters show him taking pleasure in being hated for his political beliefs, proudly telling de Beauvoir that they had the same enemies (Mills and Mills, 2000: 333).

His intellectual life was equally interesting; as a 28-year-old in his first grant application he had the audacity to declare that he did not take American sociology seriously and preferred to write for 'little magazines' because they dealt with the right topics and were not misled by crippling academic prose (quoted in Gitlin, 2000: 231). Becker (1994) describes him as a smart ass who could be difficult. Mills certainly saw himself as an outlander in the discipline of sociology as well and he presented himself as loftily above the academic game. Yet paradoxically he was not beyond playing it himself. He took great pride is writing to his parents about his earlier appearances in print, telling them in a letter that copies of his articles in the *American Journal of Sociology* and the *American Sociological Review* could be seen in their local library (Mills and Mills, 2000: 42). He was also very proud – and had a wont to tell people – that he was the youngest assistant professor at Columbia at 28 years of age, when the average age was 45 (letter in Mills and Mills, 2000: 82). The irony here is that Columbia treated him disgracefully by not giving him a full professorship until late or even allowing him to teach graduate students when at the height of his reputation.

He had a tendency to tell his students to think big, and it was a large landscape on which he worked. His first studies were in

American pragmatic social philosophy, economics and sociology, illustrating at the beginning a dislike for narrow disciplinary boundaries. Doctoral research drew him to two pantheons of the 'long century' of nineteenth-century sociology, Marx and Weber, both representatives of a tradition in which sociology was inseparable from history, economics, politics and human affairs. In the first three years of his career at Maryland, before moving to Columbia, he worked with Hans Gerth as a translator of Weber's work into English (for a study of the Gerth–Mills relationship, see Oakes and Vidich, 1999). They sought to rescue Weber's broad sociological repertoire from early translations by Talcott Parsons and Edward Shils, which tended to eschew Weber's writing on politics, history and economics for his work on values and social action. This caused considerable outrage to Shils, who wrote what Becker (1994) calls a vicious denunciation of *The Sociological Imagination* in a book review for *Encounter*, referring to it as 'imaginary sociology'. Shils clearly felt personally wounded and used unprofessional abuse in his letters of complaint to Gerth about their 'alternative' translations (see, for example, letters in Mills and Mills, 2000: 73, 76). Mills wrote to Gerth alleging that Shils said he hated them (Mills and Mills, 2000: 76) and thereafter Mills believed that Shils did what he could to undermine his career, alleging that Shils turned Daniel Bell against him (Mills and Mills, 2000: 123), although their diametrically opposed views of Cold War America probably do more to explain this than possible malevolence by Shils. None the less, this serves to illustrate that Mills developed a problematic relationship with the Shils–Parsons axis of sociology very early in his career and shows Parsons to be one of Mills's *bêtes noires*, which later influenced his depiction of the sociological imagination. Parsons referred to Mills's work has 'impressionistic' (reported by Mills in one of his letters, see Mills and Mills, 2000: 158), and book reviews of each other's work were often vituperative. Mills wrote gleefully to Robert K. Merton on one occasion asking if he had seen a critical review of one of Parsons's books (Mills and Mills, 2000: 175). Herein lies another of the contradictions in Mills's life. He hated critical reviews of his books, and although he deigned to respond publicly to most of them he was very upset and often sent private letters of complaint to editors (see a letter in Mills and Mills, 2000: 163). Yet he was a savage reviewer himself. He was aware of this within him. In one of his letters he writes of his review of Whyte's book *Organization Man*: 'I cut him down to size with some real mean cracks ... what a schlemiel. And what a thief' (Mills and Mills, 2000: 211). It is not clear from the letter whether Whyte was the *schlock* or Mills for being so self-consciously critical. However, engagement was what sociologists should be about, even if trenchantly with each other.

He 'lived' the sociological imagination in another way, for he was engaged in public affairs and used sociology as the means of analysis. Like Weber, with whose ghost Mills debated, Mills saw himself as a public intellectual (on the sociologist as public intellectual see Seidman, 1998: 173). Mills was the American Raymond Aron, a contemporary of Mill and another heir to the European classic tradition who combined sociological analysis with polemic engagement with public issues (a point made by Becker, 1994). Mills's dialogue however, came with a more radical edge than Aron's. This is reflected in a trilogy on American society: *The New Men of Power and America's Labor Leaders* in 1948, *White Collar: the American Middle Class* in 1951 (the outcome of the Guggenheim grant) and *The Power Elite* in 1956. There was no lack of interest in real-world issues in Mills's own sociological writings, although, to be fair, some of Parsons's early essays, covering the period 1938 to 1953, were equally engaged with public issues, including, for example, the emergence of Nazism (see Parsons, 1954). Less well-known books had similar motive, covering immigration from Puerto Rica, the Cuban revolution and his anxieties about militarisation, which led to a book on the causes of World War III. He also wrote an Introduction to a collection of readings from classic sociologists, entitled *Images of Man*, published in 1960 which, sadly out of print, is about the 'classic tradition' in sociology and continued his critique of sociology begun the year before in *The Sociological Imagination*. Writing to Miliband in November 1959, Mills recognised that the two were part of the same project. *Images of Man* 'is a kind of supplement or companion I guess ... I am not ashamed of it' (Mills and Mills, 2000: 281). It is relevant that the classic tradition was defined precisely by the attention given to broad public issues and to transcending narrow disciplinary boundaries. (For another discussion of the classic tradition in sociology, see Ray, 1999; Aron also gave a very well-known exegesis of this tradition; see Aron, 1965.) The readings he selected came from Marx, Weber, Durkheim, Spencer and Veblen.

It is interesting that after writing these two texts on the nature of the discipline, Mills hankered to return to the stuff of real sociology, substantive studies with a focus on public issues. In a letter to Miliband in September 1959, he wrote that he was 'sick of writing about academic stuff and want badly to get back to writing about realities' (Mills and Mills, 2000: 233). What followed was his monumental and provocative study of the Cuban revolution, *Listen Yankee: The Revolution in Cuba* – realities indeed.

Since his death on 20 March 1962 various posthumous books have been collated from his writings, including his doctoral thesis from 1945, called *Sociology and Pragmatism*, and his reputation has grown immeasurably. There are now websites devoted to his work and the most obvious is http://www.cwrightmills.org run by his three children – a father's love clearly returned. As another measure of the esteem in which he is held, the International Sociological Association undertook a poll of nominations for sociology book of the twentieth century and of Mills's books *The Sociological Imagination* featured strongly, getting nearly six times more votes than his next ranked book *The Power Elite*. The book's universal popularity is reflected in its translation into 17 languages, including Catalan and Serb. There might perhaps have been even more posthumous satisfaction for Mills in the poll. For someone born in 1916, if you like nearly at the end of the 'long century' of nineteenth-century sociology which came with the death of Weber, and for someone who persistently tried to redefine the sociological imagination in broad ways that recaptured the encompassing vision of the nineteenth-century founders of the discipline, what was more appropriate was that *The Sociological Imagination* came overall second to Weber's *Economy and Society*. To come second to Weber would have been no embarrassment to Mills. *Economy and Society* epitomises what Mills understood to be sociology's way of thinking; even more rewarding perhaps was that *The Sociological Imagination* got twice the votes of Parsons's two treatises, one on social action, the other on the social system, that epitomised what Mills took to be the subject's narrow imagination and vision.

Appropriately, Mills's thumbnail picture features in the slightly irreverent Dead Sociologists Society gallery alongside the nineteenth-century figures that gave us the discipline and whose view of the sociological imagination reflected his own: a broad encompassing discipline that was concerned with real-world events and whose discourse on public affairs ranged over history, politics, economics, ethics, philosophy and human nature (http://www2.pfeiffer.edu/~iridener/DSS/DEADSOC.html).

Narrow sociology

This view of the sociological imagination was worked out in opposition to three trends which dominated sociology at the time of Mills's writing: general theory, abstract empiricism and social administration. (In a draft of the book's contents shown to Coser, the last of the three was called social pathology, reminiscent of Durkheim not Weber.) A similar account of sociology's distorted traditions is found in E.H. Carr's famous 'What is History?' (1961), in which he describes possible relationships between the two disciplines (also see Runciman, 1999: 140*ff*). The contrast between theory and empiricism is something of a timeless dichotomy which Mills used to great effect (see Jenks, 1998, for a description of several antinomies that dominated sociology). Abstract empiricism reduced the discipline to technical problems of enumeration and analysis of quantitative data. The method of doing all this was by means of the survey and questionnaire, and its ardent exponent at the time was Paul Lazarsfeld. Lazarsfeld's subsequent depiction of sociology does not portray it in terms of a subject matter or content but a method of study and approach which he described as 'survey analysis'. Sociology's chief interest supposedly was not in concepts that describe the social world but 'variates' that measure it (1973: 12). The focus was upon the individual as the unit of enumeration and analysis, and only society in as far as clusters or collectivities of people could be collated under some measure or variable for specific research purposes. It represented dissolution of the 'social' in favour of explicating technical 'variates' or 'indicators' (on the dissolution of the social in later social theory, see Lash and Urry, 1986).

In saying this, Mills was not writing from a position of ignorance. He had used these kinds of methods himself in his 1950 study of Puerto Rican migration and for a time worked with Lazarsfeld in the Bureau of Applied Social Research. Lazarsfeld was one of two people instrumental in persuading Mills to transfer to Columbia and in a letter Mills reports on the inducements he was offered over dinner to get him to New York and what 'great fun' he had had with Lazarsfeld (Mills and Mills, 2000: 81). But it was precisely because Mills had worked on the inside of this kind of sociology that he proclaimed its vacuousness as a strong personal conviction. In a letter to Gerth, Mills wrote of his experience of doing the Bureau's kind of sociology in understated Texan tones: 'a guy ought not to get so hog wild about it' (Mills and Mills, 2000: 171). In 1952, Mills wrote to inform Gerth of his total break with Lazarsfeld, complaining that he was trying to dominate and manipulate Mills at Columbia (Mills and Mills, 2000: 172), and in letters to Miliband and Burnbaum he subsequently laid the charge that Lazarsfeld was trying to remove two of Mills's protégés from their positions at Columbia (Mills and Mills, 2000: 257).

In *The Sociological Imagination* Lazarsfeld's approach is denigrated in stronger terms as the fetishism of method: we become blind to the topic being studied as the methods suggested for studying it become the central point. Related to this complaint is the belief that often the topics studied by means of these methods are trivial, so that an exceedingly elaborate method employed with care is matched with remarkably thin results (Mills, 2000 [1959]: 52). A decade and a half after his audacious (but successful) application to the Guggenheim Foundation for a grant, Mills still believed that American sociology was not studying important topics. By 1959 he had blamed this on the fetishism of method: abstract empiricism only studies topics amenable to its methods and is unaware of the limitations this imposes on the questions asked. Methodology determines the problems to be researched and those that are amenable to statistical investigation are mostly unimportant. The final complaint Mills made against abstract empiricism was psychologism (Mills, 2000 [1959]: 67–8), which he described as the attempt to explain social phenomena in terms of the make-up of individuals. The variables and indicators used in sociological explanation are treated within abstract empiricism as features of individuals or, more properly, a sample of individuals, which divorces people from the social structure and fails to capture the effects social institutions have on people and individual behaviour. Indeed, people are often unaware of these effects and are unable to articulate some of the social forces operating on their lives. Sociology properly undertaken requires the study of people in context, placed in historical time and in a comparative and structural place (or milieu as he used to term it).

The objection Mills formed to social policy was its close connection with what in Britain was called the political arithmetic tradition of social administration and which Mills referred to as state-centred and bureaucratic practical sociology (2000 [1959]: 91 *passim*). It was like an extension of abstracted empiricism (2000 [1959]: 96, 101) in developing a bureaucratic approach to sociology's subject matter, blunting the discipline's radicalism. The examples he cites of this kind of sociology are work on the administration of social services in the welfare state, the development of management theory and work on 'human relations' (all discussed in 2000 [1959]: 92). Management theory, he wrote, can be summarised in a simple formula: to make the worker happy, efficient and co-operative we need only to make the managers intelligent, rational and knowledgeable (2000 [1959]: 92). This ignores the hierarchy of power and obedience in factories and is sociology put to serve the interests of a managerial elite (2000 [1959]: 95). In the same way, the administration of social services in the welfare state, for example, fragments an understanding of the scattered causation of social problems and is sociology done in the interests of the state. The stress on practical sociology and the development of specialist expertise – human relations experts, industrial relations centres, social research bureaux of large corporations, social research agencies in government, the police and the armed forces – is an illiberal practicality (2000 [1959]: 95) because it has turned sociologists into administrative technicians or political arithmeticians of the state. This reflects in sociology's research methods, with a focus on abstracted empiricism's collection of 'social facts' (2000 [1959]: 101), as well as in the new image of sociology, which is not, as in social anthropology's case, the handmaiden of colonialism, but now the bed-fellow of big corporations (2000 [1959]: 96). The connection was simple. Lazarsfeld provided the methodology and the state the subject matter, narrowing sociology into a bureaucratic, technical discipline examining topics of interest to management, big business, administrators of the welfare state and agencies, like the army and the police, that want to render people's concerns into features of 'human relations'.

If Lazarsfeld was Mills's methodological *bête noire*, Parsons was the theoretical equivalent, for if abstract empiricism dissolved the social, general theory dissolved the individual. Grand theory focused on 'society in general', making generalisations about societies in the abstract, stripped from historical time and place. The method of doing this was by means of general theoretical analysis, represented best at the time by Talcott Parsons – the archetypal Platitude Merchant that Runciman belittles and decries (1999: 57 *passim*). The focus was upon the social structure, and on people only as abstract 'actors' in a play scripted for them by culture, in which every move and role was moulded and shaped by forces external to them. In Parsons's terminology, people were best understood as 'personality systems'. Harold Garfinkel later referred to this representation of people as 'cultural dopes', people without voluntarism or meaning but prisoners of culture. It represented the dissolution of the individual into an over-socialised puppet, with strings pulled by society. Indeed Dennis Wrong, one of the young sociologists Mills initially refers to favourably in his letters, won spurs later as the author of a famous piece on Parsons's 'over-socialized conception of man' (1961).

Accordingly, Mills saw the development of general theory as often wasteful. However, this was the least of his complaints. General theory was verbiage – the fetishism of the concept if you like – which, when translated into plain English, was mostly trivial. Mills famously declared that the 555 pages of Parsons's *The Social System* (1951) could be rendered into 150 when put in straightforward English (2000 [1959]: 31) and he variously translated passages for effect (for Runciman's critique of Parsons's style, see 1999: 59–60). It was slight, even when properly stated in plain English, because general theories are separated from the real world, being so general as not to permit observation in historical or structural contexts. But it was slight for an even more important reason. General theory, at least in Parsons's mind, excluded certain key structural features of society thought to be fundamental to its understanding, notably power. This is a familiar mantra for critics of Parsons, but what is interesting is how Mills turns this complaint into an elaboration of his whole approach to sociology. Mills defined power in an unusual way, seeing it as the capacity to make decisions about the arrangements under which one lived (2000 [1959]: 40) rather than the ability to effect other people's arrangements (which was Weber's definition). It is not power to impose decisions on others but control over one's own life. This naturally led him to ask who is involved in making the decisions that impact on ordinary people's lives if not they themselves. Power elites, the state, politics and political parties thus become central to

Mills's understanding of the sociological imagination. He was particularly concerned to unravel how the social structure, history and the political state impact on the lives of ordinary people in their personal milieux in such a way as to denude them of power, freedom and choice.

Reasserting the sociological imagination

The sociological imagination as Mills presented it attempted a dissolution of its own, seeking to overcome the false dichotomies between individuals and society, free will and determinism, and what we now call agency and structure. It was one the first of such attempts, although syntheses of agency and structure are now *de rigueur*. Indeed, *The Sociological Imagination* has become popular again perhaps because of the modern attention on agency–structure. But this fundamentally misunderstands Mills's argument, for the sociological imagination in Mills's treatment is more than just a synthesis of agency and structure. It is about linking them with two other factors – history and politics – which gives a wider context to the intersection of individuals with society and broadens the understanding of sociology at the same time. Under Mills's arguments sociology is broadened in another way. In addition to transcending disciplinary boundaries, the sociological imagination imposes the obligation of sociologists to become engaged in explaining – if not solving – important public issues that impact negatively on the lives of ordinary people. It is integral to Mills's portrayal of the sociological imagination that its analytical insights are used to understand public affairs. It is the intersection of agency, social structure, political events and historical factors put to the service of public issues that makes Mills so fruitful for understanding the peace processes in Northern Ireland and South Africa and explains why it is he that has been revisited rather than any of the modern statements of the agency–structure synthesis, such as Giddens's (1984), Archer's (1996) or Bhaskar's (1989a, 1989b).

Having said this, *The Sociological Imagination* is a frustratingly obtuse book when it comes to explicating the alternative form of sociology. Part of the problem is the change in sociological vocabulary between then and now. There is an unfortunate tendency in much writing on the history of sociology to look for modern meaning to early terminology enabling us to find a plethora of precursors to key ideas. Much of Adam Ferguson's supposed contribution to sociology, for example, is based on projecting nineteenth-century language and meaning onto an eighteenth-century text (see Brewer, 1988; for a discussion of this general problem, see Merton, 1967). This is not the problem here, although Mills is very prescient in some of his terminology, being a precursor, for example, of the term 'postmodernism' (but, to make the point, meaning something different by it). The problem is the reverse one: the use of an idiom that is different from the contemporary one to describe essentially the same ideas. Mills's terminology is correctly appropriated by modern commentators to refer to the agency–structure debate, but it is couched in a different vocabulary. There is no doubt, however, that this was what he was referring to and he makes extensive use of the term 'social structure' in its modern meaning. But some of the other terms need their meaning explicated in order to render them appropriate to understanding Mills's account of sociological method. Moreover, Mills falls foul of the same tendency as Parsons in lacking economy in prose style. Returning the serve, it is possible to translate his arguments into succinct form without any loss of meaning; but perhaps in more than one paragraph.

If it were possible to summarise Mills's view of the sociological imagination in a paragraph it might be as follows. Sociology should hold individual biography, the social structure, history and political power in balance in the one framework. This gives social reality a three-dimensional quality. First, social reality is simultaneously microscopic, based around individuals' personal worlds, and macroscopic, in that the institutional and structural order of society impacts on people's personal milieux. Social reality is also simultaneously historical and contemporary, in that present structures, circumstances, events, processes and issues have a historical relevance that may impact on their current form and future development. Thirdly, reality is simultaneously social and political; society is deeply impacted by the operation of power within the nation state and beyond, and politics affects both the social structure and the personal biographical worlds of people, and is in turn affected by them. The sociological imagination therefore involves a co-ordination of personal biographical experience, social structural conditions, historical forces and political power and looks at the intersection of them all. This was what characterised the classic tradition of sociology and this is what the discipline's practitioners had abandoned at the time of Mills's writing. In Mills's words (2000 [1959]: 143), the lives of individuals cannot be adequately understood without reference to the institutions (political and social) and historical forces within which their biography is enacted, and societies are composed in part of the biographical experiences, historical and contemporary, of the people they comprise.

All summaries require expansion, however. It is necessary to unpack some of his terms in order to understand the force of the argument. Mills uses terminology like 'biography' and 'personal milieu' frequently. By 'biography' he means someone's set of personal and lived experiences, past and present, and by 'milieu' he refers to their personal and local social world in microcosm. These two notions are combined in a modern manner to mean what sociologists now refer to as 'agency' by people in their 'everyday life setting'. Mills also makes extensive use of the term 'social structure', which he uses in its conventional sociological sense to describe society's institutional order, although he understands this broadly to encompass military, religious, economic, political and social institutions. Translating all of this into modern parlance, people are seen to live and act within a personal milieu, which comprises their everyday life experiences and sets of troubles, yet they do not live as islands within their own social world, but have a sense of something greater than themselves through their awareness both of their social self and the social structure within which they live. This is orthodox agency–structure vocabulary: the social structure has a reality independent of the actions of individuals but people live out their biography and thereby contribute to the shaping of society. As Mills wrote, people are 'made by society and by its historical push and shove', but 'by the fact of living' people 'contribute to the shaping of this society and to the course of its history' (2000 [1959]: 6). 'The orientating conception', for the sociological imagination, Mills wrote, is 'the study of [individual] biography, of history, and the problem of their intersection with social structures' (2000 [1959]: 134).

The sociological imagination, however, is more than standard agency–structure fare. Social structures have to be approached historically, for their shape may be influenced by the past, which means that people's personal milieux and their individual biographical experiences may feel the imprint of history. One of the truisms of the discipline is that sociologists are interested in social processes for the patterns they exhibit, being concerned with historical events only for the generalisations they contain (for a good discussion of this, see Runciman, 1999: 140*ff*). Yet Mills stressed that people and societies do not exist in a vacuum but must be located in a particular context of time and space. Societies have a 'historical past' which forms part of this context and history may be relevant to understanding the shape and fashion of a society's current social structure, such as the effect of colonialism as a historical factor on the social structure of any post-colonial society. Sociologists are therefore required to 'grasp history' (2000 [1959]: 6) in addition to the intersection of individual personal biography and the social structure. The present can be so imbibed with the past that the sociological imagination overlooks history at its peril.

It is not obvious, however, what Mills means by history. He points to the commonplace that society cannot transcend its past and thus that all sociology 'worthy of the name is "historical sociology"' (2000 [1959]: 146). In only slightly less prosaic manner, history has a place in the sociological imagination because the phenomenon to be explained has to be understood at once both historically and as it currently manifests. Incidentally, this means that any worthy sociology is also comparative and should locate phenomena to be explained in a historical and comparative framework, akin to Weber (2000 [1959]: 150–1). However, Mills means something deeper than this. 'History' means stressing the specificity of the present. 'Historical specificity', a term so akin to Marx, requires the use of historical material in the analysis of the phenomena to be explained in order to establish whether it is special or unique to its current moment (2000 [1959]: 149). This is done in part to facilitate an understanding of the phenomenon by showing whether it is to be understood in terms of the specific period in which it exists. This is much more than simply providing a little dull padding by sketching the historical background to the phenomenon. Rather, the sociological imagination requires demonstrating the *relevance* of historical factors to an understanding of the phenomenon in its current form. This does not make us all historians, as if it were the mother of disciplines. History is approached by the sociologist only to establish whether or not historical materials are relevant to the present day, whether or not historical factors continue to shape the phenomenon, and if so how. When Mills therefore adds history to the intersection of biography and social structure he imposes on us the requirement to understand people's everyday lifeworld in terms of how it is impacted by the social structure in its present and historical formation and to locate their biographical lived experiences historically as well as contemporaneously. In the process we may find that history is irrelevant to the contemporary circumstance of people and societies. While everything exists in historical time, so that history can never entirely be dismissed, it is possible to discover that historical factors are only indirectly relevant (2000 [1959]: 155). None the less, the question needed to be asked.

We also have to understand these milieux and biographical experiences politically. Social structures, Mills writes, 'are usually organised under a political state. In terms of power, the most inclusive unit of social structure is the nation state' (2000 [1959]: 135). This dominating form of power is the 'major fact in the life' of ordinary people and if sociologists wish to understand social problems and structural forces as they impact on people's biographical lived experiences, the effective means of power form part of that sociological imagination. Because social structures are organised under a political state, the operation of the state influences the patterns across and within different social structures. The converse is also true, in that the dynamics of social structures can influence politics and affect the political process, in that the social structure creates some of the problems that the state has to deal with. Social structural conditions can also influence the emergence of 'skilled political actors', the men and women of genius as Sir Isaiah Berlin once referred to them, shaping their strategies for change and facilitating their political mobilisation of people and collectivities. This affects the political process and sometimes transforms it (and occasionally transforms even the state itself). This impact is not restricted to politics in the nation state, for through his analysis of the power elite, Mills recognised the internationalisation of social, economic and political processes. Thus, Mills writes in *The Sociological Imagination* that the nation state, while the generic working unit, has in some cases been superseded by the international economy and the development of international relations (2000 [1959]: 135–6). The impact of politics on the 'national social structure', as he describes the generic working unit for sociologists, can be nation state and international in its level.

This is another reason why the sociological imagination should not be reduced to agency–structure links. In Mills's hands, the sociological imagination involves a fourfold intersection rather than a dual one, between the social structure, individual biography and experience, historical events and constraints, and the political process, within both national and international domains. It was not until Giddens's theory of structuration (1984) much later that power was recognised as a dimension that needed to be incorporated into the synthesis of agency and structure.

Some observations on this programmatic statement are necessary before we begin to apply it to the case study. It is Mills's recognition of the reality of structures and processes that people live and act within that distinguishes him from the contemporary fad of postmodernism (a term he uses but in a different way). Postmodernists argue that knowledge cannot be generalised to whole societies in the form of 'metanarratives' but can only produce 'small localised narratives' of bounded and relative contexts. For example, they would argue that we cannot search for absolute truth, only truths held by people in specific localities. Mills would concord with this. But for postmodernists all structures dissolve to the person, the only thing that is real being the individual. The defining mark of sociology for Mills, however, becomes the examination of the connection between social structure and individuals' personal biography and experience. He is therefore thoroughly 'modernist', for Mills argues that there is an objective reality behind social meanings to which it is possible to obtain privileged access. And it is sociology that is thus privileged because it is able to unravel the intersection between social structure and individual biography.

This privilege is not shared widely. Ordinary people do not readily comprehend this intersection because they are fixed on their immediate lives. People live out their lives in a bounded context that Mills calls a 'personal milieu', based on their specific location in the social structure and in historical time and physical space. It is local, personal and immediate, and composed of taken-for-granted activities in familiar surroundings mostly amongst unthreatening others. In these personal milieux people do not fully grasp the big social structures, doing so only as these structural conditions impinge on their life locally and thus impose themselves on their consciousness. 'Small' people can feel swamped by 'big' institutions and process and fail to comprehend the forces operating on them and dictating to them. Yet, Mills believes there is an umbilical cord between individual biography and the social structure, which sociology can comprehend even if lay people cannot. Sociology in the service of the 'small' person unravels the connections and makes public the way in which 'big' institutions have taken over control of people's ordinary lives. This is the sociologist's 'foremost political and intellectual task' (2000 [1959]: 13). Hence it is that for Mills the central feature of sociology's subject matter is the intersection of people's personal biographies and the social structure.

One reflection of this intersection, stressed most by Mills, is the interaction between 'personal troubles' and 'public issues' (2000 [1959]: 8*ff*). The indissolubility of the individual and social structure ensures that people's private 'troubles' (such as divorce and unemployment) transfer into public issues that transcend local and personal environments to affect society generally. Conversely, public issues (such as fear of crime, anxiety over redundancy, and the consequences of high mortgage rates for homeowners) can become private troubles to affect the individual and shape their biographical experiences.

It is worth highlighting that the effect of individual biography on the social structure is not just experienced through the embodied actions and private troubles of ordinary people in local 'personal milieux', but by what Sir Isaiah Berlin called 'people of genius' who are able to affect important social changes. There are two views on their effect. These key players have influence by the fact that they represent the dominant social forces and structural tendencies of their time, so that the social structure throws up 'people of genius' who go on to effect social and cultural change. In other cases, however, some key players engage in a set of interactions that could not be predicated solely in terms of structural position. A second view, therefore, is that sometimes 'people of genius' emerge as such because they take advantage of social structural conditions to give rise to new and emergent qualities and events. However, in either case, the central feature is the intersection between the person and the social structure, with the explanation of the resultant change being incomplete without the other.

Lewis Coser's (1976: 211–13) account of the American civil rights movement acts as a good example. Coser was a close friend of Mills. He had obtained his PhD at Columbia (although not supervised by Mills) and Coser was recommended by Mills as a great prospect in a letter to Hans Gerth (Mills and Mills, 2000: 121). Mills and Coser corresponded regularly throughout Mills's life (and not just about the profession, for they shared a love of biking). While they were in Chicago on sabbatical, the two roomed together and Coser read the draft of *The Sociological Imagination*. Coser thus had sympathy for Mills's approach to sociology and this was implicit in his essay on the American civil rights movement. According to Coser, its emergence required social structural conditions, many with a historical specificity with which Mills would have agreed, such as the mechanisation of cotton production, rural depopulation of the South and urban migration, and the expansion of opportunity for Black workers arising from labour shortage in the Second World War. But it also required key individuals, whom Coser refers to as 'skilled political actors', like Martin Luther King, who were sufficiently motivated for political engagement and direct involvement, and able to exploit these structural conditions to mobilise Black people by various strategies for change which appealed to their values and interests. The success of the civil rights movement in the United States thus appears to involve a combination of historical factors, social structural conditions and the emergence of skilled political actors taking creative advantage of this confluence.

Without mentioning Mills's work, Coser's account exemplifies Mills's sociological imagination, for Coser demonstrates, for a historically specified case, how to deal with the problem, as Mills put it, of biography, history and their intersection with social structures. The limitations in Coser's explanation of the civil rights movement concern his neglect of the broader political structure in which these key players act. It is not insignificant, for example, that the social structural conditions and the emergence of 'people of genius' occurred in a political process dominated by Kennedy's presidency and his liberal agenda on a range of social issues including 'race', and in a political process affected by the connection between civil rights and anti-Vietnam war protests. This highlights the importance of political power and the state to the sociological imagination.

The Sociological Imagination was written after *The Power Elite* and the latter's politics shaped the former's view of sociology. Mills is remembered perhaps above all for his contribution to 'conflict theory' and the attack on sociological theories that presented society as harmonious and orderly. He identified the 'power elite' in American society, recognised the importance of conflict and was critical of the drift to a bureaucratic mass society in which people were manipulated by the elite through consumerism, by means of which they perpetuated amongst the masses the illusion of freedom and happiness. Mills had a pessimistic social vision in which America was drifting into a quiet totalitarianism. It is no surprise, therefore, that this affected his portrayal of the sociological imagination.

Mills argued that the intersection of personal biography, the social structure, history and politics in late 1950s America was such that ordinary people felt threatened (2000 [1959]: 11). For some, their personal troubles and society's public issues bordered on 'the total threat of panic', for others merely indifference. Overwhelmed by institutions and forces over which it appears they have no control yet in which people are embedded, at the play of big institutions and structures and the mercy of the politics of the powerful nation state, ordinary people feel panic or indifference. Uneasiness and apathy were marks of that time period and the foremost responsibility for sociologists with the proper imagination was: 'to make clear the elements of contemporary uneasiness and indifference ... It is because of this task and these demands, I believe, that ... the sociological imagination [is] our most needed quality of mind' (2000 [1959]: 13). The diagnosis is almost Weberian: increasing rationalisation in society occurs at the expense of human freedom:

> Great and rational organizations – in brief bureaucracies – have increased but the substantive reason of the individual at large has not. Caught in the limited milieux of their everyday lives, ordinary men [and women] often cannot reason about the great structures – rational and irrational – of which their milieux are subordinate parts ... These milieux are themselves increasingly rationalized. Families as well as factories, leisure as well as work, neighbourhoods as well as states – they too tend to become parts of a functionally rational totality. The increasing rationalization of society, the contradiction between such rationality and reason,

the collapse of the assumed coincidence of reason and freedom – these developments lie back of the rise into view of the man who is increasingly uneasy. (2000 [1959]: 168–9)

This diagnosis defines the parameters of the sociological imagination. It perforce requires the sociologist to show the intersection between the private troubles of these ordinary people and public issues in society. It is a sociological imagination that must not be so abstract that it ignores the public issues – the concerns and threats – of real people in real settings brought about by the crises of reason and freedom (2000 [1959]: 173, also see p. 187). It is a view of sociology that recognises that the personal milieux of ordinary people in which they live out their personal biography are shaped by both a history that is made 'behind their backs' (2000 [1959]: 182) and a social structure that has a life independent of their actions and experiences. It is a view of the sociological imagination that carries a political task, not merely to show the limits of human decision-making against the forces of history and the social structure, but to intervene in public affairs. It is a sociology that seeks information 'in order to know what can and what must be structurally changed' (2000 [1959]: 174). One which sees as its purpose the enlargement of human freedom and the procurement of feelings of well-being by collecting information that helps ordinary people to 'formulate the available choices, to argue over them – and then, the opportunity to choose' between them (2000 [1959]: 174). In effect, it is a view of sociology that returns it to its traditional concern with human affairs generally understood, dealing with issues about the future of humanity, with decisions that have to be made to achieve the public good (a particularly Adam Ferguson-like notion) and concern about who makes them.

Conclusion

It is views such as those Mills articulates above that brings me as a sociologist to want to understand sociologically the private troubles and public issues behind the ending of violence in Northern Ireland and South Africa. Conflict, violence and peace are important aspects of human affairs in the two societies that call for analysis sociologically. With Mills, like no other figure, issues like the ending of violence and people's prospects for the good life without the misery of terrorism, communal violence and intimidation are turned into interesting sociological issues which sociologists have a political duty to address.

It may be self-delusion or self-flattery but Mills may well have appreciated his programme being applied to this topic. He saw the value of comparative work, describing it as the most promising line of development for social science in his day (2000 [1959]: 138). He would have seen the ending of violence as just such a private trouble – public issue that the sociological imagination exemplified, since peace for him was a personal value. Or more properly, he valued the rearrangement of human affairs in accordance with the avoidance of conflict (2000 [1959]: 193) and would have seen the ending of acts of communal violence against the person as reflecting the high ideals of human freedom and reason. He was very antiviolence. In one of his letters to his parents during the Second World War (where he avoided the draft because of his high blood pressure), he wrote: 'goddamned bloodbath to no end save misery and mutual death to all civilized values' (Mills and Mills, 2000: 89). The case study therefore seems to represent just what Mills called upon sociologists to do when he wrote the final paragraph in the main text of his book:

> What I am suggesting is that by addressing ourselves to issues and to troubles, and formulating them as problems of social science, we stand the best chance, I believe the only chance, to make reason democratically relevant to human affairs in a free society, and to realize the classic values that underlie the promise of our studies. (2000 [1959]: 194)

What then does a Millsian view of the peace process look like? It is possible to distil the discussion of the sociological imagination into a set of guidelines for examining the peace process in Northern Ireland and South Africa. These are as follows.

- A sociology of the peace process should not offer a grand theory or universal scheme to understand peace processes in general, but is restricted in its applicability to specified cases that exist in real time and space.

- It is necessary to locate the peace process in Northern Ireland and South Africa in its historical past, to establish whether historical factors continue to shape the form and context of the process.
- Any account of the emergence and development of the peace process in these two countries must focus on the intersection between the social structure, individual biographical experience and the political process.
- This means in practice that it is necessary to:

   – Identify social structural conditions, and changes to long established patterns of structural differentiation, which affect the dynamics of conflict and conflict resolution, both internal to each country and internationally.
   – Outline the events and developments within the political process, nationally and internationally, which have altered the political dynamics of the conflict, and accordingly affect the political search for peace.
   – Chart the influence of individual biographical experience on the peace process, by examining: (a) the effect of key individuals who have exploited the moment and whose strategies for change and political mobilisation bear upon the peace process; and (b) the experiences of ordinary people in taken-for-granted settings whose interests and values make them open to mobilisation.

- It is important to show the interaction between local personal milieux and the social structure, by exploring how ordinary people experience the structural and political changes to their local setting, and whose response to which affects the peace process.
- The dialectic between 'personal troubles' and 'public issues' needs to be highlighted, showing how the broad social conflict translates into 'personal troubles', which themselves transform into 'public issues', and vice versa, demonstrating the effect this has on the wish to end violence and the will to make peace.

The following chapters address these issues separately. In Chapter 2 we attempt to show the relevance of history to the peace process in several ways. In particular by identifying the historical factors that explain why violence was so endemic and thus why people may have wished for it to end; and by discussing the legacy of the failure of earlier periods of reform that act as a burden on the present peace process. Chapter 3 examines the intersection of individual biographical experiences with the social structure by looking at the private troubles–public issues around violence and peace. Stress is laid upon the different experiences of violence in various milieux that mediate private troubles–public issues in such a way as to affect levels of support for the peace process. Politics is implanted on this intersection by the focus placed on the mobilisation strategies of key political actors. In Chapter 4 the political dimension of the sociological imagination is given greater attention when we look at the way in which social structural factors and political events, nationally and internationally, combined to impact on the ending of violence. These separate discussions are brought back together in the Conclusion, where there is an overall statement and assessment of the contribution Mills's view of sociology makes to our understanding of the peace process in South Africa and Northern Ireland. We also leave to the Conclusion the answer to the reverse question of what this topic tells us about the efficacy and value of Mills's conception of sociology.

2
The Historical Specificity of the Peace Process

Introduction

When trying to understand the peace process in Northern Ireland and South Africa it is tempting to emphasise exclusively the role of key people, as if they were special charismatic men and women without whom history would not exist. The peace process would thus become reduced to the effects of the biographical experiences and strategies of people like Nelson Mandela, F.W. de Klerk, John Hume, Gerry Adams, David Trimble and the rest. It is more common in the literature for developments in the political process, both nationally and internationally, to be used as the key factor, whether these developments are the move towards politics within former terrorist groups, the involvement of external governments as brokers, or shifts in voting patterns and preferences inside the two countries. Sociologists are inclined to stress exclusively structural factors, such as demographic changes, the emergence of new lines of differentiation and cleavage, and the effects locally of international economic restructuring, amongst others. However, the sociological imagination as Mills understood it requires all three to be considered in the one framework, along with historical factors, and as such it provides a rounded explanation of the peace process. We begin the explanatory process with this chapter.

However, two caveats should be declared at the outset. It is necessary to state that we are dealing with concomitants rather than causes, things that appear together rather than which can be said to have caused each other. This book will not be so bold as to suggest one set of factors is the 'cause' of all the others. Second, we are considering changes that do not work solely in the one direction, for some affect people and parties in negative ways to decrease their will to make peace. This reminds us that we are analysing an uncertain peace process that may well not yet deliver 'peace' as people would perfectly prefer it. Indeed, many of the problems that dog the peace process and which lead ordinary people to query whether peace has broken out despite the ending of large-scale communal violence, reflect the burden of the past on current events and opportunities. This last point reveals the wisdom of Mills's claim that the sociological imagination should be historically grounded. For the topic at hand, Mills's injunction requires us to specify historically the peace processes in Northern Ireland and South Africa. This is what we attempt here.

It is worth reminding readers what this means. Historical specificity requires us to show the *relevance* of history to the current moment. As Mills would have it, this means that it is necessary to locate the peace process in Northern Ireland and South Africa into its historical past as a way of specifying the present. We take this to mean that it is necessary to identify whether historical factors are important in the current process and, if so, to describe what these historical factors are and how they shape the form and context of the process. This is not done for the simple purpose of providing interesting background material and historical padding, though this is valuable enough, but rather to show the relevance of the past for understanding the contemporary situation in resolving violence in the two societies. It cannot be taken for granted that historical factors are important. As Mills wrote, phenomena 'vary in respect to whether or not understanding them requires reference to "historical factors"' (2000 [1959]: 155), and the historical nature of a given phenomenon may only be indirectly relevant to an understanding of its current form. In fact, what we shall demonstrate in this chapter is that the past is highly relevant to the peace process in Northern Ireland and South Africa. History helps us understand sociologically the nature of the social structure in each society, which made violent conflict so endemic. It therefore gives background to the emergence of the peace process itself. History also helps us understand some of the problems that continue to bedevil the peace process in the two societies. History is thus both a legacy, in that its imprint is still evident, and a burden, in that this impact is sometimes very negative on the process of ending violence.

This reflects the paradox of history in both countries. History is relevant to understanding the present, but centuries of conflict in the two societies ensure that this history is contested. History is perceived as partial and partisan. At least two factors ensure that history is always a selective version of the past. For one thing, victors write history not the vanquished. Hence, patterns of power and inequality impact on the way the past is interpreted and represented. Second, people often write the past in such a way as to comment on the present and sometimes even the future – what historians call 'presentism'. Current or future concerns shape the way in which history is approached and past events are often selected because they speak to contemporary issues. Irish history in particular is tenaciously contested because of past and present conflicts that produce competing versions of the past. And what is doubly confusing is that each version claims itself as the true one. This political *use* of history is rampant in Ireland and South Africa, but professional historians are not immune to selectivity. This must be borne in mind by the reader in the following historical references, but it is with history that we must start. In order to begin to show the relevance of history to the current peace process it is necessary first to understand the terms of the conflict.

Religion, race or politics?

Charles Wright Mills would appreciate that ordinary people, living in their personal milieu and immersed in common-sense knowledge, would develop folk models that 'explain' the conflict they are wrapped up in. These explanations are rooted in common sense and are believed to be true because they resonate with people's everyday experiences in their locality. Since ordinary people in Northern Ireland are surrounded by what appears to be objective religious distinctions, and South Africans likewise by racial ones, common sense and folk notions often render Ireland's conflict as a religious war and South Africa's as a racial one. This places the violence as in some way immutable by being rooted in innate biological differences or divinely inspired theological disputes. This points to a parallel between the two conflicts, for they are both absolutist. As I have written extensively elsewhere (Brewer,

1992, 1998; Brewer and Higgins, 1999), racism has a deterministic belief system to reinforce racial divisions based on claims about biological science rooted in the nineteenth century, as does sectarianism on claims about Scripture based in the sixteenth. Both conflicts can be presented as legitimate by being grounded in a deterministic belief system which in its own terms makes claims about inferior Black 'races' or Catholics explicable and justifiable. Moreover, these belief systems are proving to be resistant to change. Despite the passage of time, claims about biological science are still commonsensically used in folk notions of 'race' and anti-Catholicism is still claimed to be Scriptural.

Perhaps the first issue that needs to be addressed therefore is whether Ireland's historical conflict is religious and South Africa's racial or whether this disguises their inherently situational and relativist nature. Jonathan Swift, the well-known eighteenth-century satirist and Irishman, once said that Ireland had enough religion to make its citizens hate, but not enough to make them love one another. W.B. Yeats, another well-known Irishman, penned of the Irish that there is more substance in their enmities than in their love. It appears strange that a society noted in the distant past for the conversion of Europe, a land of saints and scholars, and known today for maintaining very high levels of religiosity against the modern secular trend, should be associated with enmity, hatred and conflict. This is no paradox. Religion, while not the cause of conflict, is the social boundary-marker that demarcates the groups between whom there is conflict. Likewise 'race' in South Africa. The conflict is over the legitimacy of the state and access to its political, economic and cultural resources, but religious affiliation and assumed racial differences define the boundaries of the groups who are in competition. As we shall see shortly, theology took on this role in Ireland and 'race' in South Africa because of the character of their respective colonisation, with the Reformation bringing Protestants as settlers in Ireland and imperial expansion and trade taking Whites to South Africa.

This is not to deny the meaning of these differences to the people who once held them. The religious affiliations of protagonists in Ireland once had strong theological meaning for people involved in the conflict, at the time of the Reformation and since; it still does for a few conservative evangelicals who believe they are fighting the Lord's battle when attacking Catholics. So, too, for the small group of Conservative Afrikaners and White racists in the new South Africa.

Mostly, however, religious affiliation or assumed racial group had little substance in the conflict, such that 'Protestant', 'Catholic', 'White', 'Coloured', 'Asian' and 'African' are merely labels as rough representations and approximations of contrasting positions on the legitimacy of the respective states.

An Irish example can be used to illustrate the social meaning of these terms. Sir Fred Catherwood, a well-known Christian businessman born in Northern Ireland and a former President of the Evangelical Alliance, tells a story of how Protestant women from Belfast were once besieging a British government minister in a local hotel. A spokesman for the minister said to the women that he was 'not much of a Christian, but I know that Christians are meant to love their neighbours and you want to shoot them'. The women replied quickly, 'we're not Christians, we're Protestants' (recounted in Thomson, 1996: 38). That is, Protestantism is understood by protagonists mostly in terms of its political and constitutional stance rather than its theology; the same would be so for Catholicism and for the meaning of belonging to an assumed racial group in South Africa. To Whites under apartheid their 'race' was more about power and privilege than biology. Those sensitive to the political nature of the conflict prefer to use alternative nomenclature to describe these positions, such as Republican/Nationalist for 'Catholic' and Unionist/Loyalist for 'Protestant'. This is a fine distinction and it is easy to see how some people, especially outsiders to the country, can mistakenly perceive the conflict in absolutist terms as a religious or racial one, caused by religion or racial purity, fought to defend religious or biological principles, and contested by people for whom religious affiliation or 'race' is their primary identity.

While it is not unusual for 'race' to retain its saliency in the modern world as a disguise for essentially socio-economic and political conflicts, such as in the American Deep South or Britain's inner cities, it is puzzling that religion still represents the boundaries of groups between whom there is conflict. It is unusual in the modern industrial world for conflict to be socially marked by religion, or at least for religion to remain important after the country has modernised and industrialised, since historically religion was once a powerful source of social cleavage and conflict throughout Europe and North America (on England for the seventeenth century, see Hill, 1971; Millar, 1973; Tumbleson, 1998; and the eighteenth century, see

Colley, 1992; Haydon, 1993; and in the nineteenth century, see Norman, 1968; Arnstein, 1982; Wolffe, 1991; Paz, 1992). The conundrum, then, is why religion in Northern Ireland retains its saliency as the critical social cleavage around which social division coheres. Marx gave us a glimpse of the explanation when he wrote that 'the tradition of the dead generation weighs like a nightmare on the brains of the living'. Put another way, Northern Ireland has not transcended the social divisions of the past. In some ways South Africa has the same failure in being unable in some respects to transcend the old apartheid racial divisions. The contemporary peace process therefore is heavily shaped in its form by history and many of its difficulties lie in the burden the past poses for the present. Historical specificity, in other words, is an essential part of understanding the current phenomenon.

History is relevant to the topic at hand in three ways:

- The violence that the peace process seeks to resolve needs to be located in its historical roots in order to show that the peace process did not appear in a vacuum but was itself grounded in time and space.
- Historical factors, such as the nature and character of early colonisation, the cultural reproduction through history of separate communities, and the tradition and meanings built around various historical events, help to shape the contemporary form and character of the peace process.
- At least in Northern Ireland's case, history has been reified to the point that historical tradition constrains the flexibility of the peace process and limits the opportunities for peace, which goes some way to understanding some of the current difficulties that bedevil the ending of violence.

History is thus both a legacy and a burden; it is something that continues to shape the present and often in negative ways.

The legacy and burden of history

Peacemakers in Northern Ireland and South Africa are confronted with a situation in which ancient religious or racial differences ensured the survival of separate communities. By force of law and culture, through such methods of same-religion or 'race' marriages, residential segregation, distinct cultural organisations and segregated schools, the social structure of the two societies ensured the effortless perpetuation of distinct and separate groups and communities. The various 'races' and religious groups lived in separate areas, they held to separate symbols, they contested rather than shared territory; Belfast and Johannesburg were divided cities whose geography and physical space gave vivid portrayal to the conflict. The law reinforced this under apartheid, as culture did in Northern Ireland. Those working to end the violence thus had two obstacles to overcome: the legacy of historical factors that created violence, conflict and social division, and the impact of a social structure that reproduced separateness.

To begin to understand this intersection of history and the social structure we must begin with colonialism and the particular form in took in the two societies. This is perhaps the single most important historical factor that is relevant to the present peace process and thus is the key to the historical specificity of the present. It might be thought that colonialism is the wrong concept with which to approach dominant groups who have lived in their respective societies for nearly four centuries. But the earlier colonial divisions became solidified into a particular kind of social structure that was effortlessly reproduced over time in a way that continued to make colonial divisions real up to the present day. In Mills's terms, colonialism is highly relevant when historically specifying – understanding – the current period.

Colonialism as a historical factor

It is an important warning that every society needs to be placed in the context of its own history. We will, accordingly, begin the discussion of the two societies separately, but it will be clear that they shared a similar historical path as settler societies. Colonisation took a different form in each society but this was the single overriding historical factor that helped to create the kind of social structure in which there was social division, culturally reproduced over the centuries, and around which communal violence and conflict cohered.

In Northern Ireland's case, violence, conflict and social division have their genesis in the form of social structure created in Ireland by Plantation in the sixteenth century (for general histories of Ireland,

see Foster, 1988; Bardon, 1992; Rafferty, 1994; Ruane and Todd, 1996; Brewer, 1998). Plantation describes the voluntary migration – plantation – of English and Scottish Protestants to Ireland. Plantation transformed Irish society as none of the earlier wars of conquest stretching back to the twelfth century had done, and it initiated different patterns of development on the north-east coast of Ireland – the ancient province of Ulster, which later formed the bulk of what became known after partition as Northern Ireland. Right from the beginning Ulster was different. Protestant planters saw themselves as embattled because Ulster had Catholic rebels who preyed on the Protestant settlers. The planters in Ulster came from Scotland rather than England, bringing with them Presbyterianism and its tendency to separatism, and at the beginning Presbyterians experienced their own exclusion by Anglicans. The Scots outnumbered the English in Ulster by a ratio of five to one in 1640 (Akenson, 1992: 108), and their cultural legacy is manifest today in many facets of popular culture and place name (Gailey, 1975). This separatism extended to having their own systems of social control based around the presbytery, to the point that Hempton and Hill (1992: 16) describe Ulster Presbyterians as a self-contained and regulating community and virtually independent of the wider structures of the English state. As many others have argued, Ulster Presbyterians saw their task as keeping themselves true to the Reformed theological tradition, searching out apostates within their community rather than evangelising amongst Anglicans or Catholics (Miller, 1978; Wallis and Bruce, 1986: 272–3; Hempton and Hill, 1992: 18). At the same time, as Holmes shows (1985: 45, 57), Irish Presbyterians were also prevented from establishing new congregations (Blaney, 1996: 20–40, discusses some early attempts at out-reach by Presbyterians). The notion that they were, in terms of Calvinist theology, God's covenanted 'elect' only reinforced the tendency to separatism, and has continued to do so ever since.

Throughout the eighteenth and nineteenth centuries Ireland essentially remained a Plantation society, in that the social structure created at the time of Plantation became set in stone. Its lines of differentiation remained structured around Protestant–Catholic divisions which came to represent all other lines of cleavage. Gender, 'race' and social class as alternative lines of cultural and social division were all subsumed under the ethno-religious divide that was first established in the sixteenth century. This single cleavage continued to have meaning for the position taken by the two groups towards politics, ownership of economic wealth, social status and cultural practices and beliefs. Protestant and Catholic people thus developed as solidaristic communities in the nineteenth century, which transcended internal fault lines as they confronted the other as a separate community in a zero-sum conflict in which it seemed that their interests were incompatible. This separateness was ideologically and culturally reproduced through religion, residential segregation, different schooling, endogamy and the like, but was also reinforced by economic trends and politics.

The economy of the Protestant-dominated north-east coast (which was to become Northern Ireland) developed apace from the rest of the island because of linen and shipbuilding around Belfast. Belfast was a thriving port, strategically placed to the Clyde ports and Liverpool, linking it to the centres of trade within the British Empire (for a history of Belfast, see Goldring, 1991). Belfast's strategic placement facilitated the expansion of the linen industry in Ulster and the development of associated engineering. The existence of the port led also to the development of shipbuilding as one of the premier industries in the north-east corner of Ireland. Linen and shipbuilding acted as a spur to other industries, such as glassworks, potteries and rope work, and by the mid-nineteenth century Belfast rivalled Liverpool (it was known as the Irish Liverpool) and Manchester (it was also known as the clean Manchester). Protestant industrialists claimed that it was their ascetic ethic that brought such wealth along with God's blessing on Ulster; others referred to the good fortune of a deep port close to the Clyde and the ready supply of landless Catholics dispossessed and forced to work in the factories and mills. Either way, Belfast boomed. Economic developments in the nineteenth century therefore reinforced the division of the island of Ireland into two identities, mutually sculpted in opposition to each other. The industrial heartland was Presbyterian, inclined theologically and socially to cultural separatism; the rest of Ireland was rural, traditional, seen even as backward, but defiantly Catholic. It became increasingly difficult to contain both in the one territory.

This was not an easy realisation, and three Home Rule Bills in the last quarter of the nineteenth century and the beginning of the twentieth, steadfastly opposed by Ulster Protestants, separated the island politically. After the famine in the 1840s, Irish Catholicism, now emancipated from the penal law restrictions placed upon it under the earlier Protestant ascendancy, became more confident culturally and more politically assertive. Cultural self-confidence showed itself in the grand architecture of newly built Catholic churches, designed to impress Protestant neighbours. Political assertiveness revealed itself in a strident and effective nationalism that succeeded in placing the issue of Irish Home Rule on Britain's policy agenda, although it was never successful enough for the House of Commons to vote in support. None the less, the demand for independence divided Protestants and Catholics politically. These social structural strains culminated in a bloody fight for independence following the end of World War I. This eventually developed to the point that the colonial society planted in the sixteenth century was overturned in 1921, at least in 26 of its counties, with the partition of the island into two jurisdictions – a Catholic-dominated Irish Republic and a Protestant-dominated Northern Ireland.

Partition was a journey to nationhood for Northern Irish Catholics which they vigorously contested. Two conflicts persisted after partition. Ulster's territory was contested, since partition split their homeland in half as Catholics saw it, and Catholics in the North felt like second-class citizens compared to Protestants in terms of the privileges, rights and life-chances they experienced. Catholic opposition to both partition and social exclusion brought no easy peace for Protestants, as inequality was challenged militarily by the IRA and politically by constitutional Nationalist parties. Partition may have kept Protestants from a united Ireland dominated by Catholics, but the old inequalities were transported with them into the new territory, at least initially, and with them the ancient conflicts. Catholics were offered citizenship in the new state but on terms that made their Catholicism and Irishness problematic, and their position in the social structure made them second-class citizens. Accordingly, they mostly withheld legitimacy from the state. Between 1922 and 1972, the conflict spilled over into incidents of violence by Irish Republicans demanding a united Ireland and anti-Catholic riots from those loyal to Britain. A sustained period of civil unrest occurred after 1968, when Catholic demands for civil rights were initially rejected and met with force from both the police and Protestant organisations. Violence became endemic.

Hayes and McAllister (2001b: 83) identify three kinds of violence that have been experienced in Northern Ireland's conflict since 1968: direct acts of violence, such as being the victim of a violent event and experiencing intimidation; indirect violence through having a family member, close relative or friend killed or injured; and collective violence, such as exposure to riots, the aftermath of explosions and other crowd events. Republican paramilitary groups, Loyalist equivalents and the security forces account for most of the deaths during this conflict (O'Duffy, 1995), but crowd violence has been perpetrated by both communities (including Loyalist organisations like the Orange Order and Catholic residents' groups). These kinds of violence, known colloquially as 'the Troubles', have been intense. Hayes and McAllister (2001a: 901) report that one in seven of the population has had a direct experience of violence, one in five has had a family member killed or injured and one in four has been caught up in an explosion. Extrapolating these figures to the population size of Britain it would mean 111,000 deaths and 1.4 million people injured, and in US terms it would mean more than the number of those Americans who died in World War II and nine times more than the Americans who died in Vietnam (2001a: 902). In a small country like Northern Ireland this level of violence has polarised Protestant–Catholic relations and reinforced the zero-sum framework within which both communities construct group interests. The violence since 1968 has made traditional hatreds worse and while this level of violence prompted the idea of a peace process, the legacy of hatred is that mistrust and suspicion bedevil it.

In South Africa's case the colonial experience is slightly more complicated but ends up with much the same result (for general histories of South Africa, see Davenport, 1977; Moleah, 1993; Reader, 1998). There were push and pull factors to the scramble for Africa – it was a trading post for the spice sea routes to the East, first permanently colonised by Whites for such purposes in 1652, and it provided an opportunity for settlers to escape war, persecution or poverty in Europe. It came underpinned with Christian intolerance, such that Africans were seen as the personification of evil, being licentious and lazy, and European notions of civilisation, so that Africans were seen as primitive and culturally inferior. The southern tip of Africa, most suited to European settlement, witnessed the first settlers, who were Dutch and led by Jan van Riebeeck, an iconic figure for what has been described popularly as the 'White tribe' of South Africa. The settlement had two needs: land and labour. The first led to wars of conquest and land dispossession over the indigenous population, the second to the use of slave labour from the Dutch East Indies. Slave ownership and a war frontier mentality were central experiences of the lifestyle of the early settlers, who were known as Trekboers, from the Dutch *boer* for farmer and *trek*, meaning to pull (in this case farm wagons) or otherwise known simply as Afrikaners. Raids undertaken by the dispossessed Africans and the need to ensure control over the imported slaves ensured that the Trekboers were organised as military commando communities as much as farm settlements. There were also wars with various indigenous groups adding to this mentality. Their slave-owning mentality proved enduring as well. Black people were allegedly inferior, ripe for dispossession and enslavement. Towards the end of the nineteenth century one Afrikaner author wrote that Black peoples carried the mark of Cain; it was God that had made them, as Scripture says of Cain's descendants, 'drawers of water and hewers of wood'. In effect, they were seen as divinely suited to be servants of the White 'race'. The writer doubted whether Kaffers (the derogatory term for African peoples) had a soul (quoted in Reader, 1998: 481). This did not stop the Boers engaging in furtive miscegenation, from which came what was once called the Coloured community, and many an established Afrikaner family has Black roots as a result. Then the British arrived, who took the Cape Colony from the Dutch, first by force and then treaty.

Britain wanted the Cape merely as a stepping off point for its growing trade routes. It wanted to minimise further development and instructed settlers to keep themselves absolutely separate from Africans, who were, meanwhile, subject to military campaigns by British forces to solidify earlier land dispossession. However, by 1820 Britain had started to plant settlers in the Cape, and they quickly established themselves as traders and merchants rather than farmers. Trade perforce required them to mix with Africans and official policy of disengagement locally was breached by the government's own policy of planting traders as settlers. British traders ventured from the Cape into Natal, with more military campaigns resulting to ensure British control. But the impact of British policy on the Trekboers was as influential as it was on Africans, putting an end, for example, to Afrikaner slave ownership. Given that slavery was supposedly divinely ordained, Afrikaners perceived the British government's abolition of slavery as contrary to God's law and against the natural distinctions of 'race' and religion, and led directly to the Great Trek into what came to be called the Orange Free State and Transvaal. The trek into Natal in the hope of an alliance with the Zulu nation against the British resulted in the massacre of many innocent trekkers (including the murder of Piet Retief, the leader of the Great Trek) and the infamous Battle of Blood River in revenge, which later entered the national identity of Afrikaans speakers. When in their new territories, the Trekboers met their need for labour in the same way they had in the Cape, by the seizure of Africans.

However, gold and diamonds transformed Afrikaans society out of all recognition. As far as Britain was concerned, the discovery of gold and diamonds in Afrikaner-held territory could not have been more unfortunate, so they took it over, annexing first what became known as Griqualand West (for diamonds) and then eventually moving on to the Transvaal (for gold). The discovery of gold and diamonds gave us Cecil Rhodes as a figure in Southern African history, but is more important for the profound social changes that followed the development of mining. While the prospect of wealth inflamed Rhodes's imperial designs, the mines intensified the shortage of labour, leading to the use of convict labour and the development of the migrant labour system. With migrant labour came the mine compounds, the development of African townships (called at this time 'locations') without a sustainable infrastructure as dormitories for workers, and the infamous pass laws. And as the regulation of labour increased, so did the number of offences committed by workers, leading to the development of crude forms of policing (on which see Brewer, 1994) while simultaneously increasing the supply of convict labour. The polarisation of racial attitudes went hand in hand with the implementation of this official racial segregation, which gave twentieth-century apartheid solid roots in British policy in the nineteenth century (a point made by Welsh, 1975).

The development of the South African state in 1910, with the Union of the four provinces as a way of managing co-operatively both Boer and British interests, largely left Africans by as they saw the consolidation of colonial dispossession and inequality turn eventually in 1948 into apartheid. The reconciliation of Boer and Briton under the generalship of Louis Botha and Jan Smuts resulted in a common 'native policy', but the narrower Afrikaner nationalism of people like James Hertzog, which eventually culminated in an election victory for the National Party in 1948, pushed the country's 'race' policies in an even more hardline direction. The Natives' Land Act of 1913 contained the essentials of South Africa's later apartheid social structure, where the dominance of Whites was guaranteed in law and the subjugation of Blacks enforced by might through the militarisation of policing. There was territorial segregation, with Blacks confined to designated areas and permitted into White areas only for employment. Material deprivation coincided with space and territory, as Black areas were under-resourced; education, housing, welfare, health and employment opportunities were all unequally distributed, and political power was in White hands. This was all underpinned by a system of laws and social control that enforced segregation and by a cultural and religious critique that justified inequality and injustice on racial and Scriptural grounds. While the Bible stood alone in Ireland as the justification for anti-Catholicism, biology and the Bible were in collusion to support apartheid in South Africa.

This brought conflict and violence into the centre of the society's social structure. Black political opposition has a proud history of non-violent protest (for histories of Black politics, see Karis and Carter, 1972, 1973, 1977; Gerhart, 1978; Lodge, 1983), but manifestly failed to prevent their gradual exclusion from all representative politics, first for Africans and eventually for all 'non-White' groups. Incidents of collective protest occurred, such as at Sharpeville in 1960, but the banning of the ANC shortly afterwards, and the imprisonment or exile of its leaders, effectively ended political protest in the 1960s, leading to a long quiescent period. Violence remained, however, in specific forms. There was structural violence against Black South Africans in the form of extreme social exclusion, poverty and unemployment; there was state violence reflected in the severe repression of Black people; and there was criminal violence in Black areas which experienced high rates of murder, rape and violent assault as the strains and tensions within apartheid manifested themselves in drunkenness, domestic abuse and violent crime. The political conflict that ignited in South Africa after the 1976 Soweto uprising, which spread rapidly through the urban townships (see Kane-Berman, 1978; Hirson, 1979; Brewer, 1986), gave a different kind of violence. Political violence after 1976 took five forms (see Kane-Berman, 1993; Johnston, 1997: 78): an intermittent and low-intensity campaign of insurgency by Umkhonto we Sizwe, the armed wing of the ANC (on which see Barrell, 1990); collective unrest in the townships to make them ungovernable; violence from the security forces and their surrogates, at first to confront Black protest and subsequently to disrupt transitional negotiations; politically motivated Black-on-Black violence between the ANC and Chief Buthelezi's Inkatha movement, later the Inkatha Freedom Party (on Buthelezi, see Maré and Hamilton, 1987; Mazala, 1988); and random Black-on-Black violence between warlords, criminal gangs, migrants and hostel dwellers which was linked to the pathological conditions of apartheid but also often exploited both by political groups and the security forces and their surrogates. Since the settlement, political violence has transformed into ordinary criminal violence, which has risen dramatically (see Kane-Berman, 1993; du Toit, 2001). For example, between 1983 and 1992, Kane-Berman (1993: 13) estimates there were 15,843 deaths attributable to political violence in South Africa, with two-thirds occurring since 1990, only a few hundred more than 'ordinary' murders in 1991 alone. In the same nine-year period, there were seven times more non-political murders. By 1995, 'ordinary' murders had nearly doubled compared to 1991, and came to more than the total number of deaths caused by political violence in the decade between 1983 and 1994; everyday in South Africa in 1995, 52 people were murdered in violent crime. South Africa's murder rate per 100,000 of population in 1995 was six times higher than that in the US (du Toit, 2001: 47).

Colonialism and conflict

Comparisons would be impossible if societies could be understood only in terms of their own history or if we extenuate the differences in historical detail over the parallels. It is clear that colonialism has been a shared historical experience for both societies and has resulted in significant similarities. It is worth drawing out these parallels and in the process argue against an oversimplified reductionism that blames everything on the British (the best example of this approach with respect to Northern Ireland is Miller, 1998). The interests and policies of the metropolitan core are critical factors, but it is also important to stress the effect of internal divisions within the settler group, the ambiguous links which the settlers had with Britain and the development within settlers of interests independent of the metropolitan core. Moreover, while these colonial divisions remain alive in the present, the colonial seeds were planted so long ago that it becomes difficult to see today's descendants of settlers as anything but integral parts of the society with as much legitimacy to be there as the indigenous population (although this is not to say that colonial inequalities are justified and ought not to be overturned).

Colonialism had created social formations in Northern Ireland and South Africa in which violence was an inherent feature of the social structure. As colonial societies, both societies were dominated by two relationships, an endogenous one between the settlers and 'natives' (used here as a technical term without moral judgement), and an exogenous one between the metropolitan core society and the colony. Colonisation depended on the metropolitan group having local surrogates who could assert control on their behalf. British interests in Ireland, for example, required Protestant control in Ireland and thus Protestant dominance, as they did in pre-Union South Africa with respect to English-speaking Whites compared to Afrikaans speakers and other 'races'. The broad exogenous relationship therefore ensured that, internally, the social structures of Ireland and South Africa were dominated by the endogenous one between settlers and 'natives': 'Protestant'–'Catholic' was the sole relationship of significance in Northern Ireland, matched by 'White'–'non-White' in South Africa. But the broader relationship between settlers and the metropolitan core negatively affected the internal one in many ways. Settlers were caught between 'natives' and the metropolitan society, making them cling tenaciously to that which identified them with it, their Protestantism and political union with Britain in the case of Ireland and notions of whiteness and 'race' in South Africa (on 'settler ideology' in twentieth-century Ulster, see Clayton, 1996, 1998). But the relationship of local settlers with the metropolitan core was always unstable because of the changing position of the colony in the exogenous relationship as the metropolitan society acted in terms of its interests rather than those of the settlers, even to the point of the core occasionally responding to the demands of 'natives' and withdrawing wholehearted support from settlers. British support for Catholic emancipation, Irish Home Rule and its more liberal 'race' policies in South Africa are historical examples of ambivalence towards settlers.

Divisions amongst settlers complicated group relations as members of the dominant group responded differently to the interests of the metropolitan core and the force of pressure of the demands from 'natives' for reform. This resulted in a paradox that dogged settlers. In terms of their relationship with 'natives', some local settlers felt a sense of superiority, ascendancy and dominance, while the colonial relationship with the metropolitan society gave them a sense of grievance, threat and fear. And while some settlers sympathised and identified with 'natives', and used their status with the metropolitan core as an opportunity to put pressure on other sections of the dominant group, they were always in a minority. (This is obvious from what we know of liberal Whites in South Africa, but the small group of Protestant home rulers and nationalists is perhaps less well known, see Loughlin, 1985; Hyndman, 1996.) Superiority and suspicion mixed in equal proportion amongst the majority of Protestants in Ireland and most Whites in South Africa, ensuring that anti-Catholicism structured group relations in Ireland and racism in South Africa.

The alliance between settlers and the metropolitan society was therefore always fraught and fragile as the interests of the British in Ireland and South Africa changed. By the nineteenth century, however, the structure of dominance could not be easily altered without provoking major Protestant or White resistance. In the former case it led to resistance to Irish Home Rule, in the latter to the Great Trek by Afrikaans speakers to avoid Britain's more liberal policies on slavery. However, the metropolitan core did not consider the respective groups equal in their ability to influence British interests and policy, and the respective conflicts had differing capacities to be carried over to Britain to affect the stability of its social structure and political process. In effect, the metropolitan society jettisoned South Africa's Black population when, after the Boer War, it permitted union of the four provinces under White hegemony. Catholic emancipation in Ireland, however, had greater capacity to destabilise Britain itself, and the metropolitan society responded differently to demands for reform in Ireland. Yet Ulster Protestants were culturally and physically closer to Britain than South Africa's White communities (Afrikaners were very distant), and their ability to shape British policy produced the familiar cycle of Catholic protest, British reform and Protestant reaction (emphasised by Ruane and Todd, 1996: 12). Partition of the island of Ireland was the consequence of this cycle.

Yet, ironically, partition reinforced the parallel between the Union of South Africa (founded in 1910) and Northern Ireland (founded in 1922). The metropolitan core had formally withdrawn from involvement in South Africa, and effectively did so in Ulster by leaving Protestants and the Stormont government alone to pursue their own version of the ascendancy. The descendants of settler groups in both countries thus had free rein to control and structure group relations. The Protestant ascendancy under Stormont rule in Northern Ireland, and the tightening of the race laws in South Africa before and after the introduction of apartheid by Afrikaner nationalists, amounted to a return to the deprivations of earlier colonial exploitation and subordination, although it was worse in South Africa (on apartheid, see Posel, 1991; for the debate about how much discrimination there was against Catholics, see Whyte, 1983; Brewer, 1998: 87–127). Both societies became polarised around their zero-sum conflicts, which turned increasingly bitter and violent. The history of both societies is a one of communal violence, political protests and state repression. Forms of 'internal colonialism' like these sat uneasily with the trend of decolonisation in the mid- to late twentieth century, and the pressure for change in the two societies increased rather than lessened as minority groups appealed to international norms and pointed to cases of reform elsewhere. The demand for peace was voiced internally and internationally. Thus, another historical factor relevant to specifying the character of the current peace process is earlier attempts at peacemaking.

Earlier reform processes

The current peace process can be historically specified in two senses. The first is by placing it in the context of social structural conflicts that encouraged the use of violence, which explains why the ending of violence became an important public issue. Second, it can be located historically in the context of earlier failed attempts at reform, since the current peace process has been shaped also by the experience of earlier failures to end violence. The failure of two instances of internal reform can be briefly highlighted – O'Neill's premiership in Northern Ireland and the Bantustan policy of homeland development in South Africa – to show how the legacy of failure acts as a constraint on the present peace process.

Old-style racial segregation, taken further under apartheid after 1948, was comprehensively rethought in the late 1950s with the development of eight Bantustans or African homelands (Africans now became known as Bantu rather than Kaffers). It was no longer supposed to be racial inequality but 'separate development'. It was presented as the creation of separate structures for Africans – schools, hospitals, towns and national homelands – but amounted to an attempt to impose total racial separation. People were forcibly removed to their new national homeland and given permission to enter South Africa (that is, 'White' areas) only for employment and under severe restriction. The introduction of Bantu self-government in the homelands was presented by the National Party government as giving Africans political representation in their own parliaments to compensate them for denying this right in South Africa. Similar motives existed for the development of Bantu education and all the other separate structures in the homelands. An important consequence for the urban townships followed from the transformation of apartheid into 'separate development', for they became seen as transitional areas, dormitories for workers in White areas, and people living there lost their rights to permanent residence. This created severe infrastructural problems and under-resourcing in the townships which are a lasting legacy. Africans were to have rights but could exercise them only in their 'own' areas. That these structures were always underfunded by the government and incapable of delivering the necessary service to the massive numbers of dispossessed Africans removed to the Bantustans or left in the townships ensured that they gave Africans virtually no rights at all. As far as minority group members were concerned, the Bantustan policy amounted to no reform at all. Not unnaturally, the example shows that reform, if it is to be successful, needs to genuinely address the inequalities and life-chances of the dispossessed, or otherwise it fails to address the structural causes of conflict or stop the violence. It led directly to the Sharpeville massacre and built up pressure that exploded in the 1976 uprising and all that followed.

Captain Terence O'Neill, on the other hand, was genuinely committed to introducing reforms that were real. The lesson his failure teaches is that reform failed because other sections of the dominant group would not support change and the paramilitary groups responsible for violence were excluded from the process. O'Neill was a liberal Unionist, representative of the enlightened Protestant tradition, progressive in religion and politics, and someone who wanted to transcend the old style in both. He assumed the post of prime minister in 1963, at a time when other progressive Unionists were calling for modernisation in religion and politics. Younger Unionists demanded change. In 1962 Bob Cooper, then involved with the Young Unionist Council, was critical of the 'ageing tired men' who dominated Ulster politics, who were embedded in the past, 'men who cannot look forward with hope and who are forced to look back with nostalgia' (cited in Brewer, 1998: 103). Lord Brookeborough resigned the following year and O'Neill, as his successor, reflected a new approach, bemoaning the lost opportunities and wasted time of Brookeborough's premiership. It was a tragedy, O'Neill later wrote, that Brookeborough did not try to persuade his 'devoted followers to accept some reforms' (quoted in Bardon, 1992: 621). He once referred to 'small-minded men' who had removed rights from Catholics 'during the first years of Northern Ireland's existence', and who did nothing to make Catholics 'feel wanted or even appreciated'. Reform was O'Neill's watchword: on taking office he said that his task was 'literally to transform Ulster' by bold and imaginative measures. He wished to transform Ulster economically, and introduced economic planning, and politically, by building 'bridges between the two traditions in our community'. Reconciliation was declared policy and Catholics were now part of the one community not alien outsiders to it. The old rhetoric and shibboleths were jettisoned in favour of an inclusive style, which opened up the promise of better Protestant–Catholic relations. The practical reforms did not, unfortunately, match the change in government rhetoric, but even the change in discourse went too far for some Protestants who wanted to hear the old anti-Catholic and Orange shibboleths, and to keep the traditional power and ascendancy they reflected. O'Neill was accused of being a traitor, of 'committing spiritual fornication and adultery with the anti-Christ' (cited in Brewer, 1998: 104), and the Royal Ulster Constabulary (RUC) discovered that the Ulster Volunteer Force (UVF) was plotting to assassinate him. Leading members of the UVF have admitted with hindsight that the resurrection of the organisation in the 1960s was in order to oppose O'Neill rather than the IRA: 'his overthrow was to take the shape of violent incidents in Belfast and Northern Ireland to hype up communal and political tension' (see Gusty Spence, quoted in Garland, 1997: 7; also see Garland, 2001). O'Neill was vilified mercilessly by the Rev. Ian Paisley, whose anti-Catholicism led him to form his own political party (Democratic Unionist Party) in opposition to liberal O'Neillism and his own church in opposition to liberal Protestantism (the Free Presbyterian Church), since both supposedly supped with the antichrist. The old sectarian and anti-Catholic forces within Protestantism and Unionism ruled the day, leaving O'Neill to lament on his resignation in 1969: 'I have tried to break the chains of ancient hatreds. I have been unable to realise [what] I had sought to achieve ... but one day these things will and must be achieved' (O'Neill, 1969: 200).

What is relevant about these historical references is that the reform attempts rebounded as minority group protests continued (for example, the Sharpeville protests in South Africa in 1960 and the civil rights movement in Northern Ireland) and the resistance of some sections of the dominant group to change was enhanced. This gave the push to conservative opposition in Northern Ireland (such as the development of Paisleyism and the Loyalist paramilitary organisations) and increased suppression of the minority (such as the long period of suppression and quiescence in South Africa after Sharpeville). This was broken in South Africa only in 1976 by the Soweto uprising. In Northern Ireland's case, it was the IRA who inherited the mantle after the failure of the civil rights movement in 1968–9 with their subsequent prolonged terrorist campaign. Such wide-scale communal violence intensified the internal pressure for change in both societies. This internal pressure was reinforced by increased international interest and, in Ulster's case, the renewed attention of the metropolitan society. (However, international focus was always more directed on South Africa because Ulster was seen as an internal UK problem and its conflicts, when they exploded in 1968–9, took much of the world by surprise.) However, given the zero-sum nature of these conflicts, inasmuch as the reform process responded to minority group violence, the reluctance of the dominant group to engage in a peace process was fed lest they be seen to be giving in to bullying. The faltering fortunes of early peace processes were much the same in both places because of this.

After the 1976 Soweto uprising in South Africa, the new Botha government introduced several reform packages from 1978 onwards, covering township amenities and rights, local government, policing and economic access by Black groups, amongst others. Attempts were made to address the difficult position of urban Africans, who had been the ones in revolt but whose passivity was essential for continued labour supply. For example, limited sections of the population were given permanent residence rights in the townships, the urban townships were given local councils to help in their administration, some of the restrictions on Black workers in urban areas were lifted, and new police forces composed of local people were established in the townships. This essentially tinkered with the peripherals of apartheid but did nothing to address White political control of the state and monopoly of its mechanisms of force. Piecemeal reform of the peripherals none the less encouraged the oppressed population to believe they could obtain more and set in train various changes that encouraged Black politics (see Brewer, 1986), and by the mid-1980s the state had lost control of the townships. The pace and direction of reform did not meet Black demands and communal violence took the country into the mire. It was this that de Klerk inherited when P.W. Botha resigned and which shaped the peace settlement in South Africa (for a chronology of the negotiations between 1990 and the first non-racial election of 1994 see Mattes, 1994; Sparks, 1995).

In Northern Ireland's case, early peace processes were essentially externally led, imposed by the metropolitan society who wanted to be rid of the problem of terrorism and the related burdens it imposed on Britain, including economic costs. The metropolitan core responded to 'the Troubles' by immediate reform of the RUC through the Hunt Report, and by taking back some powers of the Unionist-dominated councils in housing allocation, all of which eventually culminated in 1972 in the abolition of Stormont and the introduction of Direct Rule. Top-level institutional rearrangements took place to try to address the structural inequalities and injustices in Northern Ireland through the 1973 Sunningdale Agreement which introduced limited power-sharing, although violent public opposition from Protestants led rapidly to its collapse. Government-led reform attempts were tried and failed again with the 1985 Anglo-Irish Agreement, which met with vociferous Protestant opposition. Even though the paramilitary groups responsible for much of the violence were excluded from the process, the dominant group remained intransigent. The failure of significant sections of the settler group to be taken along with external-led initiatives inevitably doomed them to failure. Meanwhile, Republicans were moving forward from a reliance on physical force only very slowly. (On the IRA's military strategies and its tangential relationship to politics, see Smith, 1995.) Sinn Féin's early move in the 1980s was to combine the armalite and ballot box in a dual strategy, supported by Gerry Adams and Martin McGuinness, key members of the IRA Army Council, as a result of massive political support following the hunger strikes. It is reasonable to argue that the hunger strikes are the equivalent to the 1976 Soweto uprising in representing that moment of epiphany when people were converted to politics. Only slowly and incrementally was this transformed in Northern Ireland into an exclusively political strategy, since it took some time for Sinn Féin to see that the logic of the ballot box is incompatible with that of the armalite and that political violence tended to limit electoral progress.

The minority group in Northern Ireland lacked the strategic resources for change that Black South Africans possessed. The minority groups in South Africa were aided by significant external intervention, they could push the agenda rapidly because of the sheer scale of their numbers and their strategic location in the economy, and the spread of violence geographically was immense. Catholics in Northern Ireland had none of this. They were fewer in number, violence was more localised and was not supported by mainstream Catholic opinion. Moreover, Britain's reform measures in Northern Ireland led to violent backlashes by Loyalists and intensified the suspicions of other sections of Unionism. There was no equivalent brake on the momentum for reform in South Africa once the state decided to initiate a more genuine peace process. In Northern Ireland conversely, while inter-communal violence intensified the drive and commitment amongst the metropolitan core for a peaceful resolution, it delayed support for the idea of peace amongst the dominant group, slowing the emergence of the peace process compared to South Africa, making it externally led and much more fragile and problematic. The 1985 Anglo-Irish Agreement exemplified the external character of the peace process in Northern Ireland, for the metropolitan society involved another (though integrally involved) state rather than local Unionists. The later Downing Street Declaration in 1993 continued the exclusion of local Protestants from the process, since the British government simply anticipated their likely opposition. Wilford (1999) argues that one of the key elements missing in earlier reforms has been the ability of Unionist political elites to deliver the consent of their constituency for a political accommodation. Indeed, getting local Protestants on board the peace process remains one of the key problems which distinguishes the two countries, since most White South Africans are ahead of Ulster Unionists in wanting peace rather than just an end to violence.

A consideration of the failure of earlier processes of reform to end the violence has relevance to specifying the present peace process. This historical material indicates that peace processes which are to work in the way they have not in the past, require the following:

- that the process produces proposed reforms that make a genuine attempt to address the structural causes of conflict;
- that these measures include policies to address past inequalities, injustices and dispossession as well as mechanisms for ending the violence;
- that the dominant group feels able to buy into the process and not thwart it so that their political elites are able to deliver support;
- that the dominant group is willing to compromise on its former dominance;
- that the leading paramilitary groups are included in the process;
- that the minority group(s) is able to accept a second best solution that goes some way to meet the interests of the dominant group.

Conclusion

History is highly relevant to understanding – specifying, as Mills would say – the parameters of the present peace process in South Africa and Northern Ireland. Historical factors help us locate the process by showing how conflict and division were integral to each society's social structure. While this gave impetus to peace as a public issue, peace was a prisoner of the past. While an historical analysis of the failure of peace processes in the past is able to show us what features a peace settlement must have in order to work, violence, conflict and division were endemic to each society's social structure, and the history of conflict and violence in each society became a legacy that burdened the willingness of groups down the ages to compromise and change. History supplies a litany of failed attempts at reform which have hardened group attitudes, solidified positions and intensified the violence. History on its own, however, was not Mills's concern. It is important that sociology specifies the link between history and social structure. Significantly in this regard, planters of whatever religious or racial hue culturally reproduced a colonial society down the centuries. The law upheld what culture created, so that each society continued to feel the imprint of colonialism upon its social structure well after the initial settlement. This was because the original colonial divisions based around 'race' or religion continued to structure the lines of differentiation into the modern advanced industrial stage and as anti-Catholicism or racism reinforced group relations. Twentieth-century group relations were still very much locked in the seventeenth century. And as such, the patterns of inequality, dispossession, injustice and expropriation were long established, creating a history of violence and conflict in each society which itself becomes a relevant factor in historically specifying the present moment.

The history of violence in Northern Ireland and South Africa leaves two legacies that burden the current peace process. First, it has given us several failed attempts at reform which only encourage cynicism and indifference amongst many ordinary people who claim to have seen it all before. Enthusiasm for peace at the grassroots can be dampened, even damaged, as a result of the cynicism of those people who present the current process as allegedly no more than similar ventures in the past that either did not work or were supposedly manifestly unfair to one group or another. Second, the history of conflict has become reified. Past violence, and its forms of resistance, struggle and suffering, have become represented in a tradition of principles, symbols and iconography which define what each group means by its history of struggle or resistance. These symbols are rooted in, as some people would see it, the honourable sacrifice (the blood of the martyrs as Ian Paisley puts it vividly) of those who have fought on behalf of the group. These symbols limit flexibility in the peace process because they are principles not easily jettisoned without peacemakers being accused of having forgotten all that history supposedly means to the people involved in or who suffered through the violence. People have made history into a shibboleth, so that all the personal biographical experiences represented by it and captured in historical events in effect flow back and impact upon the peace process.

By concluding the discussion of the historical specificity of the peace process in such negative ways, it might reasonably be asked why the peace process in both countries has proceeded so far. Having in one sense dispatched history by demonstrating its relevance, we now must look for the answer to the intersection of the three other dimensions of the sociological imagination. We begin where Mills says sociology should start: the connection between individual biographical experience and the social structure.

3
Individual Biographical Experiences and Peace

Introduction

The problem with Mills's terminology on the whole is not that it is given modern meaning improperly as current sociological concepts are read backwards to give Mills's words meanings he did not intend. It is the reverse: he uses different and more commonplace terminology to refer to modern-day sociological ideas. This is perhaps most apparent with respect to his many references to the individual biographical experiences of ordinary people in their personal milieux. It is justifiable to read this as prosaic references to what sociologists call 'agency' by people in their everyday life setting, a setting that Schutz and the social phenomenologists call people's common-sense lifeworld. Agency does not simply refer to activity – riding a bicycle – but to action that is oriented to another, what Weber called social action, such as the cyclist taking action to avoid hitting real or imagined pedestrians, other cyclists or drivers. Action oriented to another involves the agent in applying their common-sense knowledge to guide the course of the interaction. Common-sense knowledge is that body of mutual knowledge, as Giddens calls it, which is shared by people and used by them to accomplish their everyday life activities. Agency is thus social action that has meaning attached to it based upon the agent's common-sense knowledge about all the circumstances surrounding the act, the other people involved and the common sense assumptions and mutual knowledge that bear upon the act and its setting.

'Individual biographical experience' (or agency) and 'personal milieu' (or common-sense lifeworld) were inseparable terms for Mills.

Agency always occurs in a locally bounded context for it is this milieu that gives meaning to the common-sense mutual knowledge actors possess and which they apply when acting in the social and natural worlds. As Schutz once said, the 'natural attitude' of people is to use the common sense knowledge that is grounded in their immediate locality and bounded social world as the first 'realm of relevance' to apply when framing their own agency and understanding the agency of others. It is not scientific knowledge that ordinary people use to understand and act in the world in the first instance, but common-sense knowledge that is bounded and contextualised to their everyday life milieu; or, at least, it is scientific knowledge only as filtered through common sense.

When Mills makes reference to individual biography and people's personal milieu, therefore, he is describing key sociological ideas using ordinary terminology: namely, that ordinary people live within a physically and culturally bounded space that helps to shape and give meaning to the common-sense knowledge they use to understand all the circumstances surrounding their action and that of others in this setting or beyond it. Some of this knowledge is tacit and incapable of being articulated, so that not all actors are able to be discursive and account for their agency should they need to. Some is not agency at all since the actors are not knowledgeable ones, in that their actions are not conscious or can be medicalised through illness that strips it of voluntarism. Mostly, however, ordinary people are knowledgeable actors capable of voluntaristic action. That is, they are in possession of the common-sense knowledge that enables them to act in routinised and taken-for-granted ways that are understandable to others in the same physical and cultural space and to all those others beyond it who have familiarity with that milieu (although none of this implies we must take actors' accounts unproblematically).

We know that Mills did not see this everyday lifeworld as unique to the individual. He was not a solipsist, in which the only thing real or knowable is the individual self. Milieux are personal to individuals but they are also social worlds in microcosm. People's biographical experiences may be different, their sets of personal problems, crises and troubles may be unique, but there are several reasons why their personal world is social. For one thing, Mills saw personal milieux as micro-worlds shared with others based upon people's mutual knowledge, which meant that people tended to understand the world in similar ways and act in ways meaningful and comprehensible to others. Second, people's individual biographical experiences show the impact of others throughout history, as well as the imprint of politics and contemporary social structure. Mills's conception of the sociological imagination requires that the habits, knowledge, actions, concerns and troubles that comprise the individual's biography of experiences show the effect of social structural forces and conditions, history and political events. Methodological individualism or solipsism would deny Mills the chance of addressing the individual–society link (now called the agency–structure duality), and prevent him from broadening sociology's domain by the inclusion of history and politics, all things dear to his perspective on the sociological imagination.

Conversely, Mills did not want to reduce individuals to 'personality systems' within a social world that rendered them automata or cultural dopes. This is why his starting point was with the individual, their personal biographical experiences and the lifeworld or milieu in which they lived their ordinary lives. It was a starting point at the opposite end to Talcott Parsons's mammoth treatise *The Social System* (1951). However, Mills was not a social interactionist theorist either, ideas also in common currency at this time through the writings of Herbert Blumer. He would have been familiar with the work of the symbolic interactionists – his PhD thesis was on the American pragmatists, the sociological dimensions of which Blumer also wrestled with – and the writings of the Chicago School did not feature in his denigration of 'narrow sociology'. Indeed, Blumer was one of the referees he nominated on his successful grant application to Guggenheim (see letter in Mills and Mills, 2000: 78) and had been one of the authors used by Mills to comment on *The Sociological Imagination* in draft form. Despite this, Mills would not have seen the description and charting of people's lifeworlds and personal biographical meanings as the end product for sociology, as do various versions of social interactionism. What is important for Mills is that individuals and their personal milieux and biographical experiences intersect with and are impacted by the social structure. It is this, after all, that makes his work relevant to the agency–structure debate. However, as we have stressed throughout, Mills extends the intersection to include history and politics as well. So he is concerned with the way in which people's individual biographical experiences and milieux in turn reflect upon and shape history, society and political events.

We have seen the way in which historical factors can impact on people's personal biographical experiences by charting the way in which colonialism as one historical factor affected people's personal troubles in Northern Ireland and South Africa, giving a legacy of inequality, discrimination, conflict and violence that were critical public issues that the state and citizenry had to address, giving impetus to the search for peace as a public issue. We have also seen the flow-back, that is, how people have shaped history in a way that impacts back on their biographical experiences. In Northern Ireland's case, people have reified history, making these historical events into a structure of myths, symbols and experiences of suffering and resistance that constrains the peace process. This chapter will consider another of the links Mills saw as central to the sociological imagination, the interface of individuals and the social structure, at least as Mills understood it. While the connection between personal biography and the social structure manifests itself in myriad ways, as later agency–structure theorists show, Mills particularly stressed the way in which personal troubles and public issues rebounded to highlight people's embeddedness in society but also society's embeddedness in the small lives of ordinary people. As we saw, he took this emphasis because of his concern to return sociology to an engagement with important issues in public affairs. This chapter puts these ideas into practice by addressing the connection between personal troubles and public issues in the contemporary peace process in South Africa and Northern Ireland.

The chapter will illustrate the interaction between personal milieux, individual biographical experience and the social structure in four ways. First, it will focus on what Mills considered the main mediation between individuals and society, the dialectic between personal troubles and public issues, and will look at how this dialectic affected the peace process in both societies in positive and negative ways. That peace as a public issue is premised on the violence it seeks to resolve is perhaps prosaic: the violent social conflict was experienced as personal troubles by ordinary people which transformed into public issues that gave the push to the peace process. However, in exploring the other ways in which milieu, individual biography and the social structure are related, we will see that the dialectic is much more complicated than this. The second exemplification of the intersection between milieu, individual biography and social structure that is addressed here is the exploration of how violence at the level of the social structure was experienced quite differently in terms of people's individual biographical troubles. It is different experiences of violence that largely influence some groups to consider peace as a process to end violence rather than to achieve more encompassing ideals around justice and equality. Third, it will become apparent that it is not just communal violence that is a private trouble–public issue, but also peace itself. While the continuance of violence threatens the ontological security and well-being of ordinary people, peace comes to some people at such a price that the peace process itself provokes insecurity and alarm, making peace itself a problematic public issue that in turn impacts on people's private troubles. A distinction will also be made between the individual biographical experiences of 'ordinary people' and 'key players', the men and women of genius as Berlin called them, who translate and mediate the connection between private troubles and public issues. Therefore, the final dimension addressed here is the mobilisation strategies of key individuals whose biographical experiences have enabled them to exploit the moment in a way that rebounds with the biographical experiences of those they mobilise to impact on support for, or opposition to, the peace process. By such means we also begin to address the fourth dimension to the sociological imagination, by illustrating the way in which politics intersects with individual biography and the social structure, something taken further in Chapter 4.

Personal troubles and public issues

Living as they do in their personal milieux, ordinary people do not readily grasp the broad events taking place around them and the structural forces at play affecting their lives. This applies as much to communal violence as the peace process itself. Ordinary people respond to events – whether incidents of atrocity and violence or peacemaking activities – only as they impinge on their taken-for-granted local milieu. This milieu is a comfortable, natural state in which actors engage in familiar and routine activities and develop a common-sense mutual knowledge that is their working knowledge for living. Schutz calls this people's 'natural attitude', Giddens people's sense of 'ontological security'. Giddens (1996) sees disruptions of ontological security as a chronic feature of modernity. So, it should be recalled, did Mills, whose analysis of the United States in the 1950s, in *The Power Elite*, portrayed people struggling between anxiety and apathy, indifference and insecurity. But living amidst communal violence, with centuries-old histories of enmity, seems a most severe disruption to feelings of security and well-being.

Yet one of the striking features of the violence in Northern Ireland and South Africa for so long was that it was contained geographically to specific milieux (mostly to the townships in South Africa's case and the working-class districts in Northern Ireland), allowing people in other milieux to distance themselves from it. This reduced the impact of communal violence on their personal troubles and weakened its potential disruption of their ontological security. While violence was experienced differently depending on local milieux, even in areas of high violence people tried to distance themselves from it. The sporadic nature of the violence ensured that even in milieux of high violence, many residents found ways of routinising and living with it (for a study of how policemen and women in the RUC routinized the danger, see Brewer, 1991b): they had no choice if they were to remain living in that milieu and if everyday life routines were to continue. Even in the worst times of widespread civil unrest in areas of high violence, such as the struggles to make the townships in South Africa ungovernable during the mid-1980s or during the hunger strikes in Northern Ireland at the beginning of the same decade, ordinary people tried to maintain a semblance of routine to enable them to continue their 'small' ordinary lives. People tried to get to work and children to school. Barricades were removed to permit workers to earn wages and then put back again at night; shopping had to be done and businesses tried to keep open. Hospitals, schools, unemployment offices continued to function. This is but one example of how people in milieux of high violence, like those living elsewhere, tried to normalise the violence, if only to stop themselves going mad. None the less we know that alcoholism, depression and mental illness, the usual signs of social stress, were higher in areas of intense violence, showing that it remained as a personal trouble irrespective of attempts to reduce its ontological effects.

Violence occasionally spilled out from areas of high conflict in the form of terrorist attacks, assassinations and bomb outrages in 'softer' areas – familiar more to Northern Ireland than South Africa, but present in the latter none the less. These remained powerful sources of ontological insecurity for those in 'soft' areas affected by the deaths, injuries and economic damage, but these personal troubles did not affect everyone and the attacks were soon forgotten by all those left untouched by them. (This is something that the victims or their relatives readily complain about in Northern Ireland, and was obvious amongst some people who gave evidence before South Africa's Truth and Reconciliation Commission; see Truth and Reconciliation Commission, 1998.) This explains why few commentators on both societies ever saw them as worst-case scenarios, no matter how grim the violence was at times. This led occasionally to the ironic suggestion that the violence would have to get worse before people would want peace – ironic because the killings were thought by some to have to increase before we would want them to cease. However, even in milieux where the violence was not high, it always remained a backdrop. The militarisation of law and order was obvious even behind the blinkers, restrictions on daily life imposed by the violence were experienced irrespective of local milieux, and normal social interaction brought people into normal dealings with the 'threatening other' that could be fearful. Above all, the personal troubles of those directly affected by violence or those living in milieux where violence was high made the violence a public issue. While many ordinary people, in an attempt to prevent their ontological security being affected too much by communal violence, may well have felt that it took place elsewhere and involved mainly other people than themselves, the personal troubles of those directly affected did become public issues to impact on everyone who was exposed to the public media that articulated these private troubles–public issues. Some people tried to limit even that exposure. (For example, by avoiding listening to the local news, or any kind of news, and selecting routes to work or to the shops that avoided going near areas where the evidence of conflict would penetrate.) This explains the paradox of the two places. Public and media attention focused on the violence – and much of it was outrageous and barbaric and could not be ignored – so that it dominated the public policy agenda, yet many ordinary people living through it were extolling the virtues of their respective society and declaring that it was not as bad as the public image: something outsiders could scarcely credit. This also helps to explain why people for whom peace brings a cost can claim – again with incredulity as outsiders see it – that the situation was better *before* the peace process began. Anti-Agreement Ulster Unionists and the poor South African Whites who are particularly affected by the explosion of ordinary crime and job competition, best represent those who believe peace has made the situation worse precisely because they are amongst those people relatively unaffected directly by the violence before. (Adam, van syl Slabbert and Moodley, 1997: 213, argue that these sorts of people also have a vested interest in opposing reform because they are the ones most likely to be threatened by the advancement of opposing groups.) Individual biographical experiences do not make this true for everyone, however. Jeffrey Donaldson, for example, one of the fiercest and most dangerous Unionist critics of the Northern Irish peace process, often explains his opposition to power-sharing with Sinn Féin because of the murder of family members.

Normalisation of the violence as a coping mechanism is not therefore incompatible with the idea that communal violence endangered virtually everyone's feelings of ontological security. It was this that made the ending of violence a sufficient public issue to encourage the development of the peace process. However, the mediation or intersection of personal troubles (individual biography) and public issues (social structure) is much more complex than this. The wish for the violence to stop – something that is likely to have been ubiquitous throughout the centuries for most people in both societies – is different from the will to make compromises, to barter agreements and opt for the second-best preferences that peace processes usually demand. The biographical experiences of ordinary people can be such that what is translated into a public issue is merely the demand for the violence to end rather than for an encompassing peace process to be made to start and work. While peace is clearly premised on the cessation of killings, it requires more than that. It requires that injustice, inequality, power-sharing and institutional reform become public issues as well as violence and the biographical experiences and troubles of victims. As Wolsterstorff observed in relation to 'shalom', peace incorporates well-being and a sense of flourishing, and narrow notions of peace can misunderstand the range of public issues that peace processes need to address around the question of justice, such as considerations of social redistribution, the introduction or restoration of equality and fairness in the allocation of scarce resources, and the opening up of life-chance opportunities that were once closed to some groups or people. At least two factors seem to be important in encouraging ordinary people to move beyond wanting an end to violence and towards developing a more embracing will for peace: the ways in which violence is experienced as a personal trouble; and the ways in which violence as a personal trouble is translated into a public issue.

We will leave until the next chapter the all-important question of why the translation of personal troubles into public issues should have led to a more sustained peace process now rather than in the past. In the next section we show how violence was experienced sufficiently differently by various groups in the two societies to affect the mobilisation of support for peace as a public issue. Violence was a personal trouble in Mills's terms, but people's different biographical experiences of it resulted in some of them giving a priority to stopping the killings, and others to place emphasis on a fuller embrace of peace involving reconciliation, forgiveness, compromise and a willingness to accept second-best preferences. This has affected the way in which peace has been translated into a public issue, particularly for members of those groups who have been subject to suffering the most violence.

Violence as a personal trouble and peace as a public issue

In applying the sociological imagination to the topic at hand, it is highly relevant that the pattern of violence was different in South Africa compared to Northern Ireland. Violence impacted differently on the biographical experiences of ordinary people in the two societies, leaving a lasting legacy for their respective peace processes and to some significant contrasts in the progress of the process in the two places. In effect, differences in milieux between the two societies gave contrasting biographical experiences for their citizens. Different patterns of violence caused contrasting kinds of personal troubles, which transformed the violence into different kinds of public issues in the two societies. In particular, in Northern Ireland the biographical experience of violence has tended to result in the majority of Protestants not yet being able to move to embrace peace fully in the way that most White South Africans have done. This impacts on the mobilisation of support for peace as a public issue, making Northern Ireland's peace process much more fragile.

As Sandy Johnston (1997: 72) has argued persuasively, public issues in the peace process like disarmament and demobilisation of paramilitary groups, amnesty for protagonists and the incorporation of former protagonists into the police (Northern Ireland) or Army (South Africa), have been affected by the various patterns of violence in the two places. Leaving aside for the moment the violence and deaths for which the security forces are responsible, communal violence in Northern Ireland took two forms: terrorist bomb attacks, murders and intimidation by the paramilitary organisations on both sides, and crowd violence on the streets of both communities. In South Africa, the townships erupted, but milieux where Whites lived were immune because the guerrilla organisations played a relatively small role in South Africa's conflagration, and acts of terrorism even less (see Brewer, 1986: 106–56). In Mills's terminology, the biographical experiences of White South Africans were not shaped negatively by ANC violence, resulting in less demonisation of them than of the IRA or Sinn Féin by Protestants in Northern Ireland. The Afrikaner Nationalist government's relentless demonisation of the ANC was not matched by the experience of violence amongst most White South Africans, who did not come to feel on strict military grounds that the ANC were a threat. It tended to play a bigger part in the political calculations of Whites and the ANC left no legacy militarily of White victims. The bulk of casualties were Black in intra-Black political violence; indeed, the government's strategy was to confuse the perception of apartheid's racial violence by provoking political violence amongst Black groups to present it as Black-on-Black as a way of diminishing their overall responsibility for the structural causes of violence. The White government ideologically constructed the ANC's victims as other Black South Africans. Not surprisingly, therefore, White perceptions of the ANC subsequently have not been negatively affected by their biographical experience of violence and the relative insulation of the White community from the immediate effects of political violence made it easier to deliver support for the peace process amongst the majority of the White electorate. As Johnston (1997: 84) graphically puts it, de Klerk may have taken White political fears with him into the peace process, but he did not carry the dead weight of thousands or even hundreds of White victims. This affected the sorts of public issues that the violence was translated into, making it easier for White South Africans to accept that the guerrillas' arms need not be decommissioned, effectively removing this as a public issue to potentially threaten the peace process. It also made it easier to believe that the military wing of the ANC did not pose a continued military threat and thus made Whites more ready to accept the incorporation of former guerrillas into the then South African Defence Force.

How different the situation is in Northern Ireland. The contrasting biographical experience of Northern Irish Protestants has given them sets of personal troubles that have made decommissioning, for example, a public issue that has bedevilled the peace process in Northern Ireland. Protestants have seen themselves at the brunt of Republican violence in urban milieux, through the bombing of the city centres of largely Protestant towns and other economic targets owned largely by Protestants, and subject to processes of ethnic cleansing in rural milieux through selective assassinations of Protestant farmers and small businessmen. A large number of studies on the geography of violence have shown its concentration in urban milieux (for example, see Poole, 1983, 1993), so the fear of ethnic cleansing in rural areas is symbolically real to Protestants rather than actually so, and research on the religious background of people who self-report their exposure to various types violence shows that Catholics tend to have suffered more (Hayes and McAllister, 2001a: 908–10). None the less, absolute levels of exposure to violence amongst Protestants remain very high given the intensity of the violence in such a small country.

While the IRA draws a distinction between ordinary Protestants and 'legitimate' targets, which are seen as representatives of the British state, the way Protestants define their identity makes this difficult for them to grasp. This is a distinction difficult to absorb when Ulster Protestant identity is so wrapped up with the cultural and political link to Britain (O'Malley, 2001: 280 makes the point that one of the key differences between Northern Ireland and South Africa is that national identity is the source of division in the former but is absent in the latter, something that made the nation-building project much easier in the new South Africa). IRA violence against so-called 'legitimate' targets has been experienced by ordinary Protestants as an attempt to cleanse Protestant witness from the island of Ireland. This might seem fanciful, and certainly is so in the language of extreme Loyalists and Protestant fundamentalists who talk of a Protestant holocaust, but so interconnected is Protestant identity with Britishness (see Brewer, 1998), that the IRA's anti-Britishness easily blends into anti-Protestantism as ordinary Protestants perceive it. That Republicanism believes it can make this fine distinction is irrelevant to them. Accordingly, the biographical experience of violence amongst most Protestants means that they genuinely fear that the violence may not be at an end – why otherwise, they say, does the IRA refuse to decommission? This translates into several public issues, making, for example, decommissioning, amnesties, prisoner releases and power-sharing with Sinn Féin highly contentious and controversial for most Protestants. (On Protestant opposition to prisoner releases, see von Tangen Page, 2000.) These public issues, which are so destabilising for the peace process, are rooted in the way violence has been experienced by Protestants in the North, giving most Protestants sets of personal troubles which, when translated into public issues, make the peace process fragile.

This fragility reflects in the way in which peace as a social virtue is mobilised as a public issue in Northern Ireland. Significantly in turn, the manner of this translation of violence into a public issue helps to reproduce and reinforce the fragility of the peace process. Violence as a personal trouble gets translated into a public issue by such mechanisms as media campaigns against atrocities and suspected perpetrators, by victim support groups and the peace initiatives built around specific incidents and outrages, the mobilisation undertaken by victims' families through pressure on political groups, governments and other political actors, by the broader attention given to violence and peace in the political process and in society generally through key cultural groups, such as the churches, women's groups and the like, and by public rallies and marches against violence and in support of peace. (For a discussion of peacemaking initiatives in Northern Ireland see Brewer, Bishop and Higgins, 2001; also see Knox and Quirk, 2000.) The most relevant point in this context is that while there is overwhelming consensus in wanting the violence to stop, there is no agreement on what lies next. Thus, while public rallies against an atrocity or act of sectarian violence bring thousands out in protest, the negotiated settlement known as the Good Friday Agreement is rapidly losing support among Protestants as they fear it may not deliver the end of violence. Public issues are being made of alleged IRA involvement in street protests that breach its ceasefire, of the alleged involvement of Sinn Féin politicians in acts of violence long ago, of the IRA's Catholic victims known as the 'disappeared', and of the experiences of victimhood amongst members of the dominant group. Some victim support groups, for example, are being hijacked by anti-Agreement Unionists and are being mobilised in such a way as to ensure that their experiences of victimhood are made into public issues used as obstacles to a settlement because the peace process allegedly dishonours their sacrifice or that of their murdered relative. The point being made here is that different biographical experiences of violence as a personal trouble can negatively affect the way in which peace is mobilised as a public issue, making the ending of violence the priority rather than peace itself.

There is another difference in the pattern of violence between the two societies that translates into contrasting public issues. Northern Ireland's conflict is such that all can assume the status of victim – Catholics victim of four centuries of social exclusion, Protestants and Catholics of thirty years of terrorism – and all claim the other as perpetrator (for a collection of personal accounts of victimhood in Northern Ireland, see Smyth and Fay, 2000; these parallel the South African atrocity stories in the Truth and Reconciliation Commission, 1998). Leaving aside the number of Protestant spokespeople who are now beginning to make a public issue of the claim that Catholics never experienced social exclusion in the past – an entirely indefensible argument – those Protestants who have yet to fully embrace peace tend to prioritise their own experiences of victimhood (on victimhood in Northern Ireland, see Smyth, 2000; Morrissey and Smyth, 2001). Jim Wallis, Head of the Sojourners movement in the United States, once said in a speech in Belfast that victims should not let the horror of their own suffering silence them to the pain of others and that victims also need to be accountable for their actions. Yet to hear some Unionists speak, it is as if only Protestants died and then solely at the hands of the IRA. By including the deaths of members of the security forces, Hayes and McAllister (2001a: 903–4) can rightly argue that the IRA have been responsible for most deaths in 'the Troubles', and while members of local security forces would have been overwhelmingly Protestant, and *seen* as Protestant by most members of the dominant community, who felt the police and Ulster

Defence Regiment were guarantors of their position, focusing on the deaths of civilian non-combatants gives an entirely different picture. It is reasonable to do this because the security forces were part of the problem, in the same way that deaths of members of paramilitary organisations do not give a glimpse of the innocents caught up in conflict. On this measure the majority of the non-security force deaths in Northern Ireland are of ordinary innocent Catholics murdered by Loyalists. In a comprehensive review of the 3,168 violent deaths between 1969 and the 1994 ceasefires, O'Duffy (1995) contends that 51.7 per cent were of civilians, 33 per cent security force personnel, 9.9 per cent were members of Republican paramilitary organisations and 2.8 per cent from Loyalist paramilitary groups. Of the civilians, 65 per cent were Catholic, who accounted for a third of all deaths in 'the Troubles'. Of the civilian Catholics murdered, 62 per cent were the responsibility of Loyalists. A similar proportion of Protestant civilians were killed by Republicans at 65.5 per cent, although lower in absolute numbers (Loyalists also killed 20 per cent of all civilian Protestant deaths). One point worth making here is that the paramilitary organisations were not very good at killing each other; it was the innocents in the crossfire who suffered most. The religious make-up of the innocents is perhaps also not the main point. While O'Duffy and O'Leary (1990: 332) argue that, given the Protestant population outnumbers Catholics by approximately three to two, Catholic civilians (896 deaths) have suffered both absolutely and relatively more than Protestant civilians (571 deaths), it is clear that all have suffered and culpability is spread throughout the social structure and prioritising as a public issue only one set of victims' experiences is unhelpful. The central point for the peace process is that the wide distribution of personal troubles that have been caused by violence tends to complicate any peacemaking involving victims, memory and forgiveness, for translating the victims' demand for justice into a public issue can be divisive unless it is extended to all who have suffered.

By contrast in South Africa's case, as Johnston shows (1997: 86), most victims were Black and many caused by state security forces. Between 1976, when Black political protest resumed after a long period of quiescence, and 1990, when de Klerk got serious about reform, the South African police report 623 incidents of sabotage, murder and terrorism by the ANC in which 153 people died (cited in

Johnston, 1997: 78). Compare this with the 2,031 deaths for which Republican paramilitaries were responsible in Northern Ireland, with a much smaller population density, 35 per cent of whom were civilians (calculated from figures in Hayes and McAllister, 2001a: 904). Far more ANC guerrillas were killed than others in these attacks, with estimates ranging between 500 and 694 insurgents killed and arrested between the same period (see Barrell, 1990). Security forces were more efficient killers through crude police action and brutality (on the South African police, see Brewer, 1994) and state-sanctioned death squads, whose sole purpose was to kill activists (see Laurence, 1990). However, the sheer volume of deaths due to political violence in South Africa makes it difficult to collect information on culpability with the same reliability as in Northern Ireland. Between 1988 and 1993, for example, the South African Institute of Race Relations estimates there were 16,010 deaths and only approximate classification of the perpetrators is possible. None the less figures from the South African Institute of Race Relations for 1986 suggest that security force personnel accounted for about a third of all deaths (cited in Johnston, 1997: 80; also see Kane-Berman, 1993). This gives statistical weight to the reality of Black-on-Black violence which marked the immediate post-settlement period. Yet even though both victims and perpetrators were likely to have been Black, the subordinate population universally perceived the Black-on-Black violence as an apartheid strategy. Irrespective of their 'race', the perpetrators were perceived as agents of apartheid and of a corrupt system rather than as Whites *per se*, at least outside Pan Africanist organisations. While the abolition of that system by the peace process still leaves issues of reconciliation that need to be dealt with (for analyses which claim the Truth and Reconciliation Commission has failed in this regard, see Jeffrey, 1999; Wilson, 2001), the dissolution of apartheid has confined issues of blame and responsibility to the past. Apartheid is a convenient closet into which to stuff all the problems that beset the present and thus to explain responsibility away.

In Northern Ireland by contrast, both sides think of themselves as the principal victims and blame the other for their suffering, and they carry their experiences of victimhood into the peace process (see Morrissey and Smyth, 2001). Therefore, there are many contentious public issues in Northern Ireland which divide the two communities and threaten the peace process, such as the handling of memory of particular incidents and events, the apportion of culpability and blame for the conflict, and the commemoration of the victims of both sides (who, to the other community, of course, are often perpetrators of violence). People's experiences of suffering simply get interpreted in terms of the conflict. This explains why some people on both sides in Northern Ireland feel it appropriate to deface the commemorative plaques and gravestones of the other community's victims: even the dead are not free of the strains provoked by peace. Further, Northern Ireland lacks the equivalent scapegoat to the apartheid system on to which communities can agree to dump all blame. It is perhaps a therapeutic myth that all blame can be shovelled onto the discredited apartheid system and thus into the past, but in the north of Ireland there is no consensus amongst the communities as to what abstraction can be held responsible – colonialism, the British, sectarianism, Republicanism or whatever. These merely scapegoat the other community and reproduce the division. In some of the most violent milieux, such as north Belfast, it was a case of neighbour killing neighbour and blame gets apportioned to the whole community to which they belong. This tends to frame the contentious public issues in the peace process around reconciliation and forgiveness with often vivid biographical experiences of close-at-hand violence. It is not surprising that this can weaken the commitment to peace.

The ontological price of peace

These arguments suggest what is perhaps a surprising truth: peace comes at too high a price for some people. The ontological insecurity caused by violence as a personal trouble and which gives the push to public issues around peace can be insufficiently severe as to discourage some people from fully embracing the need to compromise, and the compromises required by the peace process can cause the same severe ontological insecurity as the violence itself. The peace process as a public issue – perhaps the major issue on the policy agenda – can therefore translate into personal troubles for these sorts of people.

Peace processes require that people whose personal milieux are untouched directly by violence become sufficiently persuaded that the public issues surrounding violence, and which are premised on the personal troubles of victims directly affected by violence, require more than just an end to the violence, forcing instead a will to make the compromises that peace involves. Peace processes offer the prospect of an end to violence and the reconciliation of conflict, and thus the prospect of longer-term ontological security, but in the short term they may threaten ontological security because they require change, the overthrow of familiar ideas, routines and behaviours, all of which can be psychologically difficult. Northern Irish Protestants are not the first to have experienced this problem. With his vast experience of peacemaking in violent societies, Lederach identifies what he calls the 'identity dilemma'. People who have defined their identity for so long in terms of the enemy, in peace processes suddenly find they have to reshape their sense of who they are (quoted in Knox and Quirk, 2000: 26). There is another dimension to this problem. If people can successfully 'live with' the level of violence in Northern Ireland and it is all they have known, 'peace' itself is unfamiliar and ontologically strange. These feelings are enhanced for victims and their relatives. The public issues surrounding the search for peace and the reconciliation of ancient conflicts cause private troubles for the victims and their families. This is reinforced by the habit of peace processes to become almost the sole public issue, enveloping and encapsulating all public events. In the public domain all they hear is peace, while privately all they feel is grief. The empty chair at the dinner table once filled by someone still much loved, the constant constraint of the wheelchair, the emotional pain that gets repeated every anniversary and the persistent physical and emotional scars are daily reminders of what the violence has cost them. As Lederach argued, their hurt and bitterness can become defining features of their identity, and peace comes at a cost. The victims and their families are asked to release the bitterness, forgive old enemies and witness them now in parliament, see perpetrators receive amnesty or prisoners released, and generally move forward from their hurt, loss, and pain. Organisations representing the victims, and politicians who wish to exploit them, make public issues of these private troubles and effectively mobilise for peace on their terms alone. This is true for both sides of the zero sum divide, and for these people also, peace can enhance feelings of ontological insecurity. As Mills's argued, public issues can cause personal troubles.

The ontological insecurity and anxiety provoked by peace – whether for victims and their families or ordinary people who have just learned to live safely with violence – is only one kind of cost to peace. Research on grassroots peacemaking in Northern Ireland (Brewer, Bishop and

Higgins, 2001: 84) reveals that one of the constraints operating on peacemakers is the fear of victimisation and intimidation by unreconstructed opponents of peace who want to keep the violence going. This leads people to be accused of 'selling out' their community and makes them vulnerable to harassment and attack from paramilitary organisations on their 'own side'. Adams and Ervine, for example, have received death threats from their erstwhile colleagues. Graffiti across the towns is menacing to their personal safety and specific threats are regularly received. At one point in the negotiations leading up to the Good Friday Agreement it was said that Gerry Adams was particularly fearful of assassination from opponents within Republicanism. Significantly, this anxiety is not restricted to those who have former friends in the paramilitaries. Protestant ministers, for example, have received death threats when they have written or spoken out against bastions of Protestantism like the Orange Order or have had to confront the Ulster Defence Association (UDA) when intervening in situations of local conflict. The proclivity of Loyalist organisations for killing innocents rather than combatants makes this fear seem real. A Church of Ireland minister who wrote a critical account of his Church's role in the events around Drumcree (Storey, 2002) is under a threat from the Orange Volunteers. A Presbyterian minister in the mid-1980s had to move temporarily to England as a result of the vilification that followed from his attempt to open up relations with the local Catholic church. In more recent times, many Protestant ministers have said that when they involve themselves in peace initiatives in their hardline neighbourhoods they are more afraid of the UDA than the IRA. Some who have spoken out against the UDA have had their church buildings 'torched', and in some milieux ecumenically-minded Protestant ministers are afraid to voice support for peace publicly. This particularly affects Protestant ministers because denominational divisions within Protestantism and the lack of a parish structure means they are more isolated and vulnerable than Catholic priests to harassment from paramilitaries. (Catholic priests working for peace tend not to receive harassment from unreconstructed Republicans.) Peace comes at a huge price to these people.

Amongst ordinary people, if not peace activists, peace can also encourage feelings of powerlessness, something Mills recognised as a general feature of ordinary people in modern societies. People live in their personal milieux and experience broad social structural processes only in as much as they impinge on these milieux. 'Great changes' can thus be perceived as out of the control of ordinary people and people can feel powerless to affect them; and the changes themselves can lack support (or have just weak support) because they are easily presented as unintended consequences of forces lying outside people and which very few wanted or intended. Such powerlessness may cause apathy and disaffection from the peace process (and from the politicians who are supposed to be in control of events). For the politically disaffected, feelings of powerlessness may cause resistance to change because it cannot be understood and made sense of. Feelings of powerlessness may encourage in others, however, an over-reliance on key individuals, the men and women of the moment, who interpret the events and make sense of them for ordinary people. Through various mobilisation strategies, these 'people of genius' will take advantage of structural conditions and people's private troubles in order to make ordinary people feel in control of the peace process by means of participation in the political process (rather than withdrawal from it). This is why boycott strategies by key politicians, who threaten to leave negotiations or new forums and parliaments, are inherently paradoxical and always self-defeating if the peace process keeps moving on.

This is not to imply, of course, that all key individuals will use strategies to mobilise ordinary people for peace. The biographical experiences of these key individuals may make some completely opposed to the process, others to any deal which involves a second-best solution for 'their' group, others to any process that requires greater sacrifice than merely the cessation of violence, and so on. But they do so by means of mobilisation strategies that take creative advantage of opportunities and which involve participation in the political process. The biographical experiences of key individuals, which shape their mobilisation strategies, are therefore also important to a sociological understanding of the peace process; and, again, these individual biographical experiences pull the peace process in different directions.

Key individuals and the peace process

It is not the intention in this section to give a description of the biography, background and personal contribution of the many individuals who have motivated the peace process in South Africa or

Northern Ireland. There are too many and it would end up as biography not sociology. There are now many autobiographies by key personnel that do this well (see, for a selection Mandela, 1995; Adams, 1996; de Klerk, 1998; Hume, 1996; Major, 1999; Mitchell, 1999; Mowlam, 2002). Nor, as Runciman (1999: 154), warns us should leaders be interviewed for their subjective accounts since, he writes, those people who are best placed, by virtue of their roles, to understand how society works are often those least likely to know why it changes because they often have unrealistic views about people in less powerful roles or inflated views about their own abilities and achievements. Most important, this would not be what Mills intended when he gave attention to people's individual biographical experiences. The capturing of these experiences, as we saw, was only the starting point for sociology not the end goal. The purpose, as Mills saw it, was to show how biographical experiences link with wider forces to produce outcomes for society and the individual. Moreover, we will adopt the familiar elision in sociology by focusing on social types rather than specific individuals. The types of key individual used here are classified according to the mobilisation strategy they use to appeal to the biographical experiences, social structural interests and political positions of ordinary people. In doing this we find that three types of key individual and their associated mobilisation strategies have heavily influenced the peace process in Northern Ireland and South Africa. These are unreconstructed opponents of peace, dominant group peacemakers and subordinate group peacemakers.

Unreconstructed opponents of peace come in two types, 'hard' and 'soft'. Peace is a virtue so unrivalled in its social good that it is almost impossible for people to declare publicly that they want the violence to continue, although some by their actions perpetuate it. Paramilitary groups not under ceasefire are at the extreme end of this position. Most key individuals who are unreconstructed opponents of the process publicly state that they oppose the peace process not the end result, preferring to see peace achieved in other ways than the agreed settlement and normally in ways that are more solidly on their own terms. The 'hard no' group comprises key people who mobilise on a return to former group dominance, represented by old-time apartheid or Protestant ascendancy. However, since a return to the past is favoured by only the most antediluvian, it is more likely these days for opponents of the peace process to be of the 'soft no' version, mobilising on an unwillingness to compromise on group interests and a rejection of any second-best solution. In the latter case, these mobilisation strategies can be found on either side of the communal divides in both societies as representatives of the dominant group become reluctant to share power and resources, and representatives of the minority groups to release their preferred solution. Their biographical experiences and background ensure that old loyalties loom large – whether to dead comrades, past shibboleths and ideology, to ancient covenants and notions of land and sovereignty – and these key players become reluctant to compromise.

The litany of names of these key people is long, the most obvious being leaders of the Afrikaner right wing up to South Africa's first non-racial election – people like Constand Viljoen and Ferdi Hartzenberg, and the Pan Africanist Congress of Azania, which campaigned during the election on 'one settler, one bullet' and urged White repatriation. (For a Black Consciousness critique of the new South Africa see Kunnie, 2000.) The military group, the Azanian People's Liberation Army, justified the continuance of armed struggle and was responsible for a few deaths of White people in the period up to the election. Neither did well in the 1994 election. Guelke refers to the White right wing as passive during the election (1999: 67), and their three notable acts – the assassination of the communist leader Chris Hani, the putative 'invasion' of Bophuthatswana and the raid on the building where peace negotiations were taking place – backfired to make them marginal to the electoral process (1999: 68; on the White right wing up to and during the 1994 election, see van Rooyen, 1994). In Northern Ireland key individuals of this type are in fundamentalist Protestantism and unreconstructed Unionism, such as Paisley, Donaldson and McCartney, and unreconstructed Irish Republicans like Ruairi O'Bradaigh. 'Not an inch', 'not a bullet' or 'not a blade of grass' is the cry of their mobilisation, although by the time of the 1994 election in South Africa, which marked the implementation of non-racial democracy, the demand of these people in South Africa was for a form of White *volkstaat*. At best these key people seek only the cessation of violence or peace on such narrow terms as in effect to result in no justice or fairness to other groups at all. Where these key individuals have the means of physical force – like the Afrikaner Weerstandsbeweging, the Afrikaner

Volksfront, the Orange Volunteers, the Red Hand Defenders or the 'real' and continuity IRA – their influence on peace is negative and violence may continue or be renewed (on Afrikaner Weerstandsbeweging violence see Guelke, 1999, Jackson, 1998). Guelke (1999: 85) draws a useful distinction between right-wing Afrikaner violence and Loyalist acts of terrorism. The White right had no tradition of violence historically – they had the state's security forces to take up their challenges anyway – and was widely perceived to be politically marginal. On all counts, the Loyalists count for much more in Northern Ireland.

However, events in South Africa offer one reassuring lesson for Northern Ireland. The violent groups on the Afrikaner right wing have since the 1994 election assassinated a former leader of the Dutch Reformed Church, but are quickly dissipating the longer Whites perceive South Africa's non-racial democracy to work; or at least, the longer the problems that beset the new South Africa (such as the explosion in violent crime) are seen by Whites as unrelated to the transition to non-racial democracy. This is much the same for those paramilitary groups in Northern Ireland that have actually bought into the peace process: a kind of legitimacy for the peace process through its efficacy. Where paramilitary support for the peace process is conditional on peace working, as it appears to be for the rank-and-file IRA, added danger is given to all of the problems that bedevil the process. This conditionality also tends to give validity to fears amongst the dominant group that Republican violence may not be at an end.

The difference between 'hard' and 'soft' opponents of peace in Northern Ireland is only roughly the equivalent of the now familiar contrast between 'ethnic' and 'civic' Unionists (first established by Porter, 1996). That there are divisions may seem unusual given Protestants share a strong emotional loyalty to the Reformation faith. However, Bruce (1999; also see Bruce, 1986, 1994, 1998) has shown that while evangelicalism is the sacred canopy that helps to unite Protestants as an ethnic group, its lends itself to at least three different political positions – ethnic unionism, civic unionism and pietistic retreat from politics. The first two positions are most relevant to the peace process. Ethnic unionism emphasises the common ancestry and culture of the group, seeing Ulster Protestants as a distinct people specially favoured by God and divinely planted to the land

and given sovereignty over it. In this view the Bible is a weapon as powerful as the Loyalists' armalite or pipe bomb in upholding the position of Protestants. A peace process that destroys Protestant ascendancy is antithetical to Protestant group interests and contrary to God's plan. Civic unionists by contrast do not recognise that Protestants deserve special prominence in the counsels of heaven or the state; all citizens are equal and deserving. The demands this makes of the peace process is that it must be fair to all citizens and not privilege Catholics. Ethnic unionism tends towards the 'hard no' position, but civic unionism supports both the 'soft no' position, in which the Good Friday Agreement is denounced as one-sided, and supporters of the current peace process who see the Agreement as not perfect but the best compromise possible. This ambiguity within civic unionism explains why other writers knowledgeable about modern-day Unionism prefer to contrast types of discourse within Unionism rather than discrete types of group (see Ruane and Todd, 1999). The one language is open, inclusive and universalistic in its appeals to reform, the other exclusive, partisan and traditional. Unreconstructed opponents of the process use the latter discourse, irrespective of whether they are 'hard' or 'soft' objectors to peace.

The second type of key individual is the person within the dominant group who is prepared to negotiate, compromise and seek a second-best solution that involves the cessation of violence and institutional rearrangements to effect reconciliation and the resolution of conflict. Their discourse is open, inclusive and universalistic. F.W. de Klerk and David Trimble are the two most obvious examples amongst mainstream politicians, although there are many others. There are also examples of radical transformations of former extremists into key people working towards negotiation, such as Gusty Spence and David Ervine, former long-term prisoners belonging to the UVF in Northern Ireland, and Magnus Malan, Constand Viljoen and Barend du Plessis, members along with de Klerk of the apartheid state who moved towards dismantling it (although younger National Party Turks like Roelf Meyer soon replaced them to take the peace process further). Spence and Ervine, leading Loyalists in Northern Ireland, developed a peace vision while in prison and emerged from their sentences with a commitment to exclusively political means. It is clear from their account of this experience that they were conscious of human and political failures in previous military strategies.

The continuance of violence and conflict was seen as exacting too high a cost in human terms for the cannon fodder who do the killing and military strategies had failed to address the structural causes of conflict (on Spence, see Garland, 1997, 2001). Prison experience is sometimes salutary for paramilitary members and convinces them of the value of exclusively political means, and in Northern Ireland, at least for Protestants, there is the prospect of religious conversion in prison. Getting God functions a little like getting formal education for Republican prisoners in being a life-changing experience that can influence people to non-violence. (On the role of education in the political shift of Republican prisoners see McKeown, 2001.) God was not a possibility for them: Moen (1999) estimates that only one in twenty Republican prisoners in the Maze was Christian; those who attended Mass regularly in the blanket protest did so only to be able to meet and talk with other prisoners.

Amongst Protestants however, conversion can in some cases be to a conservative evangelical faith that is very anti-Catholic, such as the late Billy Wright, whose 'conversion' in prison did not stop his Loyalist Volunteer Force killing innocent Catholics: his religious mentors were only prepared to admit that he had 'back slid', but had not lost his grace once he was 'born again' (see Brewer, 1998: 161). In an interesting account of religion among Loyalist terrorists, Bruce (1999: 5; also see Bruce 2001) argues that he knows of only two who were committed Christians before and during their paramilitary involvement, but he also admits that since the 1994 ceasefire, small Loyalist splinter groups have sprung up with a more definite evangelical ethos. The leader of the Orange Volunteers, for example, was a Pentecostal pastor, notorious for blessing the guns and pipe bombs before the combatants went out to try to kill Catholics. One act by the Volunteers was a co-ordinated arson attack on twelve Catholic churches, which he defended on grounds that the Catholic Church is the bastion of the antichrist (Bruce, 1999: 6; on the myth of the antichrist in Protestant culture, see Higgins, 2001; Higgins and Brewer, 2002). The pastor was imprisoned for ten years for carrying pipe bombs in the boot of his car. One factor Bruce overlooks, however, is the way in which conservative evangelical religion provides a moral critique of Catholicism that easily spills over into anti-Catholic violence amongst the rabid and irrational. The relative absence of a religious background amongst convicted Loyalist terrorists hardly does justification to the backcloth effect that anti-Catholic religious rhetoric has on the immature and gullible. Of course, religious conversion can also be to a more ecumenical and liberal theology; and these converts tend to look back and see the distorted elective affinity between a conservative evangelical ethos, Loyalist culture and the descent into violence. One such convert, now working actively for peace, recounted his biographical experience:

> Both my parents were lapsed Christians, although they made sure the children went to church every week. I found this experience an ordeal and hated Sundays with passion. Church was boring and meaningless to me in my young life and the Christian message I heard in Church only reinforced the anti-Catholic message I was receiving from the Unionist/Loyalist society around me. I left school in 1969 at the age of 15 with no academic qualifications. That summer the violence came to the streets of Northern Ireland and at this young age I felt the sectarian feelings rise in me. Within a few years the violence escalated. I became involved with the Ulster Volunteer Force, which is one of the main Loyalist paramilitary organisations. In July 1975 I was arrested by the security forces and sentenced the following year to life imprisonment. As I settled into the routine of imprisonment, very slowly I started to question my beliefs and values. For the first time in my life I actually read the Bible. As I read about the life of Jesus I came to a conclusion that grows stronger with each passing day – that Jesus preached a message of non-violence and that those who follow Him are called to be peacemakers in this world. It is easy to preach the message of peacemaking, harder to practise it, yet God wants us to live it in our everyday lives. I learnt this in prison and have tried to follow it since. (quoted in Brewer, Bishop and Higgins, 2001: 1–2)

What is not immediately apparent is why such stalwarts of past ascendancy and dominance as de Klerk and Trimble should become enthusiasts for change. De Klerk was a former leader of the hardline Transvaal caucus of the National Party before becoming President (it is said that he carried no racial scars because he was the first Afrikaner leader not to have had parents interned in British concentration camps in the Boer War). Trimble is remembered for dancing hand-in hand with Paisley down the Garvaghy Road to celebrate the victory of mob violence when Orangemen were allowed to march from Drumcree church; an event which won him the support of right-wing Unionists and assisted him in becoming leader. However, both later came to display unexpected and surprising courage, without which there would have been a much delayed peace process, and perhaps no peace process at all, since the travails of structural conditions move slower than the speed with which de Klerk and Trimble took the lead in moving the rump of their parties towards reform. It was precisely because their individual backgrounds and biographical experiences were unimpeachable in right-wing terms that they were able to take doubters along. And both were successful in presenting the peace process to many confused, bewildered and powerless people in a way that it made sense for them to support change. (Marks (1998: 21) makes the point that Afrikaners have a political tradition of going along with leaders who are seen as dominant and patriarchal.)

Their mobilisation strategies appealed to altruistic notions such as fair shares for everyone irrespective of group membership, the attraction of an end to violence and of the prospect of permanent peace for everyone, and international norms of civil and human rights. Universalistic and inclusive language was used to support the principle of reform. Appeals were also made to naked self-interest, such as the economic benefits of peace and the economic costs of continued conflict. Group survival played a role too. Although this was more overt in de Klerk than it is in Trimble, both key leaders successfully mobilised by appeals to dominant group interests. De Klerk took advantage of structural and political circumstances to argue that the release of Mandela, the legalisation of the ANC and the whole socio-political and constitutional reform process were the best way to protect White interests and the last chance to strike a bargain favourable to them (Giliomee, 1990: 309; also see Giliomee, 1992). Structural and political circumstances threatened a deterioration in the position of Whites and de Klerk's quality as a key leader was to persuade Whites to negotiate peace before their position grew worse (see Schrire, 1992, 1994). Brendan O'Leary (1998, 1999) argues much the same for Trimble (Smooha, 2001: 327 also makes the point that some Unionists came to see that a majoritarian political system could no longer guarantee the exclusion of Catholics and that power sharing was the lesser evil; also see McGarry, 1998: 866). According to

O'Leary, Trimble has taken advantage of the moment to mobilise ordinary people by arguing that the Good Friday Agreement is the best way to protect Union with Britain, that generosity to Nationalists now avoids a more serious situation emerging later, and by encouraging the belief amongst his supporters that if Catholics are treated well now, they will give up on the idea of national unification. The concomitant is that Protestants are not mobilised on appeals to complete unification with Britain, which O'Leary sees as having little space within mainstream Unionist strategies because it is associated with right-wing Unionists like McCartney and the old Loyalist paramilitaries, both of whom Trimble feels need to be distinguished politically from his mainstream position. In short, Trimble's quality as a key individual is to believe that Protestant group interests are best served by cutting a deal now. This is not inconsistent with Trimble's seemingly constant threats to withdraw as First Minister from the institutions established by the Good Friday Agreement since this is a tactic forced by his weak position against the anti-Agreement Unionists. They assuredly believe that it is not in Protestants' best group interests to accept the Good Friday Agreement and in times of instability in the process they make headway in persuading a sizeable number of ordinary Protestants of the same view, weakening Trimble's position.

The third type of key individual is the person in the minority group who makes sense of the changes in people's personal milieux by various mobilisation strategies which encourage them to give up on long-standing goals and move away from the all-or-nothing mentality associated with zero-sum conflicts. Opposition within each society always contained key people who were willing to do this long before representative leaders within the dominant group were prepared to talk to them. John Hume is only the best known of such key individuals amongst Nationalists in Northern Ireland with a long-standing commitment to constitutional methods; Desmond Tutu, Allan Boesak and Nthato Motlana, amongst others, come to mind in South Africa's case as key non-violent opponents of apartheid. Their commitment to peace has perhaps always been taken for granted. Where key leaders have control over paramilitary forces, as in Buthelezi's case, or are the political representatives of paramilitary groups, like Adams and McGuinness, the shift is all the more remarkable. But these former militarists should not receive all the accolades.

The commitment to constitutional means by key minority group members has been influential in the peace process in two ways. The first, ironically, is by their failure. Whether they were persuaded to participate in piecemeal reforms that were always going to be inadequate (for example, Buthelezi's incorporation into the Bantustan policy in South Africa) or used constitutional forums to argue for more radical change (for example, John Hume and the Social, Democratic and Labour Party), constitutional opponents in Northern Ireland and South Africa had long been arguing for non-violent means without much effect on the state's reform agenda, in lessening the level of conflict or in reducing the use of violence by other members of the minority groups. However, it is possible to contend that they have also made a more positive contribution by extending political education amongst the marginal and excluded and by always ensuring that the essentially political nature of minority group demands were not ignored in the state's law-and-order response to the military tactics of non-constitutional opponents.

None the less, a major impetus to the peace process came with the conversion to political means amongst militarists, such as when Sinn Féin abandoned their dual strategy of the armalite and ballot box to concentrate solely on the latter. Key individuals who were once wedded to unconstitutional means in an all-or-nothing conflict but who have now opted to bargain a second-best solution, like Adams and Mandela, have been critical to the emergence of the peace process. The IRA, for example, has always been caught in the tension between the universalistic Enlightenment discourse of the French Revolution and the ethnic particularism of appeals to Irish Catholicism. But since the hunger strikes in 1981 it became more secular at the same time as which the position of the Catholic Church in Ireland weakened under the effects of secularisation, child abuse scandals and anti-clericalism. Adams, although himself a practising Catholic, has been successful through Sinn Féin's political strategy in modernising the IRA around an equality agenda rather than traditional appeals to cultural nationalism. In his memoirs (Adams, 1996), he writes of the seminal influences on his life, such as experiences of early childhood poverty. He mobilises IRA supporters by urging that the Good Friday Agreement offers them equality now and the promise of possible unification sometime later, with Protestant consent. Hence the terminology has changed from a united to an agreed Ireland. Like other of these leaders, he was always a reluctant militarist anyway. Writing in *Republican News* from inside prison under the pseudonym 'Brownie', Adams, while concerned to keep the movement in tact, was none the less critical of the IRA's exclusive military strategy and urged the political route. Mandela's advocation of armed struggle was always half-hearted and came only after the use of constitutional means was closed off by the state. (On the limitations of terrorism as a tactic in South Africa's liberation struggle see Brewer, 1986: 138–48; cf. Barrell, 1990. On Joe Slovo's recognition of the limits of sabotage, see Guelke, 1999: 52.) For example, Mandela quotes himself later as saying at his trial: 'the hard facts were that fifty years of non-violence had brought the African people nothing but more and more repressive legislation and fewer and fewer rights... It was only when all channels of peaceful protest had been barred to us that the decision was taken to embark on violent forms of political struggle' (Mandela, 1995: 433). To someone like O'Malley (2001: 283), this only reinforces the IRA's lack of political legitimacy and moral standing compared to the ANC, since once it was an enthusiast for physical force.

The prison experience has been seminal too. Most of the former combatants from amongst the minority groups who gave up their support for a military strategy to work for peace were imprisoned or interned – Gerry Adams, Nelson Mandela, Walter Sisulu, Gerard Kelly, Martin McGuinness, Danny Morrison and Martin Meehan. They left jail committed to non-violence in the future and exclusively political means of protest, something they shared with militarists on the other side (like Spence and Ervine in Northern Ireland). Mandela's official biographer, for example, wrote that Mandela saw prison as a microcosm of a future South Africa, where reconciliation would be essential to survival (Sampson, 1999: 222). Through his exposure to Afrikaans-speaking guards, Sampson writes, Mandela came to see Afrikaners as Africa's first 'freedom fighters' and he argues that Mandela first came to understand Afrikaners better in prison. They were 'all sorts of people whose hands are dripping with blood', but his jail years told Mandela that Afrikaners can 'move 180 degrees' as his biographer quotes him as saying; 'courageous people', Mandela said, 'do not fear forgiving for the sake of peace' (1999: 236). Ex-Republican prisoners say much the same. Moen (1999), for example, argued that prisoner-guard relations in the Maze prison were normalised during the 1990s and the prisoners developed good working relations with them which they carried on the outside. Senior prison negotiators, for example, with experience of working out the relationship between the prisoners and guards, when released were amongst the group of senior political negotiators on the outside. Using strategies adopted first in prison, most Republican prisoners turned attention to the political process when released.

Lofty appeals to high ideals should not disguise the self-interest in the mobilisation strategies of key leaders in the minority groups who pushed for peace, for people were also mobilised on grounds that it was in their group interests to bargain a settlement now. In South Africa, for example, the incorporation of members of the South African Communist Party and the paramilitary Umkhonto we Sizwe into the peace process depended much on the leadership skills of key individuals like Nelson Mandela, Cyril Rhamaphosa, Thabo Mbeki and Joe Slovo. It has been remarked that the key decision was the ANC's realisation that armed struggle and the internal campaign to make the townships ungovernable would not defeat the government politically or overcome the might of the South African Defence Force (O'Malley, 2001: 283). Indeed, with apartheid imploding from within, armed struggle was unnecessary and it is more likely the case that they successfully mobilised ANC membership and other radicals and militarists to work for a peace deal by arguing that it was better to enter the system in the early 1990s, when the economy was still strong and the state not entirely ruined by violence rather than prolong the armed struggle and risk inheriting an irreparably damaged state and economy. Thus, it was as much in Mandela's interest to end the violence as de Klerk's, although neither proved immediately successful in this and South Africa's peace process struggled for a short while under the potentially destabilising effects of politically motivated violence (as currently Northern Ireland's peace process does).

It is worth commenting on the achievement of these key people in persuading members of the subordinate community to abandon long-cherished preferences and objectives. In South Africa's case majority rule has not diminished the high level of inequality which remains for the bulk of the Black population. It is popularly understood that economic apartheid has remained (Kunnie, 2000). The abolition of apartheid has not seen the dismantling of the shacks and shantytowns, the ending of unemployment or much redistribution in terms of housing, welfare, education and other important elements of social capital. Crime levels are high in the townships, especially violent crime, with 26,637 non-political murders in 1995 alone (du Toit, 2001: 47) and the rural areas are still severely underdeveloped. While Spence (1999) argues that Black South African had low expectations of redistribution with majority rule, the ordinary Black South African's experience of relative poverty is as vivid as in the worst days of apartheid; the leafy Johannesburg suburbs through which they pass to work (if they have a job at all) contrast so boldly with the squalor of the townships. To get Black South Africans to buy into a deal which reproduces many of apartheid's social and economic inequalities for the price of institutional reform of politics and policing is remarkable and is testimony to the importance to subordinate groups of feeling culturally that they belong and that they are no longer perceived or treated as second class. South Africa's feat therefore, is to deliver support for a peace process amongst minority group members who experience next to no change in their immediate social and economic lives.

The achievement of Northern Ireland's peace process is to persuade sufficient members of the Catholic community that the changes they experience in their daily lives are sufficient replacement for other goals. Discussion in the North has tended to focus on what Protestants see themselves giving up and thus has become concentrated on the issue of Protestant alienation from the peace process. Much of the debate about police reform and bans on a few selective Orange marches, for example, is couched in these terms (see, for example, O'Neill, 2000) and community relations are perceived by Protestants to have worsened during the peace process (see Hughes and Donnelly, 2002). Aughey (2001: 217; also see Aughey, 2000) usefully summarises the 'losses' Protestants perceive they have suffered in the Good Friday Agreement to persuade Republicans away from violence. These include: having to share power with Sinn Féin, Sinn Féin's access to the House of Commons without signing the oath of allegiance to the Crown, prisoner releases, the reduction in troop levels and the implementation of the Patten Report on reform of the RUC. To these one could add the reform of the criminal justice system and the introduction of a Human Rights ethos and an equality agenda in public policy. Looked at from the perspective of the subordinate group however, the Good Friday Agreement locks Republicans into the principle of consent, by which Protestants have a veto on territorial reunification of Ireland, it has Sinn Féin participating in and publicly supporting and defending what is in effect a partitionist settlement, it has Republicanism rejecting the physical force tradition in Irish politics, to which they have been wedded for so long, giving up not only arms in two acts of decommissioning but also the cultural symbolism of resistance by force of British influence on the island of Ireland, and it has Republicanism working alongside British interests and personnel to implement a deal that falls well short of a United Ireland. Republicans have 'lost' on two principles dear to them: 'Brits out now' and immediate Irish unification. If Republicanism could be understood in terms of its own traditions and background, it would be seen that these are massive steps. Its history of military struggle makes both the ceasefire and disarmament ground-breaking, and Sinn Féin's reluctance to negotiate with the British in the past (noted by Arthur, 1995: 50–1) has been successfully overturned. These risk fissures developing in the Republican movement but none the less Sinn Féin remains one of the strongest supporters of the Good Friday Agreement. When Unionism has threatened to collapse the institutions established under the Agreement, it has been Sinn Féin arguing to continue – in effect working for the survival of a partitionist settlement which sections of Unionism want to bring down. In their wildest hopes, Unionists in the past would not have thought this attainable. Yet this is what Sinn Féin has delivered. However, zero-sum conflicts tend to render compromises into concessions so that gains become turned into losses. But if we shift focus to what Catholics might be perceived to have given up, it is a remarkable achievement by key minority group leaders to get the bulk of Catholics to accept these second-best preferences. Even though a third of Catholics have traditionally preferred to remain within the United Kingdom, the constitutional preferences of the majority were in favour of territorial reintegration and unity, especially in the medium to long term (Breen, 1996). That only 1 per cent of the Catholic electorate therefore voted against the Good Friday Agreement in the 1998 referendum (Hayes and McAllister, 2001b: 81) is remarkable for the level of support it shows for second-best preferences amongst the minority group.

In Northern Ireland's case, the cessation of violence by the main paramilitary groups and two gestures towards decommissioning by the IRA, offers an opportunity to pursue peace while not under duress, although Protestant fears that the violence may not be over, when coupled with continued street protests by both communities, hardly reduces the pressure-cooker atmosphere existing during the peace process. However, the symbolic significance of this space is, ironically, reinforced by the immense and widespread public abhorrence at atrocities committed by unreconstructed Republicans, such as the 1998 Omagh bombing, and widespread condemnation of the flash-point incidents of violence that break out on the streets in a few areas of Belfast. It is perhaps worth being reminded, therefore, that the level of violence leading up to South Africa's first non-racial elections was as intense as in the struggles to end apartheid, and has since subsided very significantly (although not completely; see du Toit, 2001). The paradox in Northern Ireland's case compared to South Africa is that while violence continued apace in South Africa up to the non-racial elections in 1994 without derailing the peace process, even the suspicion by Protestants that the cessation of violence by the IRA in Northern Ireland is not genuine is potentially derailing the process. (The evident continuance of Loyalist violence is not impacting on the attitudes of most Catholics towards the peace process.) It is worth recalling that the ANC announced only the suspension of armed conflict not its renunciation, and post-settlement violence was at a much higher level than before the peace process began, without affecting the settlement. The IRA have delivered more – in terms of decommissioning, in stopping their violence and in reconciliatory reassurances – but mere suspicion among Protestants that the war is not over is having far greater effect in destabilising the Good Friday Agreement. This, however, only reinforces the importance of the key individuals from the subordinate community in Northern Ireland continuing to persuade paramilitaries away from violence.

It must be admitted that Adams's mobilisation strategy has resulted in greater support amongst Catholics for peace as a full commitment than has Trimble's amongst Protestants. Trimble has been unable to face down his right-wing opponents in the way that de Klerk did. The Conservative Party in South Africa took up a position very like Paisley and the DUP's in Northern Ireland, arguing against the reform process because it supposedly sold out the interests of the ethnic group and exacting a toll in by-elections amongst people persuaded enough to vote against the mainstream political leaders. De Klerk opted to go for a referendum amongst the White electorate in which he threatened it was either the agreement or the apocalypse. Over 900,000 Whites voted with the Conservative Party but, having gained support, de Klerk never looked over his shoulder again. Trimble never stops looking back to what the DUP is doing, because, unlike the Conservative Party, the DUP has not gone away. The Conservative Party's charismatic leader, Andries Treurnicht, died in 1993 and the leader of the Right was then an ex-military man, Constand Viljoen, who was politically inept (and came to argue for the nonsense of a separate White homeland). In contrast, the DUP has not faded because Protestant support for the agreement was always reluctant and half-hearted, unlike the bulk of White South Africans, two-thirds of whom voted with de Klerk. This is reflected in Protestant voting patterns in the referendum on the Good Friday Agreement. Although it was ratified by 71 per cent of voters, only a narrow margin of Protestants supported it – 57 per cent compared to 43 per cent against (see Hayes and McAllister, 2001b: 80). What is more, a further 16 per cent of Protestants who voted for the Agreement were uncertain and indicated in a sample survey that they had considered voting no (Hayes and McAllister, 2001b: 80). Sinnott (1999) gives a different interpretation of this floating support, arguing that it reveals 'no' voters to be more fixed in their partisanship and wedded more strongly to traditional zero-sum mindsets. The 'yes' voters wavered understandably because of the massive distance they were travelling away from traditional positions. However, since the referendum it is feasible to argue that Protestant support has become even more wavering. Alcock (2001), himself one of the negotiators of the Agreement and a supporter of Trimble, explains this in terms of failure of the process to halt Irish irredentism; that is to say, it is rooted in the traditional fear that the Irish government will take over the North. Adams's critics within Republicanism are therefore more marginal than are Trimble's within Unionism, and it is often said that the crisis in Northern Ireland's peace process is really a crisis within Unionism over cutting a deal with Sinn Féin. Catholics voted overwhelmingly for the Good Friday Agreement and this does not appear to have diminished despite the travails in the process since. There is obviously greater support for peace as it is defined in its broadest terms, to touch on equality, justice and fairness as well as the ending of violence.

With Protestant misgivings, it was perhaps naïve not to anticipate that they would find dealing with Sinn Féin hard to stomach, all the harder when street violence still sporadically erupts. Yet it is with Sinn Féin that they have to deal. It is a reality the world over that blooded hands have to be shaken. John Paul Lederach makes the point that one of the general principles in peacemaking is that peace processes are significantly enhanced by the experiences of what he calls 'insider partials' who have a 'past' (Lederach, 1995, 1997). By 'insider partials' Lederach means former militarists and combatants who now work actively for peace, the very people Protestants object to dealing with. In a useful review of peace and conflict resolution organisations in Northern Ireland, Cochrane (2001: 138) discusses the paradox that many of those who today are committed to peace were themselves once actors in the conflict. What led them to participate in the conflict in the 1970s – the defence of their community (against the British or against the IRA) – led them to want to rebuild their community in the 1990s. These former militants have biographical experiences as 'insiders' that can be used to develop authority and legitimacy amongst combatants, turning them towards non-violence. Grassroots peacemaking tends to involve a lot of these sort of people (as well as others with biographical experiences of conflict that urge them to peace, such as victims). But it tends to be the case in Northern Ireland that each side refuses to accept the other's 'insider partials' while endorsing their own. Witness the failure of the Orange Order to meet leaders of residents groups or Sinn Féin politicians despite the benefits for peace that this would bring. It is also fair to say that Catholics show more tolerance of the peacemaking vocation of former Republican activists than do Protestants of Loyalist ones. This is perhaps because of the saliency of religion in Protestant culture which causes different perspectives on the notion of sin and forgiveness. Protestants tend to treat former Loyalists differently only where under religious conversion in prison they are 'born again' since this is seen to involve repentance. Republicans who work for peace (or other former Loyalists) who have not been 'born again' are condemned by their past. Therefore, irrespective of the peace vocation Republican 'insider partials' have or how hard they now work for peace, Protestants tend to condemn them for their failure to seek forgiveness. This is why theology plays a role in Northern Ireland's peace process in a way it did not in South Africa, for theological issues around sin and repentance mediate the translation of private troubles into public issues for many people. The simple word 'sorry' would say so much to these people.

Conclusion

Individual personal biography was the starting point for Mills's understanding of sociology and its effect on the peace process cannot be emphasised strongly enough. Key individuals, for example, have played an important role in mobilising towards peace, without which the slow travail of political and structural circumstances may never have produced peace, or done so only decades later. However, the biographical experiences and personal troubles of the many ordinary people mobilised in this way are equally important to an understanding of the peace process. Ordinary people in their personal milieux have responded to ontological insecurity and private troubles in ways that make them amenable to mobilisation by the different strategies of key individuals. The wish for the violence to end, rooted in people's personal troubles, was translated into public issues around peace. In this respect South Africa is ahead of Northern Ireland, not just in terms of having earlier negotiated a settlement, but also in terms of the level of commitment to the process amongst ordinary people. Individual biographical experiences, particularly in the way violence in Northern Ireland was experienced by Protestants, have ensured that many have only a weak commitment to the process and some not at all. Social structural conditions have been experienced differently in people's personal milieux ensuring that some people's set of personal troubles are translated into public issues that threaten the stability of the peace process. Public issues around amnesty, decommissioning and victimhood result in a more fragile process in Northern Ireland than South Africa. Peace is as much a source of ontological insecurity for them as communal violence, and key individuals opposed to the peace process mobilise effectively on this insecurity. However, to stress only the anxieties of the former dominant groups is to use the same mantra as unreconstructed opponents of peace. This understates many achievements in the peace process. There are, for example, key people who mobilise tirelessly for peace who successfully persuade ordinary people to support the process based on different sets of biographical experiences and personal troubles that motivate them to embrace peace fully. As we have seen, what is perhaps most remarkable about both peace processes is that the second-best solutions encapsulated by their negotiated settlements should have won the support of the majority of people in the subordinate and formerly excluded groups. Black South Africans, for example, continue to accept the settlement despite little advancement in their lives.

None the less, it is inadequate to explain the emergence and progress of the peace process solely in terms of the personal qualities of key people, although there is a natural tendency to make reference to the charismatic qualities of someone like Mandela, or ordinary people's personal troubles that made them want the violence to end. People have wished for the violence to end ever since it began, and while political leaders do mediate the private trouble – public issue duality by mobilising in the public arena around the small-scale biographical experiences and troubles of ordinary people, we do not exemplify the sociological imagination if we reduce the emergence and oscillating progress of the peace process to the special personal qualities of political leaders as they resonate with the wishes, biographical experiences and private troubles of ordinary people. Individual biography was not the end point of Mills's sociological imagination. The sociological imagination culminates in locating individual lives in their broader context. In this regard, the key leaders who won their constituencies for peace were responding to the opportunities afforded by social structural changes and to developments and events in the political process. The biographical experiences and private troubles of ordinary people, which assisted in their mobilisation around peace as a public issue, need to be connected to political events and social structural conditions. We look at the intersection of the social structure and politics, as key dimensions of the sociological imagination, in the next chapter.

4
The Intersection of Politics and the Social Structure

Introduction

To understand the purpose of this chapter we first need to recap. When applied to unravelling the current peace process in Northern Ireland and South Africa, Mills's sociological imagination adds to our understanding of the topic by forcing us to accept the historical relevance of seventeenth-century colonialism to the contemporary period. While charting the historical specificity of the current peace process is a prerequisite to understanding it, the impact of history is relevant only through the mediating effect of the social structure, this intersection – between history and the social structure – being something Mills recognised as essential. Colonialism became represented in a particular kind of social structure, which reproduced over the centuries through law and culture patterns of social cleavage and differentiation that made violent conflict endemic. The biographical experiences of ordinary people living in the two societies therefore felt the imprint of history in the form of sets of personal troubles and feelings of ontological insecurity caused by the conflict that translated into public issues around peace broadly understood or the more narrow concern to end violence. It is through this private trouble–public issue duality, according to Mills, that the social embeddedness of people's lives is disclosed. Mills states as a commonplace that people act in and are acted upon by society, as the private troubles–public issue duality reflects. The peace process in Northern Ireland and South Africa is a good illustration that private troubles and public issues are in a recursive relationship. But it is one mediated by differences in personal milieux, such that people's biographical experiences of violence and personal troubles can be sufficiently diverse to produce varying levels of support for peace as a public issue. And for some people, the peace process brings its own ontological insecurities and this public issue therefore causes them private troubles. This is particularly the case for victims and their relatives and tends to rebound on the peace process by affecting the ways in which peace is translated into a public issue. The biographical experiences of some people translate into public opposition to peace *per se* or to the particular peace settlement negotiated in each country. None the less, significant numbers of people have been mobilised to support the peace process through the strategies of key individuals. These mobilisation strategies, rooted in part in the leaders' own biographical experiences, attempt to make sense of the changing conditions that ordinary people experience in their daily lives, or indeed fail to experience given their expectations, in such ways as to encourage support for the peace process. While unreconstructed opponents of the peace agreements exist in both Northern Ireland and South Africa, their influence has diminished in South Africa the longer the peace settlement seems to work, or at least, the longer the problems that beset the new South Africa are not perceived to be the fault of the transition. Anti-agreement feeling is stronger in Northern Ireland, but the strategies of key individuals in the majority and minority groups have persuaded significant numbers that their best interests are served by cutting deals now.

There is an important begging question here: why now? Violence down the centuries has always caused personal troubles for ordinary people living in Northern Ireland and South Africa, and there have been recurring Siren voices calling for peace. Key individuals mobilising for peace worked tirelessly and putative peace processes have been tried and failed in the past. The question is not why peace became a public issue now, for it has always been a public issue, at least for a substantial minority of people. The critical question is why the two peace settlements succeeded now in the way peace processes did not in the past. If violence has always been a source of ontological insecurity, why is it only now that peace settlements have been introduced that have effectively and dramatically reduced, if not entirely eliminated, communal violence? For the answer we must turn to the final dimension of the sociological imagination as Mills portrayed it: the intersection between politics and the social structure. This chapter argues that private troubles and public issues are framed by a different nexus between politics and the social structure. It is not the intention of this chapter to isolate events and developments in the political process from social structural changes occurring in the two societies, as so often happens. There are many excellent accounts by journalists and political scientists of the political developments leading up to and surrounding the negotiated settlements in each country (in South Africa, see Mattes, 1994; Schrire, 1994; Sparks, 1995; Guelke, 1999; on Northern Ireland, see Rowan, 1995; McKittrick, 1996; de Breadun, 2001; Mallie and McKittrick, 2001). Some even compare the unfolding of political developments in the two places (Guelke, 1994; Arthur, 1995; Knox and Quirk, 2000; Weiss, 2000). Interestingly, there are no equivalent studies of the social structural factors that lie behind the push to peace (there are, of course, only a few sociological accounts of Northern Irish society; see Clancy *et al.*, 1986, 1995; Coulter, 1999): this only confirms that political scientists have stolen a march on sociologists in analysing the process. It is not that these political developments are devoid of sociological relevance. I have argued elsewhere (Brewer, 2001: 779) with respect to Northern Ireland that sociology can be said to have failed by its neglect of the sociological dynamics girding the country's political process. The peace process in Northern Ireland caused sociologists consternation. Without a complete and coherent account of the genesis, character and dynamics of Northern Ireland's social structure, social change took sociologists by surprise, much as it did in South Africa. In part this is to be explained by the rapidity of the events surrounding the settlements, but it also reflects sociology's disciplinary difficulties in understanding the role of politics and those key individuals who, while falling short of the sociological category of charismatic, none the less played a critical role in initiating and mobilising around the peace process. This led me to observe: 'any account of the transformation of Northern Ireland into a post-violence society that fails to establish the link between social structural transformation, political events and the role of key individuals will be deficient' (Brewer, 2001: 780).

Mills saw this intersection very clearly and made it a critical dimension of the sociological imagination. Moreover, he saw that politics was not restricted to the nation state and that international events and processes needed to be folded into sociology's way of thinking. In line with Mills's injunction for the sociological imagination to address real issues as they affect ordinary people, this chapter will not discuss this connection as a general principle but explore the social structure – politics intersection with respect to the following issues as they impacted on the peace process: demography; economic changes in the social structure; the development of civil society in response to the democratic deficit; changes to the patterns of social differentiation in particular local milieux; and the impact locally of international social and political processes. Each justifies a chapter on its own so it is with a broad brush that the canvas is covered.

Demography

Demographic changes have had a major bearing on the peace process in the two societies, introducing significant changes into the social structure, which bore heavily on the political strategies of the respective groups. Let us first address South Africa by giving some bald figures. South Africa is a huge country in size and population. In 1994, South Africa's Central Statistics Service (soon to become Statistics South Africa) estimated the population as 40.28 millions. By 2002 the *World Gazetteer* was projecting it at 45.12 millions. The World Bank estimated that between 1980 and 2000 the rate of population growth had been 2.2 per cent per annum (which compares with 0.3 per cent in the United Kingdom for the same period). In terms of its composition, the 1996 census showed that 76.7 per cent of the population described themselves as African, 10.9 per cent White, 8.9 per cent Coloured and 2.6 per cent Indian (the remainder described themselves as 'unclassified', which shows the remarkable depth of racial identity). The population is very young, with 18 per cent of the total population aged 20–29; 5–9-year-olds are the largest sector of the African population. The population is not evenly spread. The population density of South Africa's nine provinces in 1994 not surprisingly showed a skew towards the urban areas on the Rand, with Gauteng having a population density of 365.7 per square km compared to Northern Cape's 2.1; Kwa Zulu-Natal was second highest at 92.3.

Various things followed from this demographic profile that impacted on the political process. For a very long time before the current peace process, South Africa's rate of population growth, for example, was higher than the average growth rate of its stagnant economy. The World Bank estimated that it was only by 1999–2000 that the annual growth rate in the Gross Domestic Product was above the average annual population growth rate for the period 1980–2000. Before the dismantling of apartheid, international pressure from sanctions (and the threat of further sanctions) added to fears about diminished economic growth and the inability of the economy to permit the funding of apartheid society. As a result, the state was readily losing its ability to provide services to the Black population in the form of housing, jobs, hospitals, schools and all the other elements that comprise what John Rawls called social justice. Because population growth was not evenly distributed between the groups, with expansion largest amongst the African population, which already formed a numerical majority, inevitable strain was placed on the infrastructure of township and homeland life. As one simple measure, it was estimated by Central Statistical Services in 1998 (http://www.statssa.gov.za/women&men/intro.htm) that over half the population were still having to draw water, but the racial composition was revealing: 71 per cent of Africans did not have water in the home, 28 per cent of Coloureds and 3 per cent for Whites and Indians. The life-chance opportunities available to Black people were also restricted because of the unavailability of resources to meet demand. The World Bank provides figures that glimpse the scale of the problem: the infant mortality rate per 1,000 live births in 2002 was 63 (6 in the UK), the under-five mortality rate was 79 (7 in the UK). Life expectancy for males in 2000 was 47 and 49 for females (75 and 80 respectively in the UK). The adult literacy rate on the other hand is high in South Africa, at 85 per cent of females over the age of 15 years and 86 per cent of males. Between 1989 and 1994, the World Bank's Development Report estimated that an annual average of one quarter of the population in South Africa lived on less than one US dollar a day, higher than in Tanzania, Sri Lanka and the Dominican Republic, yet at the other end, 47.3 per cent of national income was owned by the highest 10 per cent of the population, one of the largest proportions amongst developing countries (World Bank, 1997). The level of frustration and discontent felt amongst the Black population at unfulfilled demands and expectations can be imagined.

The state faced considerable political instability arising from the impact these demographic trends had on the social structure (and as they affected the biographical experiences of ordinary people in their local milieux). The provision of housing, health, schooling, roads, sewage, and so on, became social problems with enormous political effect because they were wrapped up with the issue of White control of the political process. The failure to receive running water, adequate roads or sewerage, well-equipped schools and hospitals, and so on, was experienced by the majority of the population as a failure of a political system from which they were excluded. What is more, Whites were a very small numerical minority. Their population trends were First World not Third World and the decline in immigration from White Europeans arising from economic stagnation and anti-apartheid pressure meant little replenishment from outside (except of poor Whites from Portugal's former colonies in Southern Africa). While the level of population growth amongst Whites was always insufficient to enable Whites to service themselves, it eventually became too low to enable Whites to run the country, work the economy, service the state, provide policing, defence and the other normal functions of any society, without the need for massive Black labour and personnel. Black South Africans were brought into the police, the factories, the offices and the boardrooms because South Africa could not survive by relying on the demographic patterns of its small White population. Apartheid was thus subject to strain by the tensions created between a racial ideology that dictated separation and the demands of a modern state and economy that needed to incorporate its Black citizens.

It took some time for the National Party to realise this politically. After the 1976 Soweto uprising the state first opted for a strategy of economic liberalisation for Black people while maintaining White political control. However, this strategy itself created social structural anomalies that intensified Black unrest, since it increased the size of the Black middle class, and particularly encouraged the development of an African bourgeoisie with political expectations (on the history of the African bourgeoisie, see Kuper, 1965). This increased the inequalities experienced by the majority of the Black population and their sense of grievance, and it failed to address the true character of Black demands – which were political, requiring participation in the political process on an equal basis. (It is this fact which has sustained the ANC government since because the failure of economic redistribution is compensated by the success in meeting Black political demands.) But the National Party's strategy also failed because, demographically, there was not enough population growth amongst Whites to maintain political control of the state and its monopoly of the means of force without massive state-led violence and repression. This repression was only counter-productive in the long term, not only for its internal effects but for its spur to international pressure on the apartheid state because of international norms of human and civil rights.

Demographic patterns are different in Northern Ireland's case, but the principle remains the same: demographic changes have social structural effects, which themselves bear on the political process to encourage the search for a political settlement. Northern Ireland is a small country in size and population compared to South Africa. The 2001 census shows its population to be 1.68 million, less even than Greater Soweto in Gauteng province, with a population density of 114 per square km, making it still fairly rural. The population density of Greater Belfast is much higher, with nearly half of the region's total population. There is very little need to explain in detail the different demographic patterns compared to South Africa. Historically, Protestants have always been a numerical majority in Northern Ireland, able to service the economy and state (or statelet as some prefer), but in terms of the United Kingdom as a whole, Protestants were never privileged economically; on most economic measures the region of Northern Ireland is the worst in the United Kingdom (see Wichert, 1991: 66). The region's Gross Domestic Product is 74 per cent of the European Union average, although this disguises the huge subsidies Northern Ireland gets from Westminster, said to be £3.3 billion in 1992–3 (Tomlinson, 1995a, 1995b). Catholics occupied an economic niche that created institutionalised disadvantage in terms of access to jobs and housing (but not schooling and infrastructure), and thus local privilege for most Protestants. The 1991 census, for example, showed that the unemployment rate for men was 2.2 times higher for Catholics than Protestants; the equivalent figure for Catholic women was 1.8. And this differential remained true for each level of educational qualification (Knox and Quirk, 2000: 52; for classic discussions of Catholic institutionalised disadvantage, see Cormack and Osborne, 1991; Smith and Chambers, 1991).

The Catholic birth rate is higher than the Protestant rate and always has been, but Catholic demographic patterns did not threaten the advantageous social structural position of Protestants until recently. By 1991 the census was beginning to index a changing Northern Ireland. While Protestants still outnumbered Catholics, at 50.6 per cent of the population compared to 38.4 per cent (11 per cent refused to reveal their religion or said neither), there were more Catholics than Protestants amongst the younger age cohorts. When they are eventually released, the 2001 figures are expected to show that the Catholic population has risen dramatically to 45 per cent (McGaffrey, 2002). Catholics now form a majority in Northern Ireland's three largest cities – Belfast, Armagh and Derry – and in thirteen of the 26 local council areas. Demographic differences are magnified in the youngest age cohorts. Northern Ireland's population overall is a very young one. In the 2001 census, 24 per cent of the population was under 16 years of age, but young people are differentially spread in the social structure. In the 1991 census, for example, of those under ten years of age, 46 per cent were Catholic and 41 per cent Protestant, although the parents of another 13 per cent refused to classify themselves (Prendergast, 1999). It was projected that by the 2001 census the number of Catholic school children would exceed the figure for Protestants and comprise 57 per cent of all school children (Prendergast, 1999), all eventually able to vote on reaching the age of majority and contribute further to Catholic population growth. The Department of Education's annual school census (which has been running since 1999) puts the current figure for Catholic schoolchildren much lower at 50.6 per cent, which is still higher than the Protestant figure of 42.5 per cent (Bonner, 2002).

There are deep elements of continuity as well as change in these demographic patterns. Although the Catholic birth rate has traditionally been higher, it is falling as middle-class Catholics adopt fertility patterns in line with their class position and as more Catholics feel able to contravene the Church's teaching on contraception. The Catholic birth rate per 1,000 live births fell from 25.4 in 1971 to 19.5 in 1991 (McGaffrey, 2002), but the Protestant birth rate is falling as well; the number of children in primary school fell by 4.7 per cent between 1999 and 2002 but the differential remains the same in favour of Catholics. Moreover, the moderating effect of Catholic emigration is now lessening. In the past, the effects of Catholic fertility trends were moderated by the rate at which Catholics left. Employment discrimination and an unfavourable cultural and political environment meant that the boat to England or Scotland was a popular choice for unskilled Catholics, especially for seasonal labour, while the Irish Republic drew Catholic graduates on a more permanent basis. However, changing demographic patterns evidenced in recent years are extenuated by two further developments. The first is the emergence for the first time of a significant Protestant emigration from Northern Ireland, representing the exodus of Protestant undergraduates to mainland universities escaping 'the Troubles', rarely to return. Research which tracked the 1991 cohort found that nearly one in four entrants to higher education left to study in Britain, of which two-thirds were Protestant, and only one-third of the whole group returned (reported in McGaffrey, 2002). Since the trend was first noted in the mid-1980s, it is estimated that 60,000 young people, disproportionately Protestant, have been lost to the local economy (McGaffrey, 2002). Second, Catholics are not only staying in the North, there is evidence that some of them who left in the past are now returning (Prendergast, 1999). It is estimated that Catholics will become an overall majority sometime between 2025 and 2037 (although it will take longer for them to become an electoral majority).

The knock-on effects of these demographic trends in other areas of the social structure have been profound. The majority of students in Northern Ireland's universities are now Catholics – the lowest take-up in universities is from working-class Protestants – and Catholics are now better positioned than unskilled Protestants to benefit from the expansion in the economy, especially to meet the growth of jobs in information technology and computing, sectors of the local economy that have seen expansion under economic restructuring. This adds another dimension to the feeling of alienation amongst working-class Protestants and to their sense that the Good Friday Agreement is prejudicial to their group interests. Educated and skilled Catholics are coming on the labour market in increasing numbers precisely at a time when fair employment legislation and an equality agenda are governing employment practices in the private and public sectors. Catholic – Protestant relations are not the only ones affected by demography. Demographic shifts have increased the marketability and size of the Catholic middle class, which has moved from essentially servicing its own community to a wider role in the local state and economy, while offering little economic opportunity to the larger number of Catholics entering the labour market with fewer skills and qualifications. It remains the case that few of the increases in Catholic representation in white-collar, managerial and professional jobs are above their representation in the economically active population (Knox and Quirk, 2000: 52), but demographic patterns have helped to shape different economic positions within the Catholic community. (This is why some commentators explain Catholic economic disadvantage in terms of the larger number of Catholic entrants to the labour market without skills and qualifications rather than in terms of discrimination, although this is vigorously disputed; see the disagreements between Cormack and Osborne, 1991; Smith and Chambers, 1991).

One obvious consequence has been the weakening of the numerical dominance of the Protestant electorate. As O'Leary put it, Northern Irish politics are impacted by a 'minority that might become a majority, and a majority that might become a minority' (2001: 53). The Nationalist vote has risen dramatically in line with the rise in Catholic birth rate as more young Catholics are enfranchised. In the 1993 local elections, the combined vote for Sinn Féin and the SDLP was 34 per cent, rising to 37 per cent in the 1996 Forum elections, 38 per cent in the 1997 local elections, 40 per cent in the 1997 Westminster elections and the 1998 Northern Ireland Assembly elections, and 45 per cent in the last European elections (Prendergast, 1999). It is no coincidence that the decade which has seen the largest expansion in the Nationalist vote is also the period in which Sinn Féin have gone political and reaped the electoral benefits. However, the effect of demography on electoral considerations is mediated locally by various factors contingent in those milieux which in some wards constitute almost a haemorrhage. For example, in some urban working-class areas where Protestants once dominated, the flight to the suburbs intensifies the impact of demography on both the local social structure and local politics. The staunchly Loyalist Shankill district of Belfast is reputed to have had its population drop from 46,000 to 6,000 over the last century. This shift is not just of Protestants avoiding the violence, but also reflects patterns of social mobility as the Protestant middle class grows.

Many of the incidents of flash-point violence that still persist are rooted in changing population dynamics in the districts of north and east Belfast. In one such area, Ballysillan, a hardline Protestant political representative, Nelson McCausland, said: '[there is] a sense of fear within the Unionist community... The sort of talk we hear from Nationalist politicians about their growing communities sounds triumphalist. That frightens people... Unionists are now being forced to become much more forthright about the concerns they have' (*Irish News*, 2 March 1999). In 2001 the area witnessed the Holy Cross atrocities. Local Protestants violently objected to Catholic children walking to school through what was once a solidly Protestant area and threw pipe bombs at screaming primary school children.

While demography forces upon Unionists the realisation that there will not be enough Protestants to go back to old-style ascendancy, the effect of Northern Ireland's population dynamics works in a more complicated fashion than for Whites in South Africa. Through differential migration and fertility rates for Catholics and Protestants (mortality rates are much the same), Unionists know that Catholics will become a numerical majority some time in the future. Just when is open to dispute, but the fact of it is not. Trimble's political adviser responded to the 2001 census projections by arguing that Catholic population growth will slow (cited in McGaffrey, 2002), but this will only affect the time scale. A united Ireland by consent may thus be voted in naturally in the course of time unless, as Unionists see it, they can provide sufficient number of Catholics with a stake in the Union. Trends in the constitutional preferences of Catholics show that this is not an unreasonable expectation, with one third of Catholic respondents in the 1994 Northern Ireland social attitude survey preferring retention of the Union (Breen, 1996: 41). This appears to be a fairly stable proportion: in a BBC survey on 17 October 2002 38 per cent of Nationalists indicated they preferred a United Ireland (see BBC, 2002). Breen has also shown that middle-class Catholics do not become *less* Nationalist as they become socially mobile (1998: 12), so economic liberalisation without a political settlement will do nothing to buy off middle-class Catholics – a truth evident from South Africa. The key political decision for the majority of Unionists was thus when best to strike the deal: too soon and they risk alienating Protestants who are resistant to change; too late and they risk alienating Catholics from the idea of a partitionist political settlement. Pro-Good Friday Agreement Unionists see it as opportune to bargain now.

Republicans are not blind to demography either. A debate has been going on within the movement on how best to exploit the opportunity afforded by Catholic demography. Gone are appeals to a traditional cultural nationalism, suited to a rural conservative Catholic society, in favour of a modern equality agenda, suitable to contemporary Catholic employment trends. Moen (1999) reports how, in the Maze, Republican prisoners developed a charter for all those who wished to remain on the Republican wings which included statements against sexism and racism and a commitment to politics. There is also a suspicion that the Catholic population is war-weary – although this weariness has always existed without it much affecting the IRA – however, it is reputed that the IRA recognises that a military victory is unattainable although it is unable to admit it publicly. Certainly, stalwarts in the IRA have become critical of what they refer to as ceasefire soldiers, Young Turks without experience of fighting the war or doing time in prison, and who urge the continuance of the military campaign. It is not necessary to speculate that the IRA are war-weary, for population dynamics encourage Sinn Féin to the idea of the long march. Sinn Féin believe that the political process will deliver their goal of unification by normal means if they can ensure that sufficient Catholics vote for their form of Republicanism. Political violence alienates middle-class Catholics, and the electoral base of Sinn Féin is too narrow for them to wait long enough for their constituency to grow to a majority without the need for the Catholic middle class to become Sinn Féiners. The key political decision for the majority of former militarists and others in Sinn Féin thus becomes when best to stop the violence: too soon and they reduce their effective leverage on the British state, too late and they risk alienating middle-class Catholics whose vote they need in the long march. Sinn Féin has persuaded most of the IRA that it is opportune now to cease the armed struggle. The corollary is that Sinn Féin's capacity to inherit the demographic legacy depends on the IRA remaining on ceasefire during the vicissitudes of the peace process when the new institutions are prorogued under Unionist pressure. Sinn Féin knows that any return to violence will frighten off middle-class Catholics and delay the day when they can obtain an electoral majority demographically. Just how many Young Turks in the IRA will remain politically attuned to this is perhaps the key question.

The differences with Loyalist paramilitary organisations could not be greater. In an unpublished conversation with the author in 2002, John White, once a leading figure in the UDA, and a close confidant of 'mad dog' Johnny Adair, reputedly one-time leader of the killing machine that goes under the name of the Ulster Freedom Fighters, said: 'Many UDA activists are not as politically aware of IRA activists, and working-class Loyalist areas have not seen the same political and community development. Many UDA men don't even vote and there is no political vision.' He also admitted that many do not want to give up the conflict because it is a disguise for their criminal activity and thus provides them with a living. (On Loyalist criminal activity, see Bruce, 1995.) It is also a source of social status and masculine pride in an otherwise helpless and demoralising situation within the ghettoes (as is youth gang violence in the new South Africa). Police and the media in Northern Ireland displayed a moral panic about crime with the introduction of the IRA ceasefire in 1994. In fact, the crime rate in Northern Ireland is very low and there is no evidence of any unusual increase in crime accompanying the transition (Brewer, Lockhart and Rodgers, 1997, 1998, 1999). In recent years, the annual increase has been in double figures, although this is not out of kilter with increases in Great Britain, but between 1999–2000 it fell by 1.2 per cent. That there was none the less a moral panic about crime reflected the key assumption about crime causation: the paramilitaries are hoods and fronts for organised crime, and once no longer involved in political violence disclose their true colours. This was never an accurate view, with the exception of the UDA. The point being made here is that with no electoral mandate to inherit because of Protestant demographic trends and no hope of any rise in births, the UDA and its offshoots continue with political violence to disguise their ordinary crime.

Economic changes and the social structure

The key to the effect which demography had on South Africa's social structure was its intensification of economic factors affecting everyone's life-chance opportunities. South Africa's economy was not able to meet the state's expectations of it. It faced a series of problems, most of which have been carried into the post-transition period – lack of international competitiveness of South African goods as a result of high levels of domestic protection; low productivity; low training and skills levels; unemployment and reduced need for labour amongst new firms; low rates of domestic saving; balance of payment constraints, with domestic production being import-driven; and the vulnerability of South Africa's export economy, essentially raw materials and minerals, to fluctuations in world trade (see Blumenfeld, 1999). A failing economy, burdened by international sanctions and the economic costs of maintaining racial separation, created strains in the social structure which were made worse by the needs of a burgeoning Black population and the incapacity of a diminishing White population to meet its own needs, let alone those of the country as a whole.

It is not that economic factors changed so much in South Africa's case to affect society as a whole, at least not for the better; it was that continued economic deterioration had a politically salutary effect throughout South African society. The future stability of South Africa, and the capacity of wealthy Whites to continue to enjoy their economic privileges, required a political response from them that culminated in the peace process. While this left a residue of poor Whites to oppose the peace process, their clout within the social structure was marginal, being restricted to right-wing Afrikaners, poor White immigrants (mostly from former Portuguese colonies) and unreconstructed White racists in the rural hinterlands. Supporters of the peace process in White society – wealthy Whites, big business, progressive politicians – had a more integral location within the social structure and their weight carried the process. The ANC needed to inherit as viable an economy as possible if South Africa was to remain stable and at least have a chance of meeting Black expectations. This required an economic response from the ANC that culminated in support for a free enterprise economy, which itself facilitated the political process. Greater state regulation of the economy was an alternative, but the ANC opted for a business and market-friendly approach, proposing to limit government expenditure, institute tight monetary control policies by the Reserve Bank, with interest rates high and inflation low, and jettisoning its socialist rhetoric (leading to much complaint from left-wing critics; see Kunnie, 2000). Fiscal and monetary rectitude and free market terminology reassured Whites and the business sector, all of which moderated the political effects of the National Party government's demonisation of the ANC. Unreconstructed opponents of the peace process amongst the radical Black working class, like AZAPO, were not endorsed by key elements in South African society, like the business sector, White radicals and the wealthy, and were effectively marginalised. And their overt racism – one settler, one bullet – did not resonate with ordinary Black voters.

Northern Ireland's economy is also weak and replete with social structural strains that are extenuated by demographic patterns. Based formerly on the traditional industries, its economy has been in decline for the last half-century because of international economic trends and a world-wide decline in the staple industries of shipbuilding, engineering and linen. If Mills was prescient in 1959 by recognising the international dimension to local economic conditions, at the time of Northern Ireland's peace negotiations the local effects of international social processes proved critical. Global economic processes led to deindustrialisation in Northern Ireland, which weakened the relative position of Protestants and limited the capacity for employment patterns to reproduce ethnically structured and very traditional communities based along religious lines (see O'Dowd, 1986, 1995). As I have argued many times (for example, Brewer, Lockhart and Rodgers, 1997, 1998, 1999), Northern Ireland's industrialisation had taken on traditional forms, being structured by two solidaristic communities segregated by religion. Modernisation expressed itself in traditional form because it was structured by Northern Ireland's sectarian divide. Religious differences ensured the survival of separate communities, and through such cultural practices as endogamy, residential segregation, distinct social and political associations and a segregated school system, the social organisation of the two communities ensured their effortless self-perpetuation in traditional forms. Industrialisation helped maintain these traditional forms by reproducing sectarian division through largely segregated workforces and communal patterns of recruitment, often reinforced by industrial development being located in one or other of the segregated communities. Industrial development in Northern Ireland thus took place in a way that helped to reproduce two close-knit, homogeneous, traditional communities divided by religion. During the 1950s and 1960s, however, Northern

Ireland's industrial sector changed significantly with the decline in Northern Ireland's old staple industries and the growth of the service sector.

Deindustrialisation required massive economic restructuring and with the decline of the staple industries the traditional communities they helped to reproduce began to erode. Civil unrest only added to the population relocation and disruption of tight-knit local communities. The traditional forms in which industrialisation had up to that point occurred began to be replaced from the 1970s by a service and public sector that did not so readily reproduce close-knit, segregated communities. Recruitment patterns were not so communally based and tended toward the employment of women and part-time labour. The religious social boundaries which defined these traditional communities also started to change as sectarian patterns were challenged in the 1960s by the rise of the Catholic middle class, improvements in Catholic access to higher education and the emergence of campaigns for civil rights. The conflict itself wrought a burden on the country's economic problems. The level of economic restructuring necessitated by deindustrialisation was negatively affected by the violence. The search for replacement industries was severely hampered by civil unrest, and those attracted were less willing and able to engage in sectarian forms of recruitment given national and international pressure for fair employment practices and the economic incentives to conform thereto. Threats to withdraw or reluctance to relocate gave the new industries a powerful input into the reform process, although there is little evidence of this ever being used, with the exception of a few firms based in the United States concerned about the guidelines contained in the MacBride Principles. This failure of international capital to use investment as a political leverage in Northern Ireland contrasts markedly with the pressure on South Africa through sanctions.

While deindustrialisation worked its effects locally, internal processes have to be recognised as well. The British state's policy response to 'the Troubles' attempted to tackle the disparity and inequality between the communities, which had the effect of dismantling Protestant privilege. This served to reinforce those international processes, like globalisation and deindustrialisation that were affecting local tribalism. The effect of deindustrialisation on Catholics has been more positive than on Protestants, and the British state's policy response has reinforced this. Catholic labour found employment in the new industries (depending on where they were located), and the Catholic middle class had entry to government-controlled employment allowing it to expand out from its own neighbourhoods and community (something the Catholic Church in the early years of the Northern Irish state said they should not do). Residential geography changed as the Catholic middle class moved away from their own group areas in line with patterns of social mobility, making some suburbs more integrated (although working-class residential patterns have tended to polarise). In contrast, Protestant labour lost its position as an aristocracy, and the local economy could not supply the employment needs of middle-class Protestants given competition from middle-class Catholics. Many young middle-class Protestants leave to be educated in Great Britain and fail to return. The 2001 census shows that there has been an annual net loss of 5,000 young people from Northern Ireland over the last ten years, most of whom are Protestant; and there are still more people leaving than returning. The British state has become one of the major employers of Protestant labour, especially in the security industry and the public and civil service, which has the corollary of increasing the leverage of the British government whose jobs it now controls and whose exchequer is underwriting the enormous economic costs of protecting the Union. Given a British government serious about reform, Protestants are in a weak position to resist the push towards a political settlement. While this has the contrary effect on anti-Agreement Unionists, who see the British as once again duplicitous, it carries weight with Trimble and his supporters.

However, there is one effect on *refusniks* that reinforces the idea of a settlement. Economic weakness undermines any idea amongst anti-Agreement Protestants that they can threaten Britain by demanding Ulster independence. This is not economically viable: it might perhaps be no worse off than in the United Kingdom but it would certainly be dangerously weaker economically than the Republic (on the 'Celtic Tiger' economy of the Republic, see O'Hearn, 1998). This is just as unrealistic a political strategy as the *volkstaat* peddled by White South Africans opposed to the country's peace process, and only 17 per cent of Unionist respondents opted for this in a BBC poll in October 2002 (BBC, 2002). In this sense there is equivalence in the political position of unreconstructed opponents of peace in the two countries. In effect Whites had nowhere to go, no option but to embrace peace, because they could neither fight nor flee. Ulster Protestants have options only if the British state continues to underwrite them when they fail to embrace peace; and they fear that this is no longer a guarantee. The economic realities underpinning this anxiety creates tough political choices for anti-Agreement Unionists and at the moment tends to tie them in rhetorical knots as they pledge loyalty to a Crown whose government they oppose.

Another economic change with both national and international dimensions which impacts on the social structure in Northern Ireland is the narrowing of the welfare state. The British welfare state is normally mentioned as an incentive for Catholics to oppose unification. This may well affect Unionist political strategies, but not Nationalist ones. The welfare state is in economic crisis. The narrowing of the British welfare state has reduced the capacity of the state to buy allegiance (true for Protestant and Catholic alike). While this might appear to threaten the peace process, the narrowing of the welfare state has affected local communities in ways that positively reinforce it. There are two effects worth considering: its impact on the decision to leave and on the life-chance opportunities of those who choose to stay. The narrowing of the welfare state increases economic migration, affecting Protestants more than Catholics, weakening their relative economic and electoral position. There is some evidence that the proportion of Catholics who are educated at university in Great Britain is increasing (which is why there is dispute over the date when Catholics will become a numerical majority because of emigration). If this is sustained and it results in their non-return, Catholic population projections will undermine the long march political strategy of Sinn Féin. This puts increased pressure on Sinn Féin to cut a deal in order to keep Catholics at home. However, if a peace deal increases the likelihood of Catholics remaining (because they can now share political power), and persuade more Protestants to leave (because they have lost the right to sole control of the political process), the pressure on Unionists for a compromise now increases in order to cancel out the long-term effects of differential migration patterns.

Perhaps the main effect of the narrowing of the welfare state on the peace process in Northern Ireland is experienced in terms of the social problems it creates in the social structure in particular local milieux.

The narrowing of the welfare state is rooted in national and global economic processes that have caused governments universally to cut the welfare budget along with all public expenditure, yet its effects are experienced locally irrespective of the religious make-up of the neighbourhood. These social problems, ironically, have a positive effect on the peace process. The constitutional issue, for example, loses its overriding centrality in face of the concern around housing, unemployment, crime, drugs, single parents, domestic abuse, teenage pregnancies, and cuts in health and community care, school budgets and the like. These affect working-class Protestant and Catholic neighbourhoods equally, and the political agenda of both sets of politicians has been forced to address these sorts of issues. Politicians have been criticised when they appear to remain locked solely into the constitutional conflict – the new Loyalist parties, all of which support the peace process, criticise Paisley's DUP for the narrowness of their agenda, offering nothing but 'Ulster says No'. Politically expedient relationships have thus been established between some of the local representatives and community groups, who see themselves dealing with common problems. Differences on the constitutional issues can be left to one side while their other interests coalesce around social concerns. This has consequences for the way Protestants are mobilised, for traditional appeals to ethnic loyalty alone are insufficient in certain milieux.

The role of the new Loyalists is worth stressing because their political strategy is different to some traditional Unionists as a result of their experience of the local social structure in working-class Loyalist areas. To those locked in the old constitutional battle, the new Loyalist parties are accused of being communists and socialists, unable to claim the title Loyalist at all because they mobilise people on class issues and are prepared to work with Nationalists and Republicans. In not being evangelical (or even religious), the new Loyalists are not traditional Loyalists in another sense either, so accompanying political abuse are personal allegations which impugn their moral rectitude and integrity. In an interview with the author (reported in Brewer, 1998: 158), Pastor Kenny McClinton, a former member of the UVF who once advocated beheading Catholics and impaling their heads on railings in Loyalist areas, but who underwent a religious conversion to evangelical Protestantism in prison, said that the new Loyalists were a group of thugs, criminals and drug pushers, with the acronym UDP standing for Ulster Drug Party. Historically, the Loyalist paramilitaries took their political lead from mainstream Unionist politicians. In an interview with the author (reported in Brewer, 1998: 157), Gary McMichael reports that his father, John McMichael, the assassinated former leader of the UDA, became disillusioned with mainstream Unionism at the time of the 1985 Anglo-Irish Agreement, when their only response was negative (for Gary McMichael's book of recollections, see McMichael, 1999). Something was needed to replace 'Ulster says No', and the UDA produced the 'Common Sense' document (Ulster Defence Association, 1987), some of which has found its way into the Good Friday Agreement. Simultaneously, Loyalist paramilitaries who found themselves in prison and some of their comrades in the mortuary, underwent a political transformation whilst inside (see Garland, 1997, 2001). They emerged with a political agenda, pursued by new parties like the Ulster Democratic Party and the Progressive Ulster Party (PUP). And there is an element of bitterness with the mainstream Unionists whose rhetoric had led the prisoners to sacrifice themselves for no political gain, with the result there is no love lost between them. In an interview with the author, David Ervine, leader of the PUP and one of the most influential of the new Loyalists, said that Paisley 'hated his guts' (reported in Brewer, 1998: 157). In interview both he and McMichael said that politically expedient relations across the communal divide were a necessity (Brewer, 1998: 160): 'people are not the same as they were in 1920, society is not the same as it was in 1920, things have changed. And Unionists need to change with it' (Gary McMichael, in Brewer, 1998: 161).

The experiences of the local Loyalist communities they represent, suffering deindustrialisation, economic restructuring, unemployment, the narrowing of the welfare state and the economic ravages of political violence, push these parties towards compromise. It is a harder shove than on the mainstream Unionist parties. Andy White (1998: 25) reports that at the time of the Anglo-Irish Agreement in 1985, when the DUP and Ulster Unionist Party fought their local election campaigns in the Shankill on a 'Smash Sinn Féin' platform, Shankill residents had more pressing priorities, with 55.5 per cent wanting politicians to address issues like bad housing, school closures and unemployment, whilst only 21 per cent saw smashing Sinn Féin as the important issue; a further 20 per cent prioritised both together. The new Loyalist parties reflect some of these concerns while not demurring on the constitutional issue. The vicissitudes within Unionism thus need to be located in structural conditions. Northern Ireland's unemployment rate is the highest of all regions in the United Kingdom, average earnings are the lowest, something borne particularly by the poor. Gary McMicheal said of the effects this had on his political strategy: 'the Union is less important to me than serving the interests of the people of Northern Ireland. I want to help them to live together, to find an accommodation, to transcend the conflict. I have more in common with Nationalist people in Northern Ireland than I have with the British. Working-class people, irrespective of religion, have a great many problems in common, more than divides them' (interview, 15 October 1997). This look into the future also involves a backwards glance to realise that the Protestant working class benefited very little from the ascendancy: 'they might have felt they belonged in a way that the Catholic working class did not, but Stormont was a one-party state that benefited the fir-coat brigade of wealthy Protestants' (David Ervine, interview, 5 September 1997). Mainstream Unionism was powerless to halt the economic decline and incapable of stopping the violence that threatens the local social structure in Loyalist communities. In the process the new Loyalists changed their relationship with Unionism and with the British state, which under Direct Rule dispensed largesse, making them unwilling to use violence against it (Bruce, 1992: 284). Hence the new Loyalist parties are heavily opposed to violence – whether their own community's or the IRA's. On the other hand, the failure of these parties to establish much of an electoral mandate outside specific local milieux points to the scale of the problem in persuading the majority of Protestants to move toward issues of equality and justice.

Civil society and the democratic deficit

The 'democratic deficit' describes the political vacuum created in Northern Ireland and South Africa arising from the failure of democratic institutions to articulate local issues. The cause of the deficit is different in the two cases: in South Africa it was the absence of democratic institutions for the vast majority of the population because of apartheid, in Northern Ireland it was the abandonment of local representative politics after the collapse of the Stormont government. But the material effects on the peace process are similar in both countries. Let us look first at its effects in Northern Ireland.

Following the introduction of direct rule in 1972, the democratic accountability of the state was severely diminished as officials in the Northern Ireland Office replaced locally accountable representatives. Politically emasculated politicians filled this void able only to exercise veto power – the power to say no to British-led policy initiatives without carrying responsibility locally for the policy deficit this caused. Cochrane (2001: 139) describes well the effects of this democratic deficit on politics and policy in Northern Ireland.

> The introduction of what was, in effect, government by remote control, left a democratic deficit... No longer responsible for public policy or delivering services, the main political parties contented themselves in indulging in a destructive critique of government policy and each other. The seemingly endless procession of elections throughout the 1970s and 1980s, together with attempts to massage the political stalemate via inter-party talks, saw an emphasis being placed upon the constitutional future of Northern Ireland, while pressing social and economic issues slipped down the policy agendas.

It took some time therefore for local politicians to become concerned with bread-and-butter issues because they carried no responsibility for them; whatever effect the narrowing of the welfare state had on generating concern amongst ordinary people over various social problems, the mainstream politicians took aeons to move the debate from constitutional issues. They were assisted in eventually doing so not only by participation in locally accountable institutions developed through the Good Friday Agreement, but also by the pressure of many community groups in civil society.

It is a truism that peace-building is conditioned by the violence it seeks to transcend. The sporadic and low-intensity nature of the conflict in Northern Ireland ensured that the scale of the killings did not destroy civil society. In some conflicts the intermediary level of non-governmental organisations, community groups, trade unions, churches and para-church organisations has been eliminated in the massacre. This did not happen in Northern Ireland or South Africa.

The vacuum created by the democratic deficit was initially filled in both societies by a series of community action groups accountable to local people, which pursued the agenda of 'community development' in ways that moved the peace process along.

In Northern Ireland, some of these groups are neighbourhood-based, addressing locality-wide communal issues that affect their area; others deal with specific constituencies or issues, such as women's groups, victims of crime and reconciliation and peace issues. Former military activists and ex-prisoners, known as 'insider partials', vie with church people, the victims of crime, women's groups, trade unionists and community workers to push the agenda towards community development, which is code for policies of local economic regeneration, social improvement and community integration. This sector of voluntary and civil society organisations, normally referred to as non-governmental organisations, is thriving. Taylor (2001: 43) estimates that there are 5,000 voluntary and community groups, with an annual turnover of £400 million, equal to about 6 per cent of the region's Gross Domestic Product, and employing 65,000 volunteers and 30,000 paid workers, about 5 per cent of the workforce, more than in agriculture. Its success is also its weakness. The sector is only partly separate from government because, as Knox and Quirk (2000: 200) point out, British government-funded programmes dominate most of their work. To some this is 'dirty money' coming with various tags (being easily presented as British plots to woo Unionists into a united Ireland or Catholics into supporting the Union), but the work has been beneficial to the peace process for several reasons.

There have been direct political effects, by encouraging politicisation of the sector around economic and social issues rather than the constitution, which in turn has prompted the sector to develop a critical response to the ongoing political conflict (see Cochrane, 2001: 141). Many people working in the sector are aware of the negative effects of violence on their communities and many such groups therefore develop a peace agenda alongside community development. Mediators in instances of local interface conflict are often community workers and church people, part of the social fabric of the area and concerned about the effects of violence locally (see Brewer, Bishop and Higgins, 2001); indeed, many groups in civil society are formed in response to specific instances of violence or atrocity (Cochrane, 2001: 145), although these are often the most fragile since they can sometimes not sustain themselves beyond the memory (Brewer, Bishop and Higgins, 2001: 39–41). The effect that some of these community groups have had on the empowerment of women is a good illustration of their political role. It is not too much of an exaggeration to claim that local women's groups have had the most profound effect on cross-community activities of all voluntary groups in Northern Ireland (Brewer, Bishop and Higgins, 2001: 35–6). Groups such as Women Together for Peace, the Women and Peacebuilding Programme and Women's Information Group have actively sought to bring about a cessation of sectarian violence in Northern Ireland and give women a voice in society. This parallels the development of the Women's Coalition which is beginning to establish itself as a political party to contest on women's issues and non-sectarian concerns generally. These activities are beginning to make gender an important social cleavage in society, which is altering the dynamics of politics and enhancing the growth of alternative issues that cut across traditional sectarian politics. While the main political parties each have a women's caucus based on sectarian lines, it is simply not the case that most women's groups in the community and voluntary sector acknowledge the primacy of the national struggle above other issues as O'Neill alleges (cited enthusiastically by McGarry, 2001: 133).

However, the greatest effect of the community and voluntary sector on the peace process is perhaps more subtle than this and illustrates well the intersection between politics and sociology that Mills articulated. Two effects in particular are worth mentioning: the NGOs have developed a form of communitarianism by promoting active citizenship and encouraged the development of a local civic culture in face of the divided society surrounding them. Communitarianism emerged in the 1980s intended as a community response to international developments. Global economic processes led to fiscal policies that laid stress on low taxation, low inflation and low public expenditure, wrapped up in a political ideology – Thatcherism and Reaganomics – that saw this as the fulfilment of liberal theory and practice. The dominant themes of communitarianism (see Glendon, 1991; Etzioni, 1993, 1995) are that individual rights need to be balanced with social responsibilities, and that autonomous selves do not exist in isolation but are shaped by the values and culture of society. Society was said famously by Mrs Thatcher not to exist, but communitarianism argues that by participating in their communities active citizens can counterbalance the threat that our lives will become anomic and normless, self-centred and driven by self-interest. Such an argument has deep roots in sociology, going back to the tradition of civic humanism in the Scottish Enlightenment (Brewer, 1988), Durkheim and the whole community studies tradition. But it is not an argument for the retention of traditional community, with its repressive forms of social control through the patriarchal family and informal community structures, although not a few critics have interpreted it in this way. Communitarianism accepts the modern condition that we are located within a web of pluralistic communities with cross-cutting cleavages rather than a monolithic majoritarian social bloc, but in amelioration it stresses the importance of moral education, including the values of tolerance and peaceful conflict resolution, and of active participation by citizens in new kinds of public–private partnerships and local service programmes.

The activities of the voluntary sector in Northern Ireland evince just such new forms of participation, exemplified by the Northern Ireland Council for Voluntary Action (NICVA) (see NICVA, 1996). The large amount of cash from the European Union for peace and reconciliation persuaded many civil society groups to develop this agenda. It is a huge pot. The European Union's implementation of the Special Peace and Reconciliation Programmes has meant an investment in Northern Ireland in excess of £1.5 billion in support of peace and reconciliation activities in civil society, larger than the Gross National Product of many Third World countries. The important point in this context is made by Taylor (2001: 44), who argues that the EU insisted that the voluntary and community groups base themselves on the European model of social partnership and dialogue. Partnerships were required to involve three equally weighted elements – NGOs, local councillors and representatives from stakeholders in the community, business, trade unions and statutory sector. By 2001, there were 26 district partnerships, involving over 600 people in local decision-making, and many other formal partnership groups (discussed in Taylor, 2001: 44–5). 'Altogether,' the Head of the Secretariat of the Northern Ireland Partnership Board observed, 'we are witnessing an important sea change, a fundamental shift in the nature of civic responsibility and a popular demand for new models of participatory democracy' (quoted in NICVA, 1996: 5; also see NICVA, 1997; Hughes et al., 1998).

This kind of active citizenship has been important to the peace process in its own right as an alternative to traditional sectarian forms of political representation; Hughes and colleagues subtitled their study of partnerships 'The Path to Peace' (1998). But its effects have been complemented by the encouragement it has given to the development locally of a civic culture. Divided societies are antithetical to civic cultures because they are fractured into self-centred and self-interested ethnic groups, which take no collective responsibility and lack a sense of society as an integrated whole. Civic cultures by contrast are governed by the public good and underpinned by moral values that are tolerant and socially inclusive. It is at a local level, in particular milieux, that a form of civic culture has developed in the absence of such in the social structure generally, in which socially committed and accountable activists work for the collective communal good of their locality as a whole or specific client groups within it. Whether it is in churches, para-church activities, community relations initiatives, cross-community ventures, in trade unions, women's groups, and so on, by participation in the community and voluntary sector some ordinary people are coming together locally and in small and silent ways are developing a kind of civic culture based on their work. Once people working in this kind of milieu realise that these localities experience much the same problems irrespective of religion, the impetus increases to collaborate in resolving them, from which can be forged a civic society that transcends locality.

Taylor (2001) argues that such an identity is being formed, something vigorously contested by McGarry (2001: 117–18), since it would negate the need for consociational political models which McGarry favours. The argument here is that where they exist such identities are highly localised. It remains the case that the Orange Order and Gaelic Athletic Association are the largest and perhaps single most popular community groups and they are structured firmly along sectarian lines (McGarry, 2001: 117), but McGarry is wrong to claim that there are more community groups in the voluntary working for sectarian political goals than for a form of bi-communal partnership (2001: 118). At the grassroots it is possible to see the development of particular local spaces – what Mills would call milieux – in which groups are mobilising across the sectarian divide or coming together with others across that divide to push an issue which affects them both. Such local spaces are perhaps most evident in middle-class milieux where membership of community and voluntary associations is greatest; however, community development workers in the working-class districts are aplenty, although those in Loyalist areas have to work facing the opposition of the paramilitaries to the peace process. But even in these milieux there are playwrights, authors, poets and artists – Stuart Parker, Graham Reid, Gary Mitchell, Adrian Rice, David Rudkin and Sam Thompson to name but a few – who are constructing a space in which they can explore through art Protestant identity today and recast relations with Catholics in new ways. This space expands and contracts with the fortunes of the broader peace process or the outbreak of interface violence, but there are very many efforts going on quietly behind the scenes in many local areas which are chipping away at the bottom of the dividing wall, in the hope that eventually the development of trust in local civic culture will bring the edifice down. McGarry is right to contend the wall has not yet fallen, although I am not sure Taylor argued it had, but the honourable attempts locally to remove some of the bricks should not be undervalued. The faltering fortunes of Northern Ireland's peace process compared to South Africa's lies in the failure of political elites to smash its walls in the manner that apartheid crumbled; Northern Irish political elites appear still to rely on busy peace builders at the bottom.

The weaknesses in the structures and processes of apartheid politics in South Africa meant there was a similar democratic deficit in South Africa's Black townships and homelands. If economic liberalisation occurred for Black South Africans under the impulse of a modern economy, White political control was still thoroughly embedded. The exercise of Black political rights was restricted to puppet institutions, parliaments and assemblies, with little power, fewer resources and no legitimacy. Internal political opposition was outlawed, the main liberation movement exiled and close attention was given by the South African police to any activity by Black South Africans that might be construed as threatening White mastery of politics. This was simultaneously apartheid's short-term strength and long-term weakness. Under the apartheid state, social problems were absorbed under the issue of control of the political process and eventually facilitated the peace process by establishing a set of grievances that could not be dissipated by economic liberalisation, allowing the exiled political movements to link their national liberation campaigns with local issues in order to establish an electoral base.

The key to this was the role played by civil society (this is widely recognised, see, for example, Knox and Quirk, 2000: 162–94). It is now a commonplace to argue that civil society was politicised in the 1980s and helped to win the end-game in South Africa (see Cohen, 1986). The sheer scale of this middle sector perhaps could not fail to impose itself. By the early 1990s, Deegan (1999) estimates that there were 54,000 NGOs active in South Africa, with an annual expenditure of one billion Rand, virtually all from foreign funders given as aid, skills training and other resources or as part of anti-apartheid programmes. But even this does not capture the extent of the independent associations that comprise civil society, for it consists of different kinds of groups. Deegan's figures describe only the scale of externally funded groups linked to international agencies. There were groups formed around apartheid's own institutions: either those left relatively untouched by apartheid, such as the Church, which on the whole the apartheid state never repressed, or ironically, those structures established by the state as part of its economic liberalisation and reforms, such as the trade unions and the township committees. There were also autonomous organisations and bodies established by township residents themselves. All of them assisted in placing pressure on the apartheid state, helped move the Black agenda towards politics and community development and away from violence, and provided networks of political activists that the ANC could work with and use in its broader national political strategy. This reduced the need for political violence as a liberation strategy (although political competition between the parties in South Africa itself became violent, especially that between the Inkatha Freedom Party and the ANC). This network of anti-apartheid groups was also avowedly non-racial, and was successful in creating a local space, similar to Northern Ireland, in which the divided identities of apartheid society could be reconstructed to promote the idea of a common civic culture. The ANC's long honourable commitment to non-racialism ensured there was no bifurcation between civil society and the liberation movement in this respect.

This highlights the dual role played by civil society in South Africa's case. In South Africa there were two kinds of democratic deficit, which gave civil society two forms of mediation to undertake. It filled the gap between the state and the wider society, as in Northern Ireland, allowing forms of political representation and delivering services otherwise denied or neglected, but it also filled the vacuum between the external liberation movement and the mass of Black South Africans. The ANC had been banned for several years and had no overt presence in the country. Its intermittent acts of sabotage after 1976 were no substitute for political engagement. It was important that it connected with the internal protests that erupted after 1976 and began to work co-operatively with the plethora of groups that had sprung up during the ANC's exile. Big umbrella groups like the United Democratic Front, which co-ordinated many community, voluntary and political groups, not only mediated between the state and the wider society, almost acting, as Knox and Quirk write (2000: 164), like a government-in-waiting in organising protests, delivering services and representing the case for reconstruction, they also linked the ANC to the internal protest movement (see Houston, 1999 for an analysis of the UDF–ANC links). The Church also mediated both kinds of deficit. The South African Council of Churches (Protestant), the Southern African Bishops Conference (Catholic) and later even the Dutch Reform Church (on which see Kuperus, 1999), and clerics like Tutu, Boesak and Dr Beyers Naude, worked to oppose the state and in concert with the external liberation movement (on the Church in South Africa's transformation, see Prozesky, 1990). So did the trade union movement through organisations like the Congress of South African Trade Unions (whose 'White' leader eventually became a minister in the ANC government).

Three consequences for the peace process merit attention. First, civil society was able to slow the slide into violence that seemed to threaten the township protests as people's courts introduced the 'necklace' (a burning tyre filled with petrol placed round people's necks) as an informal social control and as the South African Police appeared to lose all restraint in its attempt to reassert state control. They did so by utilising both of the arenas within which they worked. They helped persuade the state to moderate its response, or, at least, that an exclusively military response was self-defeating, especially through their link to international agencies that pressured the White government through the threat of sanctions and by appeals to norms of international human rights. Internationally-linked NGOs were particularly important in this respect. And civil society helped persuade the internal movement, especially by influencing the UDF–ANC alliance which dominated the liberation struggle, that violence was self-defeating since it risked them inheriting an irreparably damaged economy. The Church was only one group of many that was particularly vocal in warning the liberation movement of the dangers of the descent into violence. Second, by filling two vacuums at once, the array of community and voluntary groups, NGOs, residents' organisations and the like linked grassroots peacemaking with top-level negotiations. The ANC took civil society with them to the negotiating table, in the sense that the vision, commitment and experience of participation in non-racial citizenship activity within civil society infused the negotiations. Indeed, Deegan (1999) argues that one of the complaints in the post-apartheid period is that many of the NGOs have not demobilised but have been co-opted by the ANC government to form 'government NGOs', where as policy advisers and consultants to the government, they risk becoming associated with the policy postponements and unfulfilled expectations of the post-apartheid period. There is a useful contrast with Northern Ireland here, where the gap between civil society peacemaking and that done around the top table by the politicians is like a chasm (Brewer, Bishop and Higgins, 2001: 86). With the exceptions of Sinn Féin and the Progressive Unionist Party, there is no integration of the activities at the grassroots with high-level negotiations, and the spirit and commitment at the bottom does not infect the top.

Third, civil society took its experience, skills and resources into the interregnum of the transition period between 1990, when de Klerk signalled the start of the reforms, and 1994, when the first non-racial election was held. This was a period when insecurities and uncertainties flourished while the negotiations proceeded and in which incidents of violence broke out, especially between the ANC, the Inkatha Freedom Party and shadowy 'third force' groups and death squads which potentially threatened the peace process (see Laurence, 1990; Kane-Berman, 1993; Jeffrey, 1995). The number of deaths in political violence doubled during the transition period (see Sisk,

1994; du Tout, 2001). The parties agreed the establishment of the National Peace Accord, which contained codes of conduct for political parties and armed groups, interim measures of reconstruction and community development, and the formation of local structures to monitor the violence and effect conflict resolution. There were regional and local peace committees – over 200 in all – which in effect drew on the expertise and resources of civil society to undertake their work, bringing together representatives of community and voluntary groups, NGOs, women's groups, the Churches, trade unions, civic organisations, resident committees, tribal authorities, as well as the police and army. Local circumstances were accorded a role in determining the make-up of the committee to ensure as wide legitimacy as possible. They tried to settle disputes and moderate the violence, and while they were never entirely successful in the Kwa Zulu-Natal region or on the Witwatersrand, the violence would have been worse without them (the Annual Reports of the National Peace Secretariat make interesting reading, see National Peace Secretariat, 1993, 1994). It was this sort of approach to active citizenship and local participation in the structures of peace-building, begun in civil society, that later informed the Truth and Reconciliation Commission.

Changing patterns of differentiation

It should be apparent from the above that the fault lines in South Africa and Northern Ireland based around ethnicity (socially marked in the former case by 'race' and the latter by religion), that shaped both their social structure and political processes, are beginning slowly to change with the emergence of new fissures. This does not mean the disappearance of ancient social cleavages – racial inequalities remain real in South Africa and the saliency of religion in Northern Ireland is high because secularisation is working only slowly and religious differences remain important (see survey evidence in Bruce and Alderdice, 1993; Brewer, 2002). It would be a fool indeed who argued that religious or racial differences no longer mattered. I concluded a review of patterns of religiosity in Northern Ireland between 1993 and 1998 with the following observation: 'there is no evidence that events during the decade around the cease-fires and peace negotiations have weakened either religious identification or the impact of religion on ethno-national identities' (2002: 38). This remains my view. I claim here only that ethnicity is not the only form of differentiation in the social structures of South Africa and Northern Ireland, and the political process is beginning to reflect this as 'own-group' interests slowly give way to cross-cutting alliances. Religion and 'race' no longer solely represent and subsume all other conflicts and this has been beneficial to the peace process. However, alternative lines of division are relatively weaker in Northern Ireland than in South Africa, helping to explain its different fortunes.

In South Africa ethnic boundaries and identities were never as clear cut as in Northern Ireland. This is ironic given that group boundaries were defined legally but identities amongst dominant and subordinate groups were blurred because of cultural divisions between Afrikaners and English speakers, the existence of 'Coloured' people as Black Afrikaans speakers, and the many ethnic groups amongst Africans. Ethnic group identities amongst Black South Africans were complicated by the existence of a significant middle class, whose creation had been a deliberate aim of state policy (see Kuper, 1965). This produced economic differences between the Black social classes, differences in consumption patterns, life-style and life-chance opportunities, and commensurate political differences over such issues as private enterprise, nationalisation and state subsidisation (and the ideological divisions within and between the parties have been, and remain, great). However, the class differences that emerged within the Afrikaans-speaking community perhaps proved more significant.

The newly elected National Party in 1948 set about solving the 'poor White problem' by massive expansion of state and public employment, with preferential treatment of Afrikaners. The eventual *embourgeoisement* of Afrikaners weakened their capacity to act as a unified ethnic group pursuing exclusively ethnic goals (see Adam and Giliomee, 1980; Giliomee, 1992). The class interests of wealthy Afrikaners urged the National Party to pursue economic growth, and the party began to rid itself of those elements within the Afrikaans community (the White working class) which caused dissonance, and brought into alliance sections of business, the English-speaking community and, eventually, sections of the Black middle class (see Brewer, 1986: 34). This new class alliance caused political problems for the National Party and the state it controlled, for it weakened ethnic solidarity amongst Afrikaners and led to divisions within Afrikaner politics (see Charney, 1984, who attributes the break-away of the Afrikaner right to class conflict). It partially incorporated some sections of the minority group, such as homeland leaders, which only set up contradictions within apartheid and fuelled opposition amongst the rest. Giliomee (1990: 309) reports that by the beginning of South Africa's peace process in 1990, many Afrikaners wished to normalise politics because their class interests had shifted their allegiances from the ethnic *volk* (and the National Party as the guarantor of the *volk*) to the state itself. A deal which left the state intact, even if under the control of the ANC, was acceptable to these Afrikaners so long as the ANC was prepared to share power within the state. (Gagiano (1990) documents this by survey evidence amongst White students.) The adoption of a new 'South African identity' post-1994, with its associated symbolic structures, like new national anthem and flag, was thus relatively easy.

The same social structural processes are not as clear in Northern Ireland. New cleavages are only now appearing within Northern Ireland around class, gender and 'race' (on racial and ethnic minorities in Northern Ireland, see Hainsworth, 1998) and are not wielding much political effect. Class differences in Northern Ireland have always existed within each ethnic bloc but have never been relevant enough to affect basic political loyalties, and class interests across the ethnic divide hardly emerged. Instances of common purpose amongst working-class Catholics and Protestants, for example, such as in the 1907 dock strike or the Poor Law riots in the 1930s, never lasted long (see Patterson, 1980; Brewer, 1998), and we know from Breen's work that social mobility amongst middle-class Catholics does not make the bulk of them *less* Nationalist (Breen, 1998) despite the myth that they become 'Castle Catholics' (a reference to Dublin Castle, former seat of British imperial power in Ireland and shorthand for pro-Union). None the less, there is evidence that ethnicity alone no longer subsumes all other lines of differentiation, although there is no sign yet that this impacts on many people's political preferences. The overwhelming number of people still vote as an ethnic bloc even though cross-cutting cleavages are beginning to appear – a situation similar to Afrikaners until the last years of apartheid. It is worth discussing these changes in social differentiation in terms of the three levels on which such contradictory evidence exists: local, national and international.

Evidence comes in part from the changes within local social structures described above, as new fissures emerge in some milieux around the increasingly diverse interests of residents. These localised 'civic cultures' create a space in which social relations are possible across the divide, and in which people can avoid their ethnic group identity for the purposes of the interaction, belong to both groups or neither, making the cleavages ambiguous as they meet across the communal divide as, for example, women, peace activists, ecumenists, environmental activists, victims of crime or parents concerned at drug abuse. Cross-community groups have taken advantage of space within local milieux (and generous funds) to flourish in both number and range of activity. A considerable amount of grassroots reconciliation, cross-community and peace work is done in the North across the sectarian divide (see Knox and Quirk, 2000: 66–85; Brewer, Bishop and Higgins, 2001; Cochrane, 2001), but since there is no tangible measure against which to test its success it is difficult to see what impact it has on politics or the social structure. This does not stop some people saying it has been unsuccessful (see Knox and Quirk, 2000: 82), although Hughes and Donnolly (2002: 40) confidently state that community relations work is having positive effects at the grass roots. Nonetheless it remains true that the major turning points in the peace process that moved it forward were either externally-led initiatives or, as Cochrane argues (2001: 151), violent atrocities. Yet the fact that a major outrage can push the peace process onward in this way shows both the abhorrence most people have for communal violence and their wish for the killings to stop. It does not yet disclose in the majority a will to take that extra step of compromise which a more genuine peace settlement requires. (This is consistent with most Protestants' individual biographical experience of violence, discussed in Chapter 3.) Moreover, the reconciliation efforts at the bottom have not altered people's social behaviour in other areas. Mixed marriage is a case in point. Taylor writes optimistically that mixed marriages have grown to one in ten (2001: 43). In fact they have grown now to nearly one in five. Evidence from the Northern Ireland Life and Times Survey shows that between 1991 and 1998, the proportion of respondents who were married or living with someone of the same religion dropped from 92 per cent to 83 per cent (Brewer, 2002: 36). Looked at with darker glasses, it still means that eight out of ten people marry or set up home with someone whose religious identity is the same. More than that, there is little intermarriage or cohabitation between denominations: 91 per cent of Catholics have partners who are Catholic, 68 per cent of Church of Ireland respondents have partners inside the denomination, as do 72 per cent of Presbyterians.

Changes to social differentiation are also the result of broader structural processes affecting Northern Ireland as a national unit, particularly the emergence of the Catholic middle class. Middle-class Catholics are no longer contained in ethnic enclaves either in where they live or work; indeed, some research shows that the proportion of Catholics under the age of 35 employed in the Northern Ireland Civil Service exceeds that of Protestants (Whyte, 1993: 112). The significance of this sector will only increase, to both Sinn Féin and the Ulster Unionists. Sinn Féin needs their support and for this it requires the IRA to stop killing. Unionists hope they will develop a stake in Union as a result of *embourgeoisement* but if this is unrealistic, at the very least the demands of this group for a political settlement that respects an Irish dimension means that some sort of peace process is required. Yet there is not much sign of common interests developing with the Protestant middle class, who remain ambivalent about the all-Irish aspects of the Good Friday Agreement, valuing it more for its devolution of control over their own affairs (Hayes and McAllister, 2001b: 85; MacGinty and Wilford, 2002).

Another structural process with potential to alter patterns of cleavage is the emergence of integrated education, but again the evidence is contradictory. There are two kinds of integrated education. The first is genuinely mixed schools, whose number had grown by 2000 to 28, an increase from 10 in as many years (Taylor, 2001: 43), although this still only comprises about 3 per cent of the school population (McGarry, 2001: 133). The other kind is growth of cross-school activity, through programmes like Education for Mutual Understanding (EMU) and Cultural Heritage. Gallagher (1994) shows that in ten years over a third of primary schools and half of post-primary schools were involved in contact schemes, but a review of EMU by Smith and Robinson (1996) revealed that schools were meeting minimal statutory requirements only. Knox and Quirk point out that while there are now 700 schools participating in other forms of ongoing contact, representing 54 per cent of all schools, the number of pupils involved is one in ten for post-primary and one in five for primary (2001: 67–8). This is ground for optimism but in the long term.

Some processes are international. The notion of 'national sovereignty' is coming under challenge amongst some supporters of Irish unity as a result of membership of the European Unity, which affects the symbolic meaning and reality of the border (on the significance of European identity as perceived by the SDLP, see Hume, 1993). These processes are affecting Protestant ethnic identity as well. Globalisation is fragmenting Protestant culture, particularly youth culture, as a result of new patterns of consumption, of both consumer goods and identities (see Brewer, 1999, 2000a: 176–80; Smyth and Cairns, 2000). Secularisation is affecting mainstream Protestant denominations (but perhaps no other) as the membership of mainline Protestant Churches declines, church attendance becomes more irregular and attitudes on moral issues become more liberal (see survey data in Brewer, 2002). Moreover, 'political Protestantism', which uses a religious label to define a political position on the constitution, is beginning to change. The Orange Order, for example, is losing membership and is finding it difficult to sustain wide-scale participation in the protest at Drumcree (only 400 turned up to support the 250-day anniversary of the protest, and senior Lodge officials complained that too many Brethren preferred watching television). The Order has come under fierce criticism from within its ethnic constituency as moderate Unionists and middle-class Protestants bemoan the disorder, violence and deaths associated with Drumcree (it is also criticised by diehards for its willingness to compromise on a few flash-point marches). A debate is clearly taking place within the Order, with people like the Rev. William Bingham questioning its practices (and his own membership) as a result of the murder of the Quinn brothers and Joel Patton (leader of the diehard 'Spirit of Drumcree' group) being expelled. The Order is also busily engaging in a process of historical revisionism in which it casts (or recasts) itself as a solely Christian organisation intending no harm to Catholics (for example, see Kennaway, 1997), although it is worth remembering that the Independent Orange Order represents more extreme Protestantism and is oblivious to the need for debate.

The contradictory nature of the evidence reveals itself in the volatility of vox pop surveys, which all goes to mirror the ambivalence of the changes in social differentiation and identity in Northern Ireland.

The 1998 election survey, for example, discovered that 62 per cent of Protestants and 61 per cent of Catholics preferred to live in residentially mixed areas, which belies the increasing segregation of housing patterns over the last three decades. Attitudes towards mixed marriages illustrate the point well (see Brewer, 2002: 36). The 1998 Life and Times Survey revealed that 43 per cent thought that most people would 'not mind' if a family member married someone from a different religion; and, as is usual in surveys like this, people are even less willing to attribute socially unacceptable views to themselves, so only 26 per cent say that they personally would 'mind a lot' or 'mind a little'. However, it is worth noting that while Catholics are the most open and liberal in response to these questions and 'Other Christians' the least, this runs completely counter to the number of mixed marriages within each, since Catholics have the least and 'Other Christians' the most (91 per cent of Catholics and 60 per cent of 'Other Christians' have partners also within the same grouping). One further example can suffice to illustrate the sociological disjuncture between attitudes and behaviour. In a poll reported in the *Irish News* (4 March 1999), 93 per cent of respondents said they supported the Good Friday Agreement, including 73 per cent of DUP voters and 93 per cent of Ulster Unionist voters; now anti-Agreement feeling is in the ascendancy in both parties.

Yet two points are worth remembering which are more positive in the long term. Most anti-Agreement Unionism is opposed to cutting a deal with Sinn Féin not to a political settlement overall. Opposition focuses primarily on the exclusion of Sinn Féin. In a public opinion poll in March 1999, one-third of Protestants indicated they objected to participation of Sinn Féin in government irrespective of decommissioning (which seems to confirm Adams's claim that decommissioning obscures the unwillingness of some Unionists to have 'Fenians' in power regardless). This appears to be a stable proportion. In a BBC poll on 17 October 2002, 37 percent of Ulster Unionist Party voters said they would not share power with either the SDLP or Sinn Féin, compared with 79.2 percent of DUP voters, while 36.6 percent said they would share power with the SDLP and another 25.5 percent with both; BBC, 2002). The IRA's alleged activities in Columbia, Castlereagh and in interface violence have probably lost Sinn Féin support amongst those Protestants who would have accepted them in power if decommissioning had gone ahead more vigorously and successfully. However, excluding Sinn Féin from the settlement is impossible politically given its mandate, and any attempt to do so would risk massive vote-switching from the SDLP to Sinn Féin (but only if the IRA's guns remain silent and were decommissioned by rust, as after all were de Valera's). If this electoral mandate strengthens, recalcitrant Protestants, like Afrikaners in the early to mid-1980s, may soon come to realise they have no choice but to work with Sinn Féin: there is nowhere else to go.

Second, whatever might be said about the failure to achieve reconciliation at the bottom as a way of challenging arguments that there has been minor social transformation in Northern Ireland (for example, McGarry, 2001: 133), it well exceeds whatever has occurred in South Africa, and its peace process proceeds apace. South Africa's settlement was an elite consensus between the ANC and the National Party and was carried through without much social transformation at the bottom. (Du Toit (2001: 143–6) discusses 'social distance' survey results to show the continued attachment to racial identities in South Africa.) Elite consensus in Northern Ireland requires co-operation with a more diverse range of parties and at present lags well behind the level of cross-community and reconciliation work in society as a whole. In the long term the politicians at the top who seem to have control of the process, haggling, indecisive and unsure, risk being out of touch with these social developments.

International dimensions

The peace process has been internationalised in a way that Mills predicted events in nation states would be. This affects both the social structure and polity of the two societies and positively reinforces the peace process. We have already addressed the international socio-economic processes that have caused profound changes in the social structure of both societies as mediated through the effects of globalisation, deindustrialisation, the narrowing of the welfare state and the blurring of the economic, if not the cultural, significance of borders. International economic and diplomatic sanctions reinforced the local effect that wider socio-economic processes had in South Africa. In Northern Ireland's case, the impact of Europeanisation affected considerations of national sovereignty as it applies in the modern context of membership of the European Union. European models of citizenship also had positive effects in local milieux.

In this section, we take further the discussion of the international dimension to the peace process by highlighting the impact of international political developments, particularly as they resonated with local social structural conditions. Let us go first to South Africa since the internationalisation of South Africa's peace process provides instructive lessons for Northern Ireland. South Africa had strong international links historically, which only intensified as wider international relations developed. The international order during the Cold War was such that the stability of Southern Africa as a whole was seen as vital to the interests of the West. There is also an important sociological dimension that should not be neglected. As a settler society with high levels of White immigration in the past, ethnic and kinship links with societies elsewhere permeated South Africa's social structure, giving Britain and Europe generally an interest in the peace process on top of any diplomatic or political concern. But these cultural ties never approached the scale where they created a political dynamic in the way that there is in Israeli–US relations because of the size of the Jewish diaspora in the United States. The material interests of investors gave much stronger connections and involvement in the place, especially from the United States and Europe. It took some time for investors to perceive that their best interests were served by reform of the apartheid state rather than shoring it up, so initially economic sanctions were negligible, then half-hearted, and only later biting; and in the early stages, the South African economy showed a remarkable ability to adapt to sanctions. Later forms of sanction were more severe under pressure from the anti-apartheid movement, particularly as their concerns fed into politics in the donor countries, notably Black American politics, as well as Western fears of the destabilising effect on the region of South Africa's collapse into war. These increased diplomatic and economic pressures affected White South Africans materially and politically. Equally important, the ending of the Cold War had its effect locally on the ANC. At one level this has led to analogies between the roles of de Klerk and Mikhail Gorbachev in moving monoliths (see Etherington, 1992: 103–4), but most crucially the ANC lost its patron. The West gave the ANC symbolic rather than material support; the latter came from the Soviet Union. Towards the end of the 1980s, a changing international context encouraged the ANC towards an accommodation. Confronted with its own severe economic problems, domestic ethnic tensions and the eventual collapse of communism, the Soviet Union firmly indicated to the ANC that its material aid would dry up and that it should negotiate with Whites (Giliomee, 1990: 306). The Bush administration told them the same (Johnson, 1990).

The end of the Cold War had its effects in Northern Ireland too. The shift within the IRA during the 1980s to an equality agenda, which occurred first in the prisons (Moen, 1999), combined with the demonstrative success of Sinn Féin's political strategy after the 1981 hunger strikes, were lessons reinforced at the beginning of the 1990s by the ending of the Cold War. This affected Republican thinking and language (see Cox, 1997; Shirlow and McGovern, 1998), pushing it away from colonial models of the British presence in Ireland to a rethink about the place of Protestants. 'The Troubles' were described using a language of rights – the lack of a just social order and civil and human rights – rather than colonial rhetoric about the British presence. Protestants were re-evaluated – no longer settlers to be driven to the sea but sharers of the island with whom an agreed Ireland needed to be finalised. And given that the Soviet monolith crumbled peacefully, there was a reassessment of the role of armed struggle. The Soviets were not patrons of the IRA as they were of the ANC, and surrogates like Libya had given them sufficient arms to make the collapse of the Soviet Union unproblematic for the supply of hardware; the fact that it fell without a bullet or bomb expended was salutary.

Again, there is an important sociological dynamic overlooked in discussion of international political developments. In Northern Ireland's case ethnic and kinship links with other societies resonated more strongly than in South Africa, such as the Irish Catholic diaspora in the United States, Protestant cultural and kinship ties with Britain and Canada, and Catholic ties with the Irish Republic. The Irish-American lobby ensured the US government involved itself heavily in brokering peace (see Guelke, 1996b; MacGinty, 1997; Wilson, 1995, 2000). The effect of the two most closely related governments is subtler. The British and Irish governments acted as patrons to their respective communities, and their unflinching support effectively blocked movement in the internal political process for a long time. The outbreak of civil unrest in 1968–9 forced Northern Ireland's conflict on the agenda of both governments, and while at one time the South thought of invading in support of embattled Catholics, it gave unstinting support to the British government's campaign against terrorism and its attempts at externally-led accommodation. However, after the failure of the Sunningdale initiative, the British government effectively withdrew politically to concentrate on defeating terrorism until the 1985 Anglo-Irish Agreement. The Agreement institutionalised the patron roles of both governments, and while the two governments presented themselves as merely holding the ring to enable the internal parties to come to a settlement, the failure of movement internally eventually forced them to become more proactive and persuasive with their respective clients. However, the lack of movement in itself does not alone explain this transformation in governmental intervention. Britain has become tired of bank-rolling Protestant insecurity, and the 1997 Labour government reduced, if not ended, the power of the Protestant veto (something which encourages Unionists and Sinn Féin alike to negotiate). The South's government for a long time felt sympathy towards a war-weary Unionist community facing a terrorist onslaught, but after their intransigence over the Anglo-Irish Agreement the South became much less tolerant of traditional Unionism (Torsney, 1998: 8). The sense that Northern Protestants had not responded to gestures, and that Republicans, North and South, showed more willingness to compromise, has seen a shift in Southern opinion towards a more overtly Nationalist position. The recognition by Southerners of the need for Protestant 'consent' to unification does not contradict this, for this is seen as acceptable as a tactic to assist the achievement of an accommodation. Thus, both patrons are urging their clients to go for reform, which simultaneously encourages the peace process and raises the opportunity costs for either client should they return to violence. And thus the internal parties now do not just address the external players, they dialogue with their opponents. They share rooms and assemblies as well as power, if only falteringly.

Conclusion

Graffiti on a gable wall in South Belfast declares in bold black letters 'Peace Now'. If we turn that into a question not a statement, to answer it we need to address the factors that help to explain why this peace process has proved so relatively successful (and it has, even in

Northern Ireland). This chapter has argued that to understand the relative success of the current process it is important to transcend several antinomies – those between politics and the social structure, the local and the national, and the national and the international. As we have seen, the sociological imagination breaches many more. It straddles the antinomies between the historical and the contemporary, as discussed in Chapter 2, and between the personal and the public, the individual and the social structural, addressed in Chapter 3. In shattering these antinomies it is easy to appreciate what an iconoclast Mills was, and how broad a discipline he hoped to make sociology.

A new nexus between politics and the social structure has emerged in Northern Ireland and in South Africa to encourage the peace process. This is evidenced in national demographic trends, economic changes, particular social transformations in civic culture and in the lines of social differentiation, which are in some instances rooted in global and international processes but in others are restricted to particular local milieux. International processes are both political (Europeanisation, the ending of the Cold War, external third-party intervention) and socio-economic (globalisation, secularisation, international economic sanctions). Local milieux are affected differently by these national and international trends, leading not only to contrasts between Northern Ireland and South Africa but above all to differences of local space within each country. In some cases local spaces are opening up in which, for example, grassroots peacemaking and reconciliation are possible, and in which new identities can be experimented with and perceived as possible or in which existing identities come to be seen as more flexible and inclusive than previously imagined. New broad social trends are evident, such as the widening of class differences within ethnic blocs and differential fertility and emigration rates. And new effects of broader trends are being experienced locally, such as the impact on people of the narrowing of the welfare state and economic deindustrialisation. We have seen how all of these developments connect to and affect the shape and fortunes of the peace process. This points to the truth of Mills's claim about the intersection of politics and the social structure. However, as we stress in the Conclusion, where we bring all the strands of the sociological imagination together, what is important about this intersection is that human agency intervenes.

Conclusion: The Sociological Imagination and the Peace Process

Introduction

It is essential to conclude this conjectural history of the peace process in Northern Ireland and South Africa with the perspective from both sides of the Janus face. The argument, it may be recalled, was two-sided, in which a specific kind of sociology was being used to see what light it might throw on the process by which communal violence is ending in South Africa and Northern Ireland, while simultaneously using this topic to illuminate the utility of a version of sociology that transcends narrow disciplinary boundaries to address the manifold ways in which history, politics and human agency connect with the social structure. To this point, the argument has concentrated on outlining what the separate dimensions of the sociological imagination taken in isolation reveal about the peace process. It is important now to bring these elements together in an overview assessment of whether the sociological imagination as Mills portrayed it particularly informs us about the emergence and progress of the process at this historical juncture. We close by addressing the reverse issue of what the peace process says for the usefulness of this approach to sociology.

Between God and chance

The peace process in South Africa and Northern Ireland is commonly described using the metaphor of a miracle (with respect to South Africa, see Guelke, 1999; for Northern Ireland, see Taylor, 2001).

These authors do not suggest that divine intervention explains the transformation, although John Whyte once wrote that it would need as much for a united Ireland ever to be realised (1990: 215). Only by analogy has God been invoked by suggesting that the scale of the change has been sufficiently dramatic and unexpected to parallel the Damascus experience. But if not God, then chance? Runciman's programme for sociology (1999), with its neo-evolutionary overtones arising from the attention given to processes of natural selection in cultural and social behaviour, requires that chance play a significant role in social change in order to parallel the contribution of random mutation in biological evolution (see 1999: 93–109; for an illustration with respect to the French Revolution, see Runciman, 1983). Fortune played its part in the peace process: good and bad. Franklin D. Roosevelt reminded us once that good luck for the early bird is bad for the early worm. Peace initiatives in Northern Ireland have been stymied in the past because of the misfortune of small majorities held by the governing party in the British parliament. Conversely, the current process in both countries has benefited immeasurably by the unexpected fall of the Soviet Union. Chance was on the side of the peace process when the National Party in South Africa dismantled White political hegemony on the miscalculation that the ANC was an ethnic party and would not attract support beyond Xhosa (a claim made by Marks, 1998: 18). It might only have been chance that prevented people in South Africa seeing through the illusion that for Whites nothing would change by the political settlement and for Blacks everything would (Marks, 1998: 17) or just bad luck in Northern Ireland that has allowed fears that the violence is not over to deafen people to the silence of the guns.

Faith, fate or fortune, however, are alliterations poor in their quality to explain the peace process. Between God and chance lies sociology. The light that Mills's conception of sociology sheds on the peace process is blindingly obvious. It rejects a monocausal explanation for one that combines individual agency, historical factors, political developments, both nationally and internationally, and social structural developments. Political scientists have stolen a march on sociologists in offering analyses of the peace process so that political developments dominate as causal factors. These vary from the charismatic skills and strategies of key leaders in negotiating political deals, such as Mandela or Mitchell, internal political developments that promoted new strategic alliances between reformist political groups or which weakened the ruling group, to international processes like the collapse of Soviet communism or enhanced external brokering by patrons. Where political scientists recognise there were other incentives to the search for a peace settlement, these are limited to economic ones. The costs of continued communal violence were counted exclusively as economic. Thus, political science explanations tell us that what bore upon political developments were factors like the rising price of paying for apartheid, the effect of international sanctions on South Africa's already weak economy, Britain's declining ability to underwrite Protestant ascendancy financially, the risks of war on the ability of weak economies to maintain privilege for key groups or the wish amongst protagonists to avoid inheriting an irreparably damaged economy ravaged by the economic costs of violence. Economic lessons were salutary to governing elites who needed to change and to violent groups who needed to abandon the armed struggle. All this is true. But it is also insufficient.

Political science approaches have the limits of any monocausal explanation. By extension, the application of the sociological imagination to understanding the peace process at least has the initial advantage of multi-causality. Chapter 1 concluded with a summary account of what a Millsian sociology of the peace process must address. This can be repeated here as a preface to assessing its achievements in enlightening us further about the process through which communal violence is ending in South Africa and Northern Ireland.

- A sociology of the peace process should not offer a grand theory or universal scheme to understand peace processes in general, but is restricted in its applicability to specified cases that exist in real time and space.
- It is necessary to locate the peace process in Northern Ireland and South Africa into its historical past, to establish whether historical factors continue to shape the form and context of the process.
- Any account of the emergence and development of the peace process in these two countries must focus on the intersection between the social structure, individual biographical experience and the political process.

- This means in practice that it is necessary to:

    - identify social structural conditions, and changes to long established patterns of structural differentiation, which affect the dynamics of conflict and conflict resolution, both internal to each country and internationally;
    - outline the events and developments within the political process, nationally and internationally, which have altered the political dynamics of the conflict, and accordingly affect the political search for peace;
    - chart the influence of individual biographical experience on the peace process, by examining: (a) the effect of key individuals who have exploited the moment and whose strategies for change and political mobilisation bear upon the peace process; and (b) the experiences of ordinary people in taken-for-granted settings whose interests and values make them open to mobilisation.

- It is important to show the interaction between local personal milieux and the social structure, by exploring how ordinary people experience the structural and political changes to their local setting, and whose response to which affects the peace process.
- The dialectic between 'personal troubles' and 'public issues' needs to be highlighted, showing how the broad social conflict translates into 'personal troubles', which themselves transform into 'public issues', and vice versa, demonstrating the effect this has on the wish to end violence and the will to make peace.

Understanding the peace process sociologically

Behind any sociological account of the peace process (or indeed, any social science depiction of events) lurks what philosophers call 'counterfactual conditionals'. Trying to imagine how events might have turned out if circumstances had in one way or another been different is an increasingly popular pastime for historians (see, for example, Ferguson's widely acclaimed analysis of the First World War, 1999: 433–62; for this and other examples see Ferguson, 1997). Sceptics in sociology dismiss it as speculative and unfruitful, involving unanswerable questions about a social world that by definition never existed, although it is possible to conceive of very limited applications in sociology (Runciman, 1999: 191*ff* considers two). There are, however, two aspects of this question that require to be separated: What if the conditions had been different? And what if we had theorised or conceptualised these conditions differently? For the sociologist dealing with real cultural and social behaviour, the relevant focus in on what has occurred and its consequences for the peace process. The first question is thus idle recreation; the second is more valid. The answer to the second is usually provided by comparisons between alternatives, either by the author drawing out the differences at the time or by others coming up with competing explanations afterwards. The former response is not proffered here (it being in my view a sufficiently complex task to erect a substantial cross-national analysis on Mills's relatively implicit perspective), but our account is open to subsequent challenge and improvement by others using alternative frameworks in the normal manner of scientific exchange. Thus, in addressing the factors that Mills's approach to sociology furnishes to explain the sequence of events that comprise the peace process, we demur from asking both what might have happened in their absence and how an alternative framework might possibly have approached the same events and factors.

The application of the sociological imagination as Mills understood it to a topic like the peace process in Northern Ireland and South Africa is appropriate for three reasons. It is in accord with Mills's personal ethical stand against violence; it is a topic of public concern and thus meets the injunction for sociology to enter the public domain and take responsibility for analysing public issues that threaten the security and freedom of ordinary people; and it is a coupling that makes sense. The two societies to which the analysis is applied are commonly held together in popular imagination and in the conceptual apparatus of the academy. The case for comparing them is based on the similarity in their social structures as settler societies, their shared history and development as divided societies differentiated by ethnicity, which, although socially marked in different ways, none the less gave them both a single line of social cleavage, and by the fact that they negotiated at roughly the same time a political settlement that has been relatively successful in ending or transforming the communal violence. However, Mills's resistance to general theory and abstract models means that the analysis is restricted to the historically specified cases of Northern Ireland and South Africa and to other cases only upon empirical investigation.

The central idea to the sociological imagination is that four dimensions of social life – human agency, history, the social structure and politics – are interconnected and impact on each other in multifarious ways. The intersection between these is the key idea, for it is the way they mediate between each other that unlocks the imagination to assist in understanding social life. It is at once both a very simple and extremely complex statement to say that everything is connected to everything else. It is simple because it is prosaic, complex because the lines of interaction can be innumerable, proving impossible to capture them all. Mills reduced the complexity by drawing attention to specific lines of connection for which *The Sociological Imagination* has become famous. For example, the intersection between individual biography (human agency) and the social structure was rendered in terms of the private troubles–public issues duality, for which the book has become particularly well known. The attention given to history was restricted to demonstrating the relevance of historical factors to gauge the phenomenon's uniqueness (specificity) to the contemporary period. Mills devoted less to politics, but noted the impact of international processes on the political unit of the nation state and of nation-state politics generally on the social structure. These particular lines of interaction only gloss the manifold ways in which these four dimensions intersect to facilitate sociological analysis.

In unravelling this four-way intersection, there is every sense in beginning with history. In Mills's mind all sociology is historical and comparative. Providing occasional historical data for background colour was not what Mills meant by this. History is something sociologists have to deal with first and perhaps dispense with thereafter. As a starting point, it is necessary for sociologists to understand the historical specificity of their topic, by which he meant assessing its uniqueness to the contemporary period by exploring whether historical factors are relevant to understanding its current form. It may be dispensed with only if historical factors can be shown to be irrelevant. Asking this question is an important counterweight to the tendency for social scientists to work in the contemporary and modern, and it adds significantly to our understanding of the current peace process in South Africa and Northern Ireland. History is relevant in several ways. The historical factor of colonialism helps us understand why there was conflict in the two societies and why it became violent. Colonialism helps to explain why their respective social structures took the form they did and why politics was reduced to a zero-sum battle between two ethnic blocs with contrary sets of political interests and preferences. History helps us understand, therefore, why peace should become a public issue for ordinary people and political groups. But there is also a historical lesson from the failure of peace processes in the past that teaches about the ingredients necessary for peace processes to succeed, helping us to see what is different about this peace process. What is unique or specific about the current peace process compared to previous ones is that this process has produced reforms that make a genuine attempt to address the structural causes of conflict; these measures include policies to address past inequalities, injustices and dispossession as well as mechanisms for ending the violence; significant sections of the dominant group feel able to buy into the process so that political elites have delivered sizeable support (although more so in South Africa than Northern Ireland); the dominant group is willing to compromise on its former political control; the leading paramilitary groups have been included in the process and support the ending of armed struggle; and the minority groups are able to accept a second best solution that goes some way to meet the interests of the former dominant group.

History on its own, however, was not Mills's concern; it was the link between history and other dimensions of the sociological imagination that mattered. In this regard, history is only relevant to specifying the present moment because of the mediating effect of the social structure. Historical forces became embedded in a particular kind of social structure in the two societies, in which there was a single line of social cleavage around which violence and conflict adhered. What historical forces first created, social forces thereafter reproduced. Planters in both societies culturally reproduced a colonial society down the centuries, with culture, custom and law upholding what colonial expropriation initially created. Historical factors like colonialism left their imprint, therefore, only because the social structure of each society reproduced the initial social divisions after the original settlement. This meant that the initial colonial divisions based around 'race' or religion continued to structure the lines of social differentiation into the modern industrial stage. As such, the patterns of inequality, dispossession, injustice and expropriation were long established in the social structure, affecting group and interpersonal relations, political partisanship and cultural association down the centuries. This ensured that anti-Catholicism or racism continued to reinforce group relations. This is perhaps unsurprising with respect to racism, but anti-Catholicism as a source of legitimation for social exclusion has proved equally tenacious in modern Ulster (see Brewer, 1998, 2000b; Brewer and Higgins, 1999; cf. Bruce, 2000).

However, it is not just the two-way connection between history and the social structure that is important. The way in which history and the social structure are related in Northern Ireland and South Africa has ramifications in politics and for individuals' biographical experiences in the two societies. It shaped politics to be about ethnic group interests rather than national ones, or at least, it elided the two so that conflict between the ethnic groups was perceived as a national struggle over political control of the territory. This reinforced the violent nature of the conflict since it appeared to be about national survival as much as personal safety. And it helped shape people's personal biographical experience, so that division, conflict, violence and victimhood were taken into the home and lived as daily experiences. This created tension between two forms of ontological insecurity that pulled in opposite directions. The insecurity, fear and threat caused by what were at times very high levels of violent conflict, pushed them towards a desire for peace, or at least in most cases a wish for the killings to stop, while fear of the ethnic 'other' ingrained and reinforced since plantation and the ontological insecurity provoked by peace itself, pulled them away from making the sorts of compromises peace settlements demand. Hence the failure of peace as a public issue to win sufficient support in the past to ensure the violence ended. Therefore, while there may have been a social and historical logic to the search for a peaceful solution because the scale and longevity of the conflict acted as an inducement to ordinary people and key leaders to try to transcend the past, previous political violence to assert dominance or resist against it, as well as earlier failed attempts at reform, were historical legacies that affected people's agency in negative ways. The selectively interpreted lessons history imparted affected people's definitions of peace, limiting their political choices, constraining their flexibility in making compromises and restricting the sorts of mobilisation they were open to around peace as a public issue.

The connections between the four elements of the sociological imagination are clear to see when examining the *status quo ante* in this way. Politics, history, social structure and individual personal experience all combined to stir the mix that were Northern Ireland and South Africa before the current peace process: they appear to have given peace no chance. In truth, what chance peace has in Northern Ireland and South Africa is precisely the result of their interaction. At a simple level, these elements created social formations in which violence was at such a level that they could not continue without the 'fatal embrace' adding to the destruction. But this is hardly sufficient as an explanation of the emergence and progress of the peace process given that equally high levels of violence existed in the past and that the pattern of contemporary violence was such that large sections of the population in particular milieux in both societies could normalise it to the point where it could be lived with reasonably well. Having dealt with history by specifying its relevance to understanding the present, we can move on to the intersection of individual biographical experience (agency), politics and the social structure as a way of explaining the emergence and vicissitudes of the current peace process.

The fulcrum on which these elements of the sociological imagination pivot is the individual. Being used to narrow forms of sociology that reduced people to 'personality systems', with little agency and voluntarism, Mills wished to bring the person back into sociology. Personal biographical experience, or what we now call agency, was his starting point and the route he took to traverse it was the private troubles–public issues duality. The personal troubles and public issues around the peace process are thus the lever to unlock our understanding of it. Although some people were admittedly capable of routinising violence, other people's biographical experience of violence created private troubles that were translated into two kinds of public issue: public calls for the violence to end and public demands for a compromise settlement. The mere fact that other people's private troubles became public issues in this way forced those fortunate people for whom violence was not a personal trouble to confront the political and media attention on violence and to think about the policies suggested at the public level either for how it might be stopped or made part of a broader peace settlement. The media revolution and public gaze meant no hiding place from violence as someone else's personal trouble or from peace as the primary public issue.

In discussing the impact of individual biographical experience on the peace process it is important to note that ordinary people's biographical experiences tend to be mediated by the agency of the key leaders whose strategies for change are the means by which ordinary people are politically mobilised in the peace process. These key leaders have been vital to the peace process. Based on their own biographical experiences – for example, as victims, ex-prisoners or as former protagonists now turned 'insider partials' – these key leaders have played an important role in mobilising for peace, without which the slow travail of political and structural circumstances may never have produced peace, or done so only decades later. Ordinary people in their personal milieux have responded to ontological insecurity and private troubles in ways that make them amenable to mobilisation by the different strategies of key individuals. While the key personnel in the process are unique as individuals, it is pertinent to categorise them into three sociological types: unreconstructed opponents of peace, peace advocates in the dominant group and supporters of peace in the subordinate groups. There are in both societies now many key leaders who mobilise tirelessly for peace and who have successfully persuaded ordinary people to support the process based on sets of biographical experiences and personal troubles that motivate them to embrace peace fully. As we have seen, what is perhaps most remarkable about both peace processes is that the second-best solutions encapsulated by their negotiated settlements should have won the support of the majority of people in the subordinate and formerly excluded groups. Black South Africans, for example, continue to accept the settlement despite little material advancement in their lives.

While many people's individual biographical experiences have challenged them towards a peace vocation – notably experiences of victimhood, imprisonment and reconciliation overtures in local spaces where they meet across the dividing cleavage – it must be remembered that Mills linked individual biographical experiences with personal milieux, so that people can have the same biographical

Conclusion: The Sociological Imagination and the Peace Process 161

experience, such as being a victim of violence or imprisonment, yet differences of milieux can result in opposite responses in the peace process. Milieux are spatial and cultural entities. They also contain a body of common-sense knowledge built up and socially disseminated in that setting. People are absorbed in their milieu and into the common-sense knowledge that pervades it. For this reason, people's biographical experiences are mediated by all that locality (what Mills called milieu) comes to mean. Variations in people's personal milieux affect the perception of their travails and the ontological insecurities they experience, which helps to explain the problems in Northern Ireland's peace process compared to South Africa. The individual biographical experiences of most Protestants, particularly in the way they experienced violence in Northern Ireland, has affected both their definition of peace, giving a priority to ending the violence rather than an embracing peace with justice and equality, and their perception of the Good Friday Agreement as being inadequate in its measures to stop the violence, resulting in only weak commitment to the process in some and in others none at all. The mediating effect of locale, common-sense knowledge and personal experience of violence ensures that some people's set of personal troubles are translated into public issues that threaten the stability of the peace process. Public issues around amnesty, decommissioning and victimhood result in a more fragile process in Northern Ireland than South Africa. Peace is as much a source of ontological insecurity for them as communal violence – so that public issues cause them private troubles – and key individuals opposed to the peace process mobilise effectively on this insecurity. The unreconstructed opponents of the process in South Africa have a much more marginal social position than in Northern Ireland, being restricted to African racist groups like AZAPO or White racists in the rural backwaters. The mobilisation strategy of both – encapsulated by 'one settler, one bullet' amongst the Azanian Peoples Organisation (AZAPO) or a White homeland amongst the White right – did not resonate with the biographical experiences of the conflict by poor Africans in milieux of poverty, wealthy middle class Black South Africans in situations of class advancement or Whites eager to ensure a stable state and economy in order to swap political disempowerment for continued economic privilege. That a major move forward in both societies none the less occurred was due to the commitment of two kinds of key leaders: former militarists who mobilised around an end to armed struggle; and politicians in the former dominant groups who mobilised on their recognition of the necessity to negotiate a settlement while they were still in a strong enough position to do so favourably.

The human agency of these two kinds of key leader, encapsulated by their biographical experiences of prison, victimhood, cross-community relations or whatever, is, however, inadequate on its own for explaining why they came to this view now rather than earlier. This is why Mills considered individual biographical experiences as a starting place not the end point. It would be misleading to explain the emergence and progress of the peace process solely in terms of the personal qualities of key people, natural though it is to focus on the charisma of Mandela or the courage of Trimble. The sociological imagination culminates in locating individual lives in their broader context. In this regard, the key leaders who won their constituencies for peace were responding to the opportunities afforded by social structural changes and to developments and events in the political process. The biographical experiences and private troubles of ordinary people, which assisted in their mobilisation around peace as a public issue, need to be connected to political events and social structural conditions. And it is the emergence of a new nexus between politics and the social structure in both societies that answers the question of why now and not before.

Human agency has played its part in giving peace a chance in both societies, whether this is the ontological insecurity of many ordinary people over the continuance of violence or the mobilisation strategies of key leaders which support the respective political settlements, but it is new developments in the intersection of politics and the social structure that assist in understanding why the public issue of peace has finally realised a settlement that has virtually stopped all communal violence. Differences in milieux are important again in helping us understand the contrasting fortunes of the peace process in Northern Ireland compared to South Africa, for some of the developments that constitute the new nexus between politics and the social structure operate more successfully in South Africa. The developments include national demographic trends, economic changes, particular social transformations in civic culture and in the lines of social differentiation. Some are rooted in global and international processes but in others are restricted to particular local milieux. International processes are both political (Europeanisation, the ending of the Cold War, external third-party intervention) and socio-economic (globalisation, secularisation, international economic sanctions). Local milieux are affected differently by these national and international trends, leading not only to contrasts between Northern Ireland and South Africa but above all to differences of local space within each country. In some cases local spaces are opening up in which, for example, grassroots and civil society peacemaking and reconciliation is possible, and in which new identities can be experimented with and perceived as possible or in which existing identities come to be seen as more flexible and inclusive than previously imagined. New broad social trends are evident, such as the widening of class differences within ethnic blocs and differential fertility and emigration rates. And new effects of broader trends are being experienced locally, such as the impact on people of the narrowing of the welfare state and of economic deindustrialisation.

It may be worthwhile to summarise at this point: indeed, Mills would suggest it is essential. *The Sociological Imagination* is notorious for Mills's enervation of narrow kinds of sociology, best represented by Parsons and Lazarsfeld. He believed that if something could not be said succinctly – and in words rather than numbers – it was either not worth saying or there was something deficient in the sociologist. There is a daunting obligation then to give a short one-paragraph summary of Mills's contribution to our understanding of the peace process in Northern Ireland and South Africa.

The sociological imagination is not a narrow disciplinary perspective but an encompassing one that approaches the peace process from four poles – history, politics, human agency and the social structure. There are interconnections between them in all directions, resulting in a multicausal rather than monocausal analysis. Through the sociological imagination we see the historical relevance of seventeenth-century colonialism to the contemporary period, but only as it became represented in a particular kind of social structure, which reproduced over the centuries through law and culture patterns of social cleavage and differentiation that made violent conflict endemic. The biographical experiences of ordinary people living in the two societies therefore felt the imprint of history in the form of sets of personal troubles and feelings of ontological insecurity caused by the conflict that translated into public issues around either peace broadly understood or the more narrow concern to end violence. It is through this private trouble–public issue duality that the social embeddedness of people's lives is disclosed. But the recursive relationship between private troubles and public issues is mediated by differences in personal milieux, such that people's biographical experiences of violence and personal troubles can be sufficiently diverse to produce varying levels of support for peace as a public issue. None the less, significant numbers of people have been mobilised to support the peace process through the strategies of key individuals. These mobilisation strategies, rooted in part in the leaders' own biographical experiences, attempt to make sense of the changing conditions that ordinary people experience in their daily lives in such ways as to encourage support for the peace process. Anti-agreement feeling is stronger in Northern Ireland, but the strategies of key individuals in the majority and minority groups have persuaded significant numbers that their best interests are served by cutting deals now. However, the sociological imagination requires that individual agency be set in its broader context. In this regard, key leaders who won their constituencies for peace were responding to the opportunities afforded by social structural changes and to developments and events in the national and international political process. Social structural and political developments facilitated new kinds of agency, opening up new choices and behaviours, changing the political strategies of two kinds of key leader, pushing former militarists against armed struggle and persuading formerly immobile political elites to change. These structural factors include demographic shifts, economic change, external intervention by third parties and the development of civic culture and new lines of social differentiation in local milieux. Irrespective of where one believes the respective peace settlements have left South Africa and Northern Ireland, without the intermeshing of individual biographical experiences and agency with historical forces, new political developments and changed social structural conditions, neither society would have reached this far.

The efficacy of Mills's sociological imagination

The purpose of applying the sociological imagination to the topic at hand has not only been to see if it helps us understand the process by which communal violence has all but ended in South Africa and Northern Ireland, but also to use the peace process to provide a test of the utility of this version of sociology when applied to issues of real public concern. This is a difficult question to answer because it requires some sense of what sociology should be about and the imposition of a gold standard against which to measure Mills's outline of the sociological imagination. It would be less problematic if the gold standard were an agreed disciplinary one, but the lack of consensus in modern sociology about the nature of the discipline ensures that personal measures are imputed. Runciman (2002), the first sociologist to be elected President of the British Academy, remarked in a speech to the British Sociological Association in April 2002 that the diversity of what sociologists do and the discipline's lack of a unifying paradigm go most of the way to explaining the subject's lack of respect in Britain compared to the United States. The discipline suffers to the extent that it is not seen as having something distinctive to offer. However, personal reflections on what is distinctive about sociology can be dangerous. Sometimes they end up saying more about the person doing the reflecting; and even if the temptation to self-aggrandisement is avoided, the person's reflections can be quite distorted by their preferences, telling us once more little about the nature of the discipline beyond its contested nature.

There are, fortunately, some points that are collectively agreed upon. The discipline began as a discursive formation, to use Michel Foucault's terminology, for commentary on and understanding about important social issues in the public domain. Irrespective of where the origins of sociology are located or in whom, the discipline was put by its various progenitors to the service of understanding profound social transformations, such as the rise of commercialism in Enlightenment Europe, the emergence of industrialism in the nineteenth century, the impact of democratisation and the French Revolution, the decline of community and traditionalism, the development of liberal utilitarianism in public policy and social life, and so on. There was, moreover, no division between the political and the social in formulating or addressing these public concerns. Rousseau's eighteenth-century discourse on the ideal set of social arrangements under the social contract also took a view on political life; Bernard Mandeville's *Fable of the Bees* was an allegory about political life as well as society. Indeed, Mandeville's subtitle to the *Fable*, 'Private Vices, Public Benefits' fits well the idea that social behaviour and political life are inseparable. Ferguson's portrayal of 'civil society' referred to governance as well as to social relations. Alexis de Tocqueville's nineteenth-century treatise on American government was also a commentary on the cultural underpinnings of politics. To go on would be to labour the point: whether we are considering Ferguson, Smith and Montesquieu in the eighteenth century, or Comte, Marx, Durkheim, Weber and Spencer in the nineteenth, politics and social life intermeshed in the public issues that motivated their work. There is another incontrovertible truth: this tradition died out with Weber, when the 'long century' of nineteenth-century sociology came to an end. The long century might be said to have started in 1767 with Ferguson's awareness of the social structure as a web of interlocking forces that shaped human affairs, or in some other eighteenth-century precursor, but it undoubtedly ended with Weber. And it was primarily through Weber that this generation shaped Mills's mid-twentieth-century agenda.

Sociology has taken tremendous leaps forward in particular historical periods. Whether considered to be the foundation of sociology or not, the eighteenth-century Enlightenment period in Scotland, France and Germany gave us the principles of scientific rationality applied to social life, the idea of social progress and the comparative analysis of society at different stages of development, and penetrating discourses on aspects of human affairs in particular societies or societies in general. The advances in knowledge were cumulative, without any one person rising high above the general contributions to knowledge. The notion of the division of labour is a case in point – Ferguson took Smith's ideas on the division of labour in the economy forward when he applied them to society in general to describe a new social condition (see Brewer, 1988), but his advances were incremental. The nineteenth century also witnessed a considerable leap forward (as Durkheim and Marx's later treatments of the division of labour symbolise). This was not just in the scale of the social transformation wrought by the industrial and French revolutions, but in the understanding of the nature and operation of the social structure as an interconnected web of functional relationships that went off in the direction of society, the economy, history, politics and human psychology (that nineteenth-century sociology was interested in psychology reflects in concepts like *Verstehen*, alienation and anomie). This was the period of sociology as a broad discipline, mother to all approaches that touched human and public affairs.

Conclusion: The Sociological Imagination and the Peace Process

After Weber's death in 1920 there were no great leaps forward perhaps until the development of what Hermino Martins (1974) calls the 'cognitivist revolution' in the 1960s, with the rediscovery of meaningful social action and poststructuralist deconstruction of the meaning of texts. During this interregnum, sociology in the United States consolidated itself around narrower approaches, such as the Chicago School (based on ethnographically rich portrayals of aspects of modern city life) and the opposite axis of Parsons–Lazarsfeld (based around general theory and abstract empiricism). In Britain sociology centred on the political arithmetic tradition (although it was never totally subsumed by it), a manifestation this side of the Atlantic of 'applied sociology' that Mills saw as equally narrow. (Abrams, 1981, laments the loss of the British historical sociology tradition.) But as Weber's co-translator (with Hans Gerth) and with a doctorate partly on Marx, Mills was familiar with the hallmark of the nineteenth-century tradition and put himself at the face of what became a rich intellectual seam to mine the classics for their sociological imagination.

He took four things from that tradition: the wish to develop sociological analyses of issues of real public concern; the necessity for sociology to approach these issues historically; the requirement to broaden sociology's scope to consider public affairs in the round rather than from its narrow disciplinary concerns; and the importance of developing a critical attitude to public affairs in order to release the potential of human reason and decision-making. The first became manifest in the focus on the private trouble–public issue duality; the second in his emphasis on historical specificity to locate the possible relevance of historical factors; the third in his stress on the intersection between the social structure, history, politics and individual biographical experience; the fourth in his focus on sociology as the liberation of human freedom, which he understood to mean facilitating people to take over control of the decisions that negatively affect their lives.

The peace process in South Africa and Northern Ireland illustrates these features well. It is an issue of tremendous public concern in both societies, dominating public affairs generally, but it is a public issue embedded in the many private troubles of the people who live there. The public issues that define the political and social agenda are grounded in the individual biographical experiences of people. Peace dominated the public agenda because of ordinary's people's experiences of violent conflict. Yet public issues can in themselves cause people private troubles, as the peace process brings costs to certain kinds of people as problematic as the experience of communal violence. Private troubles and public issues are thus in a recursive relationship in which they each affect the other, illustrating the embeddedness of people in society and society in people. However, Mills is stating the obvious here and his major contribution is the claim that this recursive relationship is mediated by personal milieux. Contingencies in the physical and cultural space and in the common-sense knowledge of the locality can impact the private trouble–public issue duality, giving people either different experiences or ways of understanding those experiences, leading to contrasting responses to the peace process. So while people are embedded in society and society in them, local space, culture and knowledge affect this embeddedness. This is the point of Mills's stress on milieux: society is not a general abstraction without physical and cultural variation or devoid of meaning-endowing people. The confrontation he urges sociologists to make with the public issues of the day therefore ends up in sociology exposing the essential connectedness between individuals and society.

The analysis of the peace process illustrates this in two ways. It highlights how history has both an objective and subjective character and it illuminates the human agency–social structure debate. These are in effect variations of the same point, since they both reflect the embeddedness of individuals and society in each other, something that Mills wished to labour. The agency–structure debate is not one that Mills was familiar with in those terms, since its lexicon postdates his death, but he was aware of the vocabulary through which the debate was normally conducted at the time: namely, couched in terms of discussions of the objectivity of history based around Marx's principle that people make history but not in ways of their own choosing. He used non-technical terms to engage with this debate, using phrases like individual biography, personal biographical experience and personal biographical milieu in ways that equate with what we now call agency in everyday life. Let us first then come to this issue with the vocabulary that Mills used before expanding to the agency–structure debate that replaced it after Mills's death.

Conclusion: The Sociological Imagination and the Peace Process 169

Mills approvingly cites Marx's dictum and extends the quip by referring to history being made behind their backs as ordinary people lose more and more control over decision-making to anonymous forces in mass society (2000 [1959]: 182). The peace process shows us that people both act in history and are acted upon by historical forces. History impacts on the personal biographical experiences of people through the way it helps to shape the social structure and polity, but it is also made by them as personal biographical experiences, social structural interests and political preferences come to define what history means to them. By becoming reproduced in a set of institutional arrangements and structures, historical forces clearly take on an objective quality to imprint themselves on individuals, although, as we have seen, this happens only through the mediating effect of the social structure. Historical factors such as colonialism have shaped people's biographical experiences and agency in Northern Ireland and South Africa via the social structure they helped to create, making ethnic dispossession, inequality and communal violence integral factors that helped to determine the biographical experiences of people living there. Simultaneously, history reflects agency. An analysis of the peace process showed that people made history into a shibboleth, so that all the personal biographical experiences represented by it and captured in historical events in effect flow back and impact upon the peace process. The litany of violent events and conflict over the centuries have produced what might be called a 'meta-history of history' as people understood and interpreted the past according to their biographical experiences and their group position in the social structure. In this way history was appropriated politically and came to affect the peace process. In effect, history has become reified. Past violence, and its forms of resistance, struggle and suffering, have become represented in a tradition of principles, symbols and iconography that define what each group means by history. These symbols are rooted in, as some people see it, the honourable sacrifice of those who have fought on behalf of the group. These symbols limit flexibility in the peace process because they are principles not easily jettisoned without peacemakers being accused of having forgotten all that history supposedly means to the people involved in or who suffered through the violence. History has become structured into a set of myths, symbols and iconography that reifies the suffering and resistance of one group or the other to constrain the peace process by imposing limits on the flexibility of negotiators and peacemakers, who can easily be accused of selling out history, dishonouring the suffering or overlooking the resistance of group members in the past. While historical factors are objective realities imposing themselves on people in the peace process, history is also used, manipulated, moulded to the social structural interests, political concerns and biographical experiences of people.

We see this symbiosis in microcosm with the example of the failure of earlier peace processes. The political conflicts over reform that dogged both societies before the final peace process themselves became burdens that impacted on people, limiting the flexibility and opportunity for compromise in the current process. But this objectification of history works through people's perceptions of the past and the selectively interpreted lessons they draw from these failed previous attempts.

If we render this point in the more familiar discourse of the agency – structure debate, the analysis of the peace process enables us to make several comments. The first is that the social structure impacts on the lives of ordinary people. This is a commonplace. Specifically in respect to the focus of this study, the lines of differentiation and cleavage inherent in the social structure in Northern Ireland and South Africa helped to shape the biographical experiences of ordinary people and create private troubles for them. Social groups formed around these social structural conditions as these social circumstances manifested themselves in particular localities and bounded contexts in both societies (giving us social classes, 'races' and groups marked by religion or other measures of ethnicity). As we saw, historical factors determined the significance placed on particular group boundary markers, with colonialism making 'race' and religion the 'master status', as Weber would say, respectively in South Africa and Northern Ireland. These groups in their social milieux developed sets of interests as a group that shaped the way in which individual members interpreted, understood and made sense of their personal biographical experiences and private troubles. People's biographical experiences and agency were understood as refracted through the social structure and its institutional order. This gave ordinary people a sense that their personal biographical experiences and private troubles were shared with others and were the collective experiences and troubles of the group as a whole in that particular milieux. People's personal stories (of victimhood, inequality, dispossession, suffering, and so on) became seen as part of a collective cultural experience and in turn came to influence how people recounted their stories and understood their troubles as typical of the group and as such interpreted as group experiences. The personal became the public; the individual experience, a collective one.

Politics reinforced the tendency to objectify the social structure. Political mobilisation strategies by key leaders made appeal to the biography and private troubles of people as collective and group experiences, such that political interests formed to coincide with these private troubles understood now as group troubles. This assisted in making private troubles into social issues within public affairs. These public issues always reproduced the social structure's social divisions, since positions were taken on them that reflected the different sets of interests that groups perceived they had based on their simultaneous collective and personal biographical experiences and troubles. Political events, circumstances and traditions came to cohere around group interests and helped to characterise the meaning of group membership, as groups came to define themselves in part by their history of political struggles or political resistance and their collective experiences as victims of violence or social exclusion. These political events simultaneously helped to shape the way in which people understood that they had collective political interests with other group members who appear to have shared the same personal biographical experiences and private troubles.

In all these ways, society took on a sense of being real and objective as personal biographical experiences and private troubles were seen as collective and people's personal milieux appeared to form a shared social world. However, people also shape the social structure. This too is prosaic. Put in general terms, the social world is what people's biographical experiences in their personal milieux make it appear to be. Concerning the focus of this study, cleavages and fissures in the social structure in South Africa and Northern Ireland were understood by ordinary people in terms of their biographical experiences and private troubles. The social structure's divisions were mediated by people's meaning-endowing capabilities, such that conflicts around 'race', religion, class or ethnicity in society came to represent what people's biographical experiences and private troubles rendered them into. Protestant home-rulers, 'Castle' Catholics, progressive and liberal Whites and Black South Africans co-opted into apartheid clearly developed interpretations of their interests different from the norm. While the institutional order imprinted itself on and constrained members of social groups, group boundaries were fluid. Social groups fractured and were subject to strain when some people's biographical experiences and private troubles lead them in different directions from other group members, such as 'poor Whites' compared to wealthy ones, unreconstructed Republicans versus Sinn Féin supporters or 'civic unionists' compared to 'ethnic' ones. This resulted in flexible and permeable boundaries of group membership and the development of different sets of interests, which shaped and reshaped the institutional order. The old ethnic blocs, for example, collapsed along with their collective ethnic interests. Middle-class Afrikaners left behind 'poor Whites' to back non-racial democracy in South Africa to preserve the state and protect their position in the economy. (This is a point emphasised in Adam, van syl Slabbert and Moodley, 1997, and was something apparent at the beginning of the reform process, see Adam and Giliomee, 1980.) Pro-Agreement Protestants back Trimble against anti-Agreement ones because they believe their best interests are served by cutting a deal with Sinn Féin now.

These examples show that it is not only group membership that is flexible under changed circumstances in the lives of ordinary people, politics reconfigures itself as people's interpretations shift. Political interests, and the institutional order built around them, can be redefined in accord with the changing biographical experiences and private troubles of people. New public issues come to be represented around the changed or changing lives of people, such that political events, circumstances and traditions came to be reinterpreted in terms of people's reformulated private troubles–public issues. Key leaders felt constrained to mobilise around, or came to enthusiastically represent the changing constellation of the private troubles of significant numbers of ordinary people and translated into public issues the interests of the new social groupings. In short, the social structure is embedded in and reproduced by the lives of ordinary people in their local and personal milieux, but, as we have seen, these lives and milieux are simultaneously shaped by the social structure.

As revealing as this is for the prescience of Mills's conception of sociology back in the 1950s, it is only one of the dimensions that broadened sociology's focus under his hand. The major contribution of Mills's sociological approach is its four dimensional character since the sociological imagination is more than the agency – structure duality. History and politics play their part in shaping the way people make sense of and understand their lives and milieux, but in turn history and politics are shaped by the way ordinary people can change the understanding of their biographical experiences and private troubles in order to transcend the past and the burden of history, and develop new sets of political interests that impact on the political process. We also know that changing social structural circumstances combined with events in the national and international political arenas to affect the peace process by encouraging significant numbers of ordinary people to re-evaluate their biographical experiences and private troubles in a direction that supported the ending of violence. The changing structural conditions within which the current peace process works, such as demographic shifts, economic changes, the emergence of local spaces in which traditional lines of social differentiation are blurred and new forms of external political intervention, gave a new dynamic to the relationship between politics and the social structure in the two societies. Not only does the peace process therefore highlight the importance of holding both politics and sociology in the one framework, the relationship between them was mediated by human agency, which confirms Mills's emphasis on the utility of combining them.

The analysis of the peace process proffered here enables us to see that one of the main values of Mills's sociological imagination is its multi-dimensional approach, revealing the embeddedness of history, politics, human agency and the social structure in each other. The peace process illustrates this in practice. New developments in the politics–social structure nexus affected the shape and fortunes of the peace process by influencing the mobilisation strategies of key individuals who pushed the peace process, and by changing the agency of ordinary people in ways that opened them up to mobilisation around the issue of peace. In one sense it appears that all there here is human agency. History, the polity and society can at one level be reduced to the activities of people. Social institutions do not act only people within them; political groups do not make choices separate from leaders and members; without the activities of individuals letting off bombs and shooting, terrorism would have no meaning. It is the agency of people, in the choices they make and the actions they perform that go to make up history, politics and the social structure. Yet this trinity also constitute themselves as objective forces external to people, over which ordinary people have no control. People act and make choices, but these are highly constrained by the context within which they display such agency. The human capacity for agency, the ability to act and to choose according to personal preferences, can be restrained by the political and social structural context. Members of political parties or social institutions, political leaders, terrorist bombers or whomsoever live and work in a broader structural context that limits their freedom of choice – sometimes giving them no effective choice. None the less, changes in the political and social context can release agency enabling and facilitating it by offering the possibility of new choices and different forms of behaviour. For example, the political disestablishment of the Church, the decline in its moral authority and the narrowing of its role in public life, which all go to make up the structural condition that sociologists understand as secularisation, permits new choices and patterns of behaviour, enabling people these days to be able to decide to stay away from church without community sanction or threats to their social position (at least not in this world). Locked as we are in a structural web, acting as agents but within constraints, new forms of agency become possible when the structural conditions change. This is what has happened in both Northern Ireland and South Africa in ways that support the peace process. For example, the major advancement in the political strategies of key leaders in the ANC or Sinn Féin and the IRA is the abandonment of armed struggle and the ending of support for political violence. This has enabled them to make major electoral gains and to mobilise significant numbers of ordinary people as a constituency in support of the peace process. However, the resonance which non-violence has for the human agency of both key leaders and their support base is premised on structural changes like the fundamental demographic shifts that occurred in Northern Ireland and South Africa which have undermined the necessity for violence. When combined with economic changes, new international developments and third-party brokering, this shift in strategy is reinforced to gird the peace process. The parallel shift in the agency of once obdurate and immovable political elites, which has successfully developed a constituency in support of change (even in Northern Ireland), is premised on structural factors like the role of external patrons in urging a settlement, civil society and grassroots progress in changing the political agenda, the blurring of the lines of differentiation and the opening up of local spaces that transcend ancient divisions, and salutary economic warnings of the cost of recalcitrance.

In short, social change, understood broadly to include social, political and economic change, made possible changes in human agency as people's private troubles and experiences changed alongside society, and changed agency, in such things as decisions about family size, emigration, involvement in community relations programmes, electoral choices, and the like, opened up further social change, and so on through the recursive cycle. The peace process thus shows society to be both a structured entity – structured socially, politically, economically and historically – and a lived experience for the individual biographical entity. The sociological imagination is devoted to working out the interaction between these entities in concrete issues that have substantive importance for public affairs in society and in ordinary people's daily lives. But there is perhaps a value of even greater import arising from this approach to sociology.

Our analysis of the peace process discloses that the sociological imagination successfully transcends many of the discipline's traditional antinomies. We can only understand the relative success of the current peace process by bringing together in one sociological framework things normally kept apart – antinomies like politics and sociology, the local and the national, the global and the nation state, the historical and the contemporary, the private and the public and the individual and the social structure. It was prescient of Mills to see the discipline in this way in the 1950s since this transcendence has now become *de rigueur* (see Jenks, 1998), although rarely are they all brought together in the one framework. Particular sociological frameworks address one or another of the dichotomies and some were transcended quite quickly after the publication of *The Sociological Imagination*. Indeed, very shortly after Mills's death, Peter Berger published his now famous *Invitation to Sociology* (1963), something of a rival manifesto for the discipline, in which he addressed the individual–society antinomy, writing about the 'individual being in society' as well as 'society being in the individual', although Berger was against broad notions of sociology's consciousness, as he referred to it, stating expressly that sociologists should not attempt to deal with the same issues as economists and political scientists. The agency–structure debate has since given us a new vocabulary with which to engage this idea and Mills's private troubles–public issues duality hardly does the agency–structure debate justice as we have come to understand it in the work of Giddens, Archer and Bhaskar. The global–local nexus has also been more thoroughly addressed in the explication of what globalisation theorists call 'glocalisation' (Alger, 1988; Sklair, 1995, 1999). The figurational sociology of Norbert Elias, for example, displays a more rigorous treatment of history from a sociological standpoint applied to concrete examples, such as the civilising process (see for example Mennell and Goudsblom, 1998). Stripped to its individual dimensions therefore, Mills's sociological imagination has been superseded on most long past, but it retains the novelty of combining them all in the one framework and linking them with the other qualities he drew from the classic tradition.

The final such quality was the stress he laid on critique; of adopting a critical attitude toward social and public affairs when they encroached on human freedom and seemed to deny ordinary people the opportunity to exercise their reason and decision-making. This ethical underpinning to sociological analysis is perhaps Mills's defining affection. Critique is more than the debunking motif that Berger (1963) says is one of sociology's four hallmarks. Mills did want to expose the underbelly of public and social affairs and unmask the façade of powerful social and political institutions, and thereby make sociology unrespectable, the second of Berger's motifs. But this was done for an ethical purpose, not for its own sake. It was motivated by a concern for the small people overwhelmed by the big institutions who when faced with structural forces and conditions they cannot understand or control withdraw either into apathy or anxiety. Mills was a member of that sub-set of American social scientists that realised modernity risked producing mass societies. Kornhauser's (1959) treatise on the politics of mass society was published the same year as *The Sociological Imagination* and while the worst fears about creeping totalitarianism did not materialise, partly because of the primacy of Mills's argument about locality and personal milieux as strong sources of identity, it affected Mills's diagnosis of the problems sociological analysis was put to serve. Mills realised that to rail against modernity was as pointless in the long run as the little Dutch child trying to stem the leak in the dyke, but he did see the possibility of sociological analysis slowing down the flood. The sociological imagination can assist in people's understanding of how society works, what structural forces are at play in people's lives and how these forces impinge on them, thus removing their ignorance. It can disclose the positive contribution ordinary people can make to public issues by showing how these issues reduce into individual personal troubles and biographical experiences, counteracting people's sense of apathy. And the sociological imagination can disclose those areas of social and public life where people can begin to take decisions that affect their lives, where their contributions and efforts can count, removing their sense of hopelessness and anxiety.

This is admittedly a romantic view, although it is one shared with subsequent sociologists imbued with a moral vision to be realised through their sociological method, whether this be the principle of empowerment in feminist methodology, Habermas's notion of emancipation (on moral vision in the sociology of Mills and Habermas, see Seidman, 1998: 171–213) or Bhaskar's stress on the promotion through social research of human freedom and dignity. Mills was a romantic – Horowitz (1985) calls Mills a utopian – in his private and professional lives, and in his proclamation for sociology he was driven by a passion as strong as that for his families, a love for the grand classic tradition in sociology where sociology was viewed as a diagnosis and palliative for the whole social condition. This may be romantic but not entirely fanciful. This analysis of the peace process demonstrates how sociology can render a seemingly structural process that is beyond people's control into one that reflects ordinary people's troubles, biographical experiences and agency. It is a process moreover, where people can be shown that they matter, a process that they can influence, negatively or positively, by the decisions they make. And were ordinary people and key leaders but to assert control in ways that eliminated the causes of conflict and its expression through violence, it could be a process the end result of which would realise greater human freedom from suffering, dispossession and violence. In the end therefore, the sociological imagination reveals the process by which violence ended in Northern Ireland and

South Africa to be an ethical process – which is its most valuable contribution. Therefore, should sociology not bother to give an analysis of the peace process? Let Mills reply:

> The problems of social science, when adequately formulated, must include both troubles and issues, both biography and history, and the range of their intricate relations. Within that range the life of the individual and the making of societies will occur; and within that range the sociological imagination has its chance to make a difference in the quality of human life. (2000 [1959]: 226)

If people could look at the peace process through the eyes of their children not their ancestors, those who are alive to inherit the future not the long dead who burden it, Mills's romantic vision for the future might be closer to reality in Northern Ireland and South Africa.

Bibliography

Abrams, P. (1981) 'The collapse of British sociology', in P. Abrams, R. Deem, J. Finch and P. Rock (eds) *Practice and Progress: British Sociology 1950–1980*. London: Allen and Unwin.
Adam, H. and Giliomee, H. (1980) *The Rise and Crisis of Afrikaner Power*. Cape Town: David Philip.
Adam, H., van syl Slabbert, F. and Moodley, K. (1997) *Comrades in Business*. Cape Town: Tafelberg Press.
Adams, G. (1996) *Before the Dawn*. Kerry: Brandon.
Akenson, D.H. (1992) *God's Peoples*. London: Cornell University Press.
Alcock, A. (2001) 'From conflict to agreement in Northern Ireland', in J. McGarry (ed.), *Northern Ireland and the Divided World*. Oxford: Oxford University Press.
Alger, C. (1988) 'Perceiving, analysing and coping with the local-global nexus', *International Journal of Social Science*, vol. 117: 321–40.
Archer, M. (1996) *Realist Social Theory*. Cambridge: Cambridge University Press.
Arnstein, W.L. (1982) *Protestant Versus Catholics in Mid-Victorian England*. Columbia: Columbia University Press.
Aron, R. (1965) *Main Currents of Sociological Thought*. Harmondsworth: Penguin Books.
Arthur, P. (1995) 'Some thoughts on transition: a comparative view of the peace processes in South Africa and Northern Ireland', *Government and Opposition*, vol. 30: 48–59.
Aughey, A. (2000) 'The 1998 Agreement: Unionist responses', in M. Cox, A. Guelke and F. Stephens (eds), *A Farewell to Arms?* Manchester: Manchester University Press.
Aughey, A. (2001) 'British policy in Northern Ireland', in S. Savage and R. Atkinson (eds), *Public Policy under Blair*. Basingstoke: Palgrave.
Bardon, J. (1992) *A History of Ulster*. Belfast: Blackstaff.
Barrell, H. (1990) *MK: The ANC's Armed Struggle*. London: Penguin Books.
Bauman, Z. (1990) *Thinking Sociologically*. Oxford: Blackwell.
Bauman, Z. (2002) Interview with Professor Zygmunt Bauman, in *Network*, vol. 83 October.
Becker, H.S. (1994) 'Professional sociology: the case of C. Wright Mills', in R. Rist (ed.), *The Democratic Imagination*. New Brunswick: Transaction Books. Also at http://www.soc.ucsb.edu/faculty/hbecker/mills.html.
Bell, C.M. (2000) *Peace Agreements and Human Rights*. Oxford: Oxford University Press.
Berger, P. (1963) *Invitation to Sociology*. Harmondsworth: Penguin Books.
Bhaskar, R. (1989a) *Reclaiming Reality*. London: Verso.
Bhaskar, R. (1989b) *The Possibility of Naturalism*. Hemel Hempstead: Harvester Wheatsheaf.

Blaney, R. (1996) *Presbyterians and the Irish Language*. Belfast: Ulster Historical Foundation.

Blumenfeld, J. (1999) 'The post-apartheid economy', paper at the conference 'South Africa: From Transition to Transformation', Dublin, 5 March.

Bonner, A. (2002) 'Catholics form the majority of school population', *Irish News*, 21 October.

Breen, R. (1996) 'Who wants a united Ireland? Constitutional preferences among Catholics and Protestants', in R. Breen, P. Devine and L. Dowds (eds), *Social Attitudes: The Fifth Report*. Belfast: Appletree Press.

Breen, R. (1998) 'Social mobility, political preferences, attitudes and behaviours in Northern Ireland'. End of Award Report to the Economic and Social Research Council, 21 April.

Brewer, J.D. (1986) *After Soweto*. Oxford: Clarendon Press.

Brewer, J.D. (1988) 'Conjectural history, sociology and social change in eighteenth century Scotland: Adam Ferguson and the division of labour', in D. McCrone (ed.), *The Making of Scotland: Nation, Culture and Social Change*. Edinburgh: Edinburgh University Press.

Brewer, J.D. (1991a) 'Policing in divided societies: theorising a type of policing', *Policing and Society*, vol. 2: 179–91.

Brewer, J.D. (1991b) 'Talking about danger', *Sociology*, vol. 24: 657–74.

Brewer, J.D. (1992) 'Sectarianism and racism and their parallels and differences', *Ethnic and Racial Studies*, vol. 15: 352–64.

Brewer, J.D. (1994) *Black and Blue: Policing in South Africa*. Oxford: Clarendon Press.

Brewer, J.D. (1998) *Anti-Catholicism in Northern Ireland 1600–1998*. London: Macmillan.

Brewer, J.D. (1999) 'Globalisation, Protestant identity and Unionist responses to the Northern Ireland peace process', paper for the first international symposium on ethnic identities and political action in post-Cold War Europe, Xanthi, 1–3 September.

Brewer, J.D. (2000a) *Ethnography*. Buckingham: Open University Press.

Brewer, J.D. (2000b) 'Understanding anti-Catholicism: a rejoinder to our critics', *Studies*, vol. 89: 243–6.

Brewer, J.D. (2001) 'The paradox of Northern Ireland', *Sociology*, vol. 35: 779–83.

Brewer, J.D. (2002) Are there any Christians in Northern Ireland?, in A. Gray, K. Lloyd, P. Devine, G. Robinson and D. Heenan (eds), *Social Attitudes in Northern Ireland: The Eighth Report*. London: Pluto Press.

Brewer, J.D. and Higgins, G. (1999) 'Understanding anti-Catholicism in Northern Ireland', *Sociology*, vol. 33: 235–55.

Brewer, J.D., Bishop, K. and Higgins, G. (2001) *Peacemaking among Protestants and Catholics*. Belfast: Centre for the Social Study of Religion, Queen's University of Belfast.

Brewer, J.D., Lockhart, B. and Rodgers, P. (1997) *Crime in Ireland 1945–95: Here be Dragons*. Oxford: The Clarendon Press.

Brewer, J.D., Lockhart, B. and Rodgers, P. (1998) 'Informal social control and local crime management in Belfast', *British Journal of Sociology*, vol. 49: 570–85.

Brewer, J.D., Lockhart, B. and Rodgers, P. (1999) 'Crime in Ireland 1945–95', in A. Heath, R. Breen and C. Whelan (eds), *Ireland: North and South*. Oxford: Oxford University Press.
British Broadcasting Corporation (2002) 'Hearts and minds poll: the details', http://news.bbc.co.uk/1/hi/northern-ireland/2335861.stm.
Bruce, S. (1986) *God Save Ulster!* Oxford: Oxford University Press.
Bruce, S. (1992) *The Red Hand*. Oxford: Oxford University Press.
Bruce, S. (1994) *The Edge of the Union*. Oxford: Oxford University Press.
Bruce, S. (1995) 'Northern Ireland: reappraising Loyalist violence', in A. O'Day (ed.), *Terrorism's Laboratory: The Case of Northern Ireland*. Aldershot: Dartmouth.
Bruce, S. (1998) *Conservative Protestant Politics*. Oxford: Oxford University Press.
Bruce, S. (1999) 'Religion, ethnicity and violence: dissecting Ulster Unionism', paper for the British Association of Sociologists of Religion conference, University of Stirling, September.
Bruce, S. (2000) 'The sociology of anti-Catholicism', *Studies*, vol. 89: 205–14.
Bruce, S. (2001) 'Fundamentalism and political violence: the case of Paisley and Ulster evangelicals', *Religion*, vol. 31: 387–405.
Bruce, S. (2002) *God is Dead*. Oxford: Blackwell.
Bruce, S. and Alderdice, F. (1993) 'Religious belief and behaviour', in P. Stringer and G. Robinson (eds), *Social Attitudes in Northern Ireland: The Third Report*. Belfast: Blackstaff.
Budge, I. and O'Leary, C. (1973) *Belfast: Approach to Crisis*. London: Macmillan.
Carr, E.H. (1961) 'What is history?' *The Listener*, 4 July.
Central Statistics Service, South Africa (1998) *South Africa: Gender Statistics*. Pretoria: Central Statistics Service. http://www.statssa.gov.za/women&men/intro.htm.
Charney, C. (1984) 'Class conflict and the National Party split', *Journal of Southern African Studies*, vol. 10: 51–74.
Clancy, P., Drudy, S., Lynch, K. and O'Dowd, L. (1986) *Ireland: A Sociological Profile*. Dublin: Institute of Public Administration.
Clancy, P., Drudy, S., Lynch, K. and O'Dowd, L. (1995) *Irish Society: Sociological Perspectives*. Dublin: Institute of Public Administration.
Clayton, P. (1996) *Enemies and Passing Friends*. London: Pluto Press.
Clayton, P. (1998) 'Religion, ethnicity and colonialism as explanations of the Northern Ireland conflict', in D. Miller (ed.), *Rethinking Northern Ireland*. London: Longman.
Cochrane, F. (2001) Unsung heroes? in J. McGarry (ed.), *Northern Ireland and the Divided World*. Oxford: Oxford University Press.
Cohen, R. (1986) *Endgame South Africa?* London: James Currey.
Colley, L. (1992) *Britons: Forging the Nation 1707–1837*. New Haven, Conn.: Yale University Press.
Cormack, R. and Osborne, R. (1991) *Discrimination and Public Policy in Northern Ireland*. Oxford: Clarendon Press.
Coser, L. (1964) 'The termination of conflict', *Journal of Conflict Resolution*, vol. 5: 347–53.
Coser, L. (1976) 'Structure and conflict', in P. Blau (ed.), *Approaches to the Study of Social Structure*. London: Open Books.

Coulter, C. (1999) *Contemporary Northern Irish Society: An Introduction*. London: Pluto Press.
Cox, M. (1997) 'Bringing in the "international": the IRA ceasefire and the end of the Cold War', *International Affairs*, vol. 73: 671–93.
Davenport, T. (1977) *South Africa: A Modern History*. London: Macmillan.
De Breadun, D. (2001) *The Far Side of Revenge*. Cork: Collins Press.
Deegan, H. (1999) 'Civil society and South Africa: beyond the transition', paper at the conference 'South Africa: From Transition to Transformation', Dublin, 5 March.
De Klerk, F. (1998) *The Last Trek: The New Beginning*. London: Macmillan.
Dickie-Clarke, H. (1976) 'The study of conflict in South Africa and Northern Ireland', *Social Dynamics*, vol. 5: 47–59.
Dickson, B. (1995) 'An ethnography of crime in Belfast: discussion', *Journal of the Statistical and Social Enquiry Society of Ireland*, vol. 27 (3): 199–201.
Dixon, K. (1973) *Sociological Theory: Pretence and Possibility*. London: Routledge.
Dooley, B. (1998) *The Fight for Civil Rights in Northern Ireland and Black America*. London: Pluto Press.
Du Toit, P. (2001) *South Africa's Brittle Peace*. London: Palgrave.
Eldridge, J. (1985) *C. Wright Mills*. London: Tavistock.
Etherington, N. (1992) 'Explaining the death throes of apartheid', in N. Etherington (ed.), *Peace, Politics and Violence in the New South Africa*. London: Hans Zell.
Etzioni, A. (1993) *The Spirit of Community: The Reinvention of American Society*. New York: Touchstone.
Etzioni, A. (1995) *New Communitarian Thinking: Persons, Virtues, Institutions and Communities*. Charlottesville: University of Virginia Press.
Farrell, M. (1976) *The Orange State*. London: Pluto Press.
Ferguson, N. (1997) *Virtual History: Alternatives and Counterfactuals*. London: Basic Books.
Ferguson, N. (1999) *The Pity of War*. London: Penguin Books.
Follis, B. (1996) 'Ulster Unionists and Afrikaner Nationalists', *Southern African-Irish Studies*, vol. 3: 171–89.
Foster, R.F. (1988) *Modern Ireland 1600–1972*. London: Penguin Books.
Gagiano, J. (1990) Ruling group cohesion, in H. Giliomee and J. Gagiano (eds), *The Elusive Search for Peace*. Cape Town: Oxford University Press.
Gailey, A. (1975), 'The Scots element in North Irish popular culture', *Ethnologia Europaea*, 7: 2–22.
Gallagher, A. (1994) 'Dealing with conflict: schools in Northern Ireland', *Milticultural Teaching*, vol. 13: 1–19.
Garland, R. (1997) *Seeking a Political Accommodation: the UVF*. Belfast: Shankhill Community Publication.
Garland, R. (2001) *Gusty Spence*. Belfast: Blackstaff Press.
Gerhart, G. (1978) *Black Power in South Africa*. Berkeley: University of California Press.
Giddens, A. (1984) *The Constitution of Society*. London: Polity Press.
Giddens, A. (1996) *In Defence of Sociology*. London: Polity Press.

Giliomee, H. (1990) 'The elusive search for peace', in H. Giliomee and J. Gagiano (eds), *The Elusive Search for Peace*. Cape Town: Oxford University Press.

Giliomee, H. (1992) '*Broedertwis*: intra-Afrikaner conflicts in the transition from apartheid 1969–1991', in N. Etherington (ed.), *Peace, Politics and Violence in the New South Africa*. London: Hans Zell.

Gitlin, T. (2000) 'Afterword', in C.W. Mills, *The Sociological Imagination*. Oxford: Oxford University Press.

Glendon, A. (1991) *Rights Talk: The Impoverishment of Political Discourse*. New York: Free Press.

Goldring, M. (1991) *Belfast*. London: Lawrence and Wishart.

Guelke, A. (1991) 'The political impasse in Northern Ireland and South Africa', *Comparative Politics*, vol. 21: 143–62.

Guelke, A. (1994) 'The peace process in South Africa, Israel and Northern Ireland', *Irish Studies in International Affairs*, vol. 5: 93–106.

Guelke, A. (1996a) 'The influence of the South African transition on the Northern Ireland peace process', *South African Journal of International Affairs*, vol. 3: 132–48.

Guelke, A. (1996b) 'The United States, Irish Americans and the Northern Ireland peace process', *International Affairs*, vol. 72: 521–36.

Guelke, A. (1999) *South Africa in Transition*. London: I.B. Taurus.

Guelke, A. (2000) 'Ireland and South Africa: a very special relationship', *Irish Studies in International Affairs*, vol. 11: 137–46.

Hainsworth, P. (1998) *Divided Society: Ethnic Minorities and Racism in Northern Ireland*. London: Pluto Press.

Haydon, C. (1993) *Anti-Catholicism in Eighteenth-Century England*. Manchester: Manchester University Press.

Hayes, B. and McAllister, I. (2001a) 'Sowing dragon's teeth: public support for political violence and paramilitarism in Northern Ireland', *Political Studies*, vol. 49: 9-1-22.

Hayes, B. and McAllister, I. (2001b) 'Who voted for peace?', *Irish Political Studies*, vol. 16: 73–93.

Hempton, D. and Hill, M. (1992) *Evangelical Protestantism in Ulster Society 1740–1890*. London: Routledge.

Hewitt, C. (1981) 'Catholic grievances and Catholic nationalism and violence in Northern Ireland', *British Journal of Sociology*, vol. 32: 362–80.

Higgins, G. (2000) 'Great Expectations: The Myth of Antichrist in Northern Ireland', unpublished PhD thesis, Queen's University of Belfast.

Higgins, G. and Brewer, J.D. (2002) 'The roots of sectarianism in Northern Ireland', in O. Hargie and D. Dickson (eds), *Researching the Troubles: Social Science Perspectives on the Northern Ireland Conflict*. Edinburgh: Mainstream Publishing.

Hill, C. (1971) *The Anti-Christ in Seventeenth-Century England*. Oxford: Oxford University Press.

Hirson, B. (1979) *Year of Fire, Year of Ash*. London: Zed Press.

Holmes, F. (1985) *Our Irish Presbyterian Heritage*. Belfast: Presbyterian Church in Ireland.

Horowitz, D. (1991) *A Democratic South Africa*. Berkeley: University of California Press.
Horowitz, I. (1985) *C. Wright Mills: An American Utopian*. New York: Free Press.
Houston, G. (1999) *The National Liberation Struggle in South Africa*. Aldershot: Ashgate.
Hughes, J. and Donnelly, C. (2002) 'Ten years of social attitudes in Northern Ireland', in A. Gray, K. Lloyd, P. Devine, G. Robinson and D. Heenan (eds), *Social Attitudes in Northern Ireland: The Eighth Report*. London: Pluto Press.
Hughes, J. Knox, C., Murray, M. and Greer, J. (1998) *Partnership and Governance in Northern Ireland: The Path to Peace*. Dublin: Oak Tress Press.
Hume, J. (1993) 'A new Ireland in a new Europe', in D. Keogh and M. Haltzel (eds), *Northern Ireland and the Politics of Reconciliation*. Cambridge: Cambridge University Press.
Hume, J. (1996) *Personal Views*. Dublin: Town House.
Hyndman, M. (1996) *Further Afield: Journeys from a Protestant Past*. Belfast: Beyond the Pale Publications.
INCORE (2000) 'Peace agreements', http://www.incore.ulst.ac.uk/cds/agreements/.
Jackson, J. (1998) 'The 1994 election: an analysis', in F. Toase and E. Yorke (eds), *The New South Africa*. London: Macmillan.
Jeffrey, A. (1995) *The Natal Story*. Johannesburg: South African Institute of Race Relations.
Jeffrey, A. (1999) *The Truth about the Truth Commission*. Johannesburg: South African Institute of Race Relations.
Jenks, C. (1998) *Core Sociological Dichotomies*. London: Sage.
Johnson, R.W. (1990) 'The politics of international intervention', in H. Giliomee and J. Gagiano (eds), *The Elusive Search for Peace*. Cape Town: Oxford University Press.
Johnston, A. (1997) 'Politics, violence and reconciliation in Northern Ireland and South Africa', *Journal of Southern African Affairs*, vol. 4: 71–94.
Kane-Berman, J. (1978) *Soweto: Black Revolt, White Reaction*. Johannesburg: Ravan Press.
Kane-Berman, J. (1993) *Political Violence in South Africa*. Johannesburg: South African Institute of Race Relations.
Karis, T. and Carter, G. (1972, 1973, 1977) *From Protest to Challenge*, 4 vols. Stanford: Hoover Institute Press.
Kennaway, B. (1997) 'What is the Orange Order?', *Lion and the Lamb*, vol. 13: 8–9.
Knox, C. and Quirk, P. (2000) *Peace Building in Northern Ireland, Israel and South Africa*. London: Macmillan.
Kornhauser, W. (1959) *The Politics of Mass Society*. New York: Free Press.
Kunnie, J. (2000) *Is Apartheid Really Dead?* Boulder, Col.: Westview Press.
Kuper, L. (1965) *An African Bourgeoisie*. New Haven, Conn.: Yale University Press.
Kuperus, T. (1999) *State, Civil Society and Apartheid in South Africa*. London: Macmillan.

Langman, L. (2000) 'History and biography in the global era: the legacy of C. Wright Mills', paper given at the American Sociological Association conference, Washington, August. http://www.anglefire.com/or/sociologyshop/langmills.html.
Lash, S. and Urry, J. (1986) The dissolution of the social, in M. Waddle and S. Turner (eds), *Sociological Theory in Transition*. London: Allen and Unwin.
Laurence, P. (1990) *Death Squads*. London: Penguin Books.
Lazarsfeld, P. (1973) *Main Trends in Sociology*. London: Allen and Unwin.
Lederach, J.P. (1995) *Preparing for Peace*. New York: Syracuse University Press.
Lederach, J.P. (1997) *Building Peace*. Washington: United States Institute for Peace Press.
Lijphart, A. (1996) 'The framework document on Northern Ireland and the theory of power sharing', *Government and Opposition*, vol. 31: 265–80.
Lodge, T. (1983) *Black Politics in South Africa Since 1945*. London: Longman.
Loughlin, J. (1985) 'The Irish Protestant Home Rule Association and Nationalist politics', *Irish Historical Studies*, vol. 24: 341–60.
MacGinty, R. (1997) 'American influences on the Northern Ireland peace process', *Journal of Conflict Studies*, vol. 19: 31–50.
MacGinty, R. and Wilford, R. (2002) 'More knowing than knowledgeable: attitudes towards devolution', in A. Gray, K. Lloyd, P. Devine, G. Robinson and D. Heenan (eds), *Social Attitudes in Northern Ireland: The Eighth Report*. London: Pluto Press.
Major, J. (1999) *The Autobiography*. London: HarperCollins.
Mallie, E. and McKitrick, D. (2001) *End Game in Ireland*. London: Hodder and Stoughton.
Mandela, N. (1995) *Long Walk to Freedom*. London: Abacus.
Maré, G. and Hamilton, G. (1987) *An Appetite for Power*. Johannesburg: Ravan Press.
Marks, S. (1998) 'Social change, order and stability in the new South Africa', in F. Toase and E. Yorke (eds), *The New South Africa*. London: Macmillan.
Martins, H. (1974) 'Time and theory in sociology', in J. Rex (ed.), *Approaches to Sociology*. London: Routledge and Kegan Paul.
Mattes, R. (1994) 'The road the democracy', in A. Reynolds (ed.), *Election '94 South Africa*. London: James Currey.
Mazala (1988) *Gatsha Buthelezi*. London: Zed Press.
McGaffrey, B. (2002) 'Census: is the gap closing?', *Irish News*, 21 October.
McGarry, J. (1998) 'Political settlements in Northern Ireland and South Africa', *Political Studies*, vol. 46: 856–70.
McGarry, J. (2001) 'Introduction', in J. McGarry (ed.), *Northern Ireland and the Divided World*. Oxford: Oxford University Press.
McGarry, J. and O'Leary, B. (1995) *Explaining Northern Ireland*. Oxford: Blackwell.
McKeown, L. (2001) *Out of Time*. Belfast: Beyond the Pale Publications.
McKittrick, D. (1996) *The Nervous Peace*. Belfast: Blackstaff Press.
McMichael, G. (1999) *Ulster Voice*. Boulder, Col.: Roberts Rinehart.

Mennell, S. and Goudsblom, J. (1998) *Norbert Elias: On Civilisation, Power and Knowledge*. Chicago: University of Chicago Press.

Merton, R.K. (1967) 'On the history and systematics of sociological theory', in his *On Theoretical Sociology*. New York: Free Press.

Millar, J. (1973) *Popery and Politics in England 1660–1688*. Cambridge: Cambridge University Press.

Miller, D. (1998) 'Colonialism and academic representations of the Troubles', in D. Miller (ed.), *Rethinking Northern Ireland*. London: Longman.

Miller, D.W. (1978) *Queen's Rebels: Ulster Loyalism in Historical Perspective*. Dublin: Gill and Macmillan.

Mills, C.W. (2000 [1959]), *The Sociological Imagination*. Oxford: Oxford University Press.

Mills, K. and Mills, P. (2000) *C. Wright Mills: Letters and Autobiographical Writings*. Berkeley: University of California Press.

Mitchell, G. (1999) *Making Peace*. London: Heinemann.

Moen, D. (1999) 'Post hunger-strike resistance to criminalisation', paper at the postgraduate conference, School of Sociology and Social Policy, Queen's University of Belfast, 5–7 November.

Moleah, A.T. (1993) *South Africa*. Wilmington: Disa Press.

Morrissey, M. and Smyth, M. (2001) *Northern Ireland After the Good Friday Agreement: Violence and Victimisation*. London: Pluto Press.

Mowlam, M. (2002) *Momentum*. London: Hodder and Stoughton.

National Peace Secretariat (1993) *National Peace Secretariat Report*. Pretoria: National Peace Secretariat.

National Peace Secretariat (1994) *National Peace Secretariat Report*. Pretoria: National Peace Secretariat.

Nordlinger, E. (1972) *Conflict Regulation in Divided Societies*. Cambridge, Mass.: Harvard University Press.

Norman, E.R. (1968) *Anti-Catholicism in Victorian England*. London: Allen and Unwin.

Northern Ireland Council for Voluntary Action (1996) *Partners for Progress*. Belfast: NICVA.

Northern Ireland Council for Voluntary Action (1997) *Partnerships – A View from Within*. Belfast: NICVA.

Oakes, G. and Vidich, A. (1999) *Collaboration, Reputation and Ethics in American Academic Life*. Urbana-Champaign: University of Illinois Press.

O'Dowd, L. (1986) 'Beyond industrial society', in P. Clancy, S. Drudy, K. Lynch and L. O'Dowd (eds), *Ireland: A Sociological Profile*. Dublin: Institute of Public Administration.

O'Dowd, L. (1995) 'Development or dependency? State, economy and society in Northern Ireland', in P. Clancy, S. Drudy, K. Lynch and L. O'Dowd (eds), *Irish Society: Sociological Perspectives*. Dublin: Institute of Public Administration.

O'Duffy, B. (1995) 'Violence in Northern Ireland 1969–94', *Ethnic and Racial Studies*, vol. 18: 740–71.

O'Duffy, B. and O'Leary, B. (1990) 'Violence in Northern Ireland 1969–June 1989', in J. McGarry and B. O'Leary (eds), *The Future of Northern Ireland*. Oxford: Clarendon Press.
O'Hearn, D. (1998) *Inside the Celtic Tiger*. London: Pluto Press.
O'Leary, B. (1998) 'The nature of the agreement', John Whyte memorial lecture, Queen's University of Belfast, 26 November.
O'Leary, B. (1999) 'The nature of the agreement', *Fordham Journal of International Law*, vol. 22: 1628–67.
O'Leary, B. (2001) 'Comparative political science and the British-Irish agreement' in J. McGarry (ed.), *Northern Ireland and the Divided World*. Oxford: Oxford University Press.
O'Leary, B. and McGarry, J. (1996) *The Politics of Antagonism: Understanding Northern Ireland*. London: Athlone Press.
O'Malley, P. (2001) 'Northern Ireland and South Africa', in J. McGarry (ed.), *Northern Ireland and the Divided World*. Oxford: Oxford University Press.
O'Neill, S. (2000) 'Liberty, equality and the rights of cultures', *British Journal of Politics and International Relations*, vol. 2: 26–45.
O'Neill, T. (1969) *Ulster at the Crossroads*. London: Faber.
Parsons, T. (1951) *The Social System*. New York: Free Press.
Parsons, T. (1954) *Essays in Sociological Theory*. New York: Free Press.
Patterson, H. (1980) *Class Conflict and Sectarianism: The Protestant Working Class and the Belfast Labour Movement 1868–1920*. Belfast: Blackstaff Press.
Paz, D.G. (1992) *Popular Anti-Catholicism in Mid-Victorian England*. Stanford: Stanford University Press.
Poole, M. (1983) 'The spatial distribution of political violence in Northern Ireland', in J. Derby (ed.), *Northern Ireland: Background to the Conflict*. Belfast: Appletree.
Poole, M. (1993) 'The spatial distribution of political violence in Northern Ireland: an update to 1983', in A. O'Day (ed.), *Terrorism's Laboratory: The Case of Northern Ireland*. Aldershot: Dartmouth.
Porter, N. (1996) *Rethinking Unionism*. Belfast: Blackstaff Press.
Posel, D. (1991) *The Making of Apartheid*. Oxford: The Clarendon Press.
Prendergast, P. (1999) 'Ulster's Doomed', *Guardian*, 13 October.
Press, H. (1978) *C. Wright Mills*. Farmington Hills: Twayne Publications.
Prozesky, M. (1990) *Christianity amidst Apartheid*. London: Macmillan.
Rafferty, O.P. (1994) *Catholicism in Ulster 1603–1983: An Interpretative History*. Dublin: Gill and Macmillan.
Ray, L. (1999) *Theorizing Classical Sociology*. Buckingham: Open University Press.
Reader, J. (1998) *Africa*. London: Penguin Books.
Rolston, B. (1995) *Drawing Support*. Belfast: Beyond the Pale Publications.
Rowan, B. (1995) *Behind the Lines*. Belfast: Blackstaff Press.
Ruane, J. and Todd, J. (1996) *The Dynamics of Conflict in Northern Ireland*. Cambridge: Cambridge University Press.
Ruane, J. and Todd, J. (1999) 'The Belfast Agreement: context, content and consequences', in J. Ruane and J. Todd (eds), *After the Good Friday Agreement*. Dublin: University College of Dublin Press.

Runciman, W.G. (1983) 'Unnecessary revolution: the case of France', *Archives Européennes de Sociologie*, vol. 24.
Runciman, W.G. (1999) *The Social Animal*. London: Fontana.
Runciman, W.G. (2002) 'Promoting sociology: how can we raise the profile?', *Network*, vol. 83, October: 16–17.
Sampson, A. (1999) *Mandela: The Authorised Biography*. London: HarperCollins.
Schrire, R. (1992) *Adapt or Die: The End of White Politics in South Africa*. London: Hurst.
Schrire, R. (1994) *Malan to De Klerk*. London: Hurst.
Seidman, S. (1998) *Contested Knowledge*. 2nd edition. Oxford: Blackwell.
Shirlow, P. and McGovern, M. (1998) 'Language, discourse and dialogue: Sinn Féin and the Irish peace process', *Political Geography*, vol. 17: 171–86.
Sinnott, R. (1999) 'Interpreting electoral mandates in Northern Ireland: the 1998 referendum', paper at the CREST/QUB conference, 'Agreeing to Disagree: The Voters of Northern Ireland', Queen's University of Belfast, 22 June.
Sisk, T. (1994) *Democratisation in South Africa*. Princeton, NJ: Princeton University Press.
Sklair, L. (1995) *Sociology of the Global System*. Baltimore: Johns Hopkins University Press.
Sklair, L. (1999) 'Globalisation', in S. Taylor (ed.), *Sociology: Issues and Debates*. London: Macmillan.
Smith, A. and Robinson, A. (1996) *Education for Mutual Understanding*. Coleraine: Centre for Study of Conflict.
Smith, D. and Chambers, G. (1991) *Inequality in Northern Ireland*. Oxford: Oxford University Press.
Smith, M.L. (1995) *Fighting for Ireland*. London: Routledge.
Smooha, S. (2001) 'The tenability of partition as a mode of conflict regulation', in J. McGarry (ed.), *Northern Ireland and the Divided World*. Oxford: Oxford University Press.
Smyth, J. and Cairns, D. (2000) 'Dividing loyalties: local identities in a global economy', in E. Slater and M. Peillon (eds), *Memories of the Present*. Dublin: Institute of Public Administration.
Smyth, M. (2000) 'The human consequences of armed conflict', in M. Cox, A. Guelke and F. Stephens (eds), *A Farewell to Arms*. Manchester: Manchester University Press.
Smyth, M. and Fay, M. (2000) *Personal Accounts from Northern Ireland's Troubles*. London: Pluto Press.
Sparks, A. (1995) *Tomorrow is Another Country*. London: Heinemann.
Spence, J. (1998) 'Conclusion', in F. Toase and E. Yorke (eds), *The New South Africa*. London: Macmillan.
Spence, J. (1999) 'Second chance for the ANC', *Government and Opposition*, vol. 34: 111–34.
Storey, E. (2002) *Traditional Roots*. Blackrock: Columba Press.
Taylor, R. (2001) 'Northern Ireland: consociation or social transformation', in J. McGarry (ed.), *Northern Ireland and the Divided World*. Oxford: Oxford University Press.

Thomson, A. (1996) *Faith in Ulster*. Belfast: Evangelical Contribution on Northern Ireland.
Tilman, R. (1984) *C. Wright Mills*. Philadelphia: Penn State University Press.
Tomlinson, M. (1995a) 'The British subvention and the Irish peace process', *International Policy Review*, vol. 5: 69–74.
Tomlinson, M. (1995b) 'Can Britain leave Ireland? The political economy of war and peace', *Race and Class*, vol. 37: 1–22.
Torsney, E. (1998) 'Defining the nation: the Republic of Ireland rediscovers nationalism', *Realms*, vol. 1: 7–15.
Truth and Reconciliation Commission (1998), *Report Vols. 1–5*. Cape Town: Juta. Also see http://www.struth.org.za.
Tumbleson, R. (1998) *Catholicism in the English Protestant Imagination*. Cambridge: Cambridge University Press.
Ulster Defence Association (1987) *Common Sense: Northern Ireland – An Agreed Process*. Belfast: Ulster Defence Association.
van Rooyen, J. (1994) 'The White right', in A. Reynolds (ed.), *Election '94 South Africa*. London: James Currey.
von Tangen Page, M. (2002) 'A most difficult and unpalatable part – the release of politically motivated violent offenders', in M. Cox, A. Guelke and F. Stephens (eds), *A Farewell to Arms*. Manchester: Manchester University Press.
Wakefield, D. (2000) 'Introduction', in K. Mills and P. Mills, *C. Wright Mills: Letters and Autobiographical Writings*. Berkeley: University of California Press.
Wallensteen, P. and Sollenberg, M. (2000) 'Armed conflict 1989–99', *Journal of Peace Research*, vol. 37: 635–49.
Wallis, R. and Bruce, S. (1986) *Sociological Theory, Religion and Collective Action*. Belfast: Queen's University of Belfast.
Weiss, R. (2000) *Peace in Their Time*. London: I.B. Tauris.
Welsh, D. (1975) 'The dynamics of racial discrimination in South Africa', *Social Dynamics*, vol. 4: 1–14.
White, A. (1998), 'The change in Loyalist ideology and strategy since the Anglo-Irish Agreement', *Realms*, vol. 1: 16–28.
Whyte, J. (1983) 'How much discrimination was there under the Unionist regime 1921–68?', in T. Gallagher and J. O'Connell (eds), *Contemporary Irish Studies*. Manchester: Manchester University Press.
Whyte, J. (1990) *Interpreting Northern Ireland*. Oxford: The Clarendon Press.
Whyte, J. (1993) 'Dynamics of social and political change in Northern Ireland', in D. Keogh and M. Haltzel (eds), *Northern Ireland and the Politics of Reconciliation*. Cambridge: Cambridge University Press.
Wichert, S. (1991) *Northern Ireland since 1945*. London: Longman.
Wilford, R. (1999) 'Regional assemblies and Parliament', in P. Mitchell and R. Wilford (eds), *Politics in Northern Ireland*. Colorado: Westview Press.
Wilson, A. (1995) *Irish America and the Ulster Conflict 1968–95*. Washington: Catholic University of America Press.
Wilson, A. (2000) 'The Billy boys meet Slick Willy: the Ulster Unionist Party and the American dimension to the Northern Ireland peace process 1993–98', *Irish Studies in International Affairs*, vol. 11: 121–37.

Wilson, R. (2001) *The Politics of Truth and Reconciliation in South Africa*. Cambridge: Cambridge University Press.
Wolffe, J. (1991) *The Protestant Crusade in Great Britain*. Oxford: The Clarendon Press.
World Bank (1997) *World Development Report 1997*. New York: World Bank.
Wright, F. (1987) *Northern Ireland: A Comparative Analysis*. Dublin: Gill and Macmillan.
Wrong, D. (1961) 'The oversocialized conceptualization of man in modern sociology', *American Sociological Review*, vol. 26: 183–93.

Index

Adair, Johnny, 121; *see also* Ulster Defence Association
Adam, Heribert, 78, 172
Adams, Gerry, 45, 67, 88, 90, 97, 98, 99, 103, 104; *see also* Sinn Féin
African National Congress (ANC), 8, 58, 80, 84, 96, 100, 104, 115, 122, 123, 136, 137, 138, 141, 147, 148, 152, 174
  economic policies of, 115, 122, 147–8
  strategy towards armed struggle, 80–1, 98–9, 100, 103, 137–8, 161–2, 174
  symbolic associations with IRA, 8
  see also Mandela, Nelson; Umkhonto we Sizwe
Afrikaner nationalism, 8, 9, 48, 56, 57, 58, 61, 62, 80, 90–2, 96, 99, 140, 141, 146
Afrikaner Volksfront, 91–2; *see also* Viljoen, Constand
Afrikaner Weerstandsbeweging (AWB), 91, 92
  use of violence compared to Ulster Loyalism, 92
agency–structure debate in sociology, x, 4, 19, 32, 33, 34, 37, 71–2, 73, 74, 156, 168, 170, 173–6; *see also* sociology
Alcock, Antony, 104
Anglo–Irish Agreement, 66, 67–8, 128, 149
anti-Catholicism, 48, 49–50, 54, 58, 64, 65, 94, 95, 158
  see also sectarianism; social exclusion
apartheid, 9, 57, 80, 100, 103, 114, 135, 136, 153
  as a therapeutic myth, 85–6

Archer, Margaret, 32, 176
armed struggle, 2, 7, 62, 80, 84, 99, 100, 137, 153, 161, 164, 174
  compared to strategy of non-violence, 97–8
  comparisons between Northern Ireland and South Africa, 8, 9, 99, 103, 161–2, 164
  in Northern Ireland, 65, 81, 85, 103, 145–6
  and new Loyalists, 129
  early Republican strategy toward, 67, 81–2
  revisions in Republican strategy towards, 98–9, 100, 101–2, 103–6, 118, 120–1, 145–6, 148, 161–2, 174
  in South Africa, 59, 80, 84–5, 103
  ANC strategy towards, 80–1, 98–9, 100, 103, 137–8, 161–2, 174
  see also African National Congress; Irish Republican Army; Provisional violence; Umkhonto we Sizwe
Aron, Raymond, 26
Aughey, Arthur, 101

Bauman, Zygmunt, 4, 19
Becker, Howard S., 20, 23, 25
Beetham, Justice Richard, 10
Belfast, 2, 18, 51, 64, 83, 86, 103, 115, 116
Bell, Daniel, 25
Berger, Peter, 4, 175, 176
  and *Invitation to Sociology*, 175–6
Berlin, Sir Isaiah, 33, 36, 75
Bhaskar, Roy, 32, 176, 177
Bingham, Rev. William, 144
Black Consciousness, 85, 91, 161

Blau, Peter, 1
Blumenfeld, Jesmond, xi, 122
Blumer, Herbert, 73
Boer War, 10, 57, 61, 95
Boesak, Allan, 97, 137
Botha, P.W., 65, 66
Bourdieu, Pierre, 6
Breen, Richard, 102, 119, 141
Brookeborough, Lord, 64
Bruce, Steve, xi, 92, 93, 94
Buthelezi, Chief, 59, 98; *see also* Inkatha/Inkatha Freedom Party

Camus, Albert,
 and the fatal embrace, 13, 159
Catherwood, Sir Fred, 49
civil rights movement
 in Northern Ireland, 54, 65, 124
 in the United States of America, 39
civil society, and the peace process, 129–39
 in Northern Ireland, 142
 in South Africa, 136–9
 see also community development
Cochrane, Feargal, 105, 130, 142
colonialism, 10, 35, 51, 86, 109, 148, 157–8, 163, 169
 and conflict, 59–62, 69–70
 in Northern Ireland, 48, 51–5, 60–1, 148, 155
 in social science, 30, 59–60
 in South Africa, 55–9, 60–1, 155
 internal, 62
communitarianism, 132–3
community development, 82, 105, 130–2, 139
 and non-governmental agencies, 132–4
conflict, zero sum, 7, 11, 12, 13, 14, 15, 53, 55, 62, 65, 97, 102, 157
 see also armed struggle; divided societies; violence
conflict resolution, *see under* peace process
Congress of South African Trade Unions, 137

consociationalism, 7, 134
Cooper, Bob, 64
Coser, Lewis, 11, 14, 20, 22, 28, 39
covenantal theology, 7, 9, 10, 52, 53, 56, 92–3; *see also* Protestantism
crime
 in Northern Ireland, 18, 121, 127, 131
 in South Africa, 58, 59, 92, 101

de Beauvoir, Simone, 23, 24
de Klerk F.W., 5, 66, 80, 84, 90, 93, 95, 96, 100, 103, 104, 138, 147
 and peace strategy, 96–7, 104, 161–2
 see also National Party
de Tocqueville, Alexis, 166
Deegan, Heather, xi, 136, 138
democratic deficit, and peace process, 129–39
Democratic Unionist Party, 65, 91, 103, 127, 128, 145; *see also* Paisley, Rev. Ian
demographic trends
 in Northern Ireland, 115–17, 148, 162
 and emigration, 117, 125, 126, 150
 in South Africa, 112, 114, 150, 162
 and immigration, 114, 122, 147
demography, and the peace process, 112–21, 150, 162
divided societies, 7, 11, 134, 155;
 see also conflict, zero-sum
Dixon, Keith, 3
Donaldson, Jeffrey, 78, 91
Durkheim, Emile, 5, 19, 26, 28, 133, 166
Dutch Reform Church, 92, 137

economy, the
 in Northern Ireland, 53, 115, 123–7
 in South Africa, 113, 121–3, 147–8
Eldridge, John, xi, 20

Elias, Norbert, 176
Ervine, David, 88, 93, 100, 128, 129;
    see also new Loyalism
ethnic boundary markers 10, 12
    in South Africa and Northern
        Ireland, 42–50, 51–4, 140–1,
        146, 158, 170, 171–2
    see also racism; sectarianism;
        social exclusion

Ferguson, Adam, x, 33, 41, 165, 166
Ferguson, Niall, 154
Foucault, Michel, 165
Free Presbyterian Church, 65;
    see also Paisley, Rev. Ian

Gallagher, Tony, 143
Garfinkel, Harold, 31
gender, 132
Gerth, Hans, 25, 29, 39, 167
Giddens, Anthony, 6, 32, 71, 72,
    76, 176
    and theory of structuration, 32, 37
Giliomee, Hermann, 12, 96, 141, 172
Gitlin, Todd, 24
glocalisation, 176
Good Friday Agreement, 2, 82, 83,
    88, 93, 97, 98, 101, 102, 103,
    104, 117, 130, 143, 145, 161
    Unionist and Republican
        approaches to, 101–3
    see also peace process; Ulster
        Unionism
grassroots peacemaking, *see under*
    peace process
Guatemala peace process, 2
Guelke, Adrian, xi, 8, 91, 92

Habermas, Jürgen, 177
Hani, Chris, 91
Hayes, Bernadette, 2, 55, 83
Hempton, David, 52
Hill, Myrtle, 52
history
    historical specificity, 35, 45–70,
        74, 156–8

and presentism, 47
reification of, 69, 169–70
see also sociology and history
Holmes, Finlay, 52
Horowitz, Irving, 20, 177
Hume, John, 45, 90, 97, 98, 144;
    see also Social and Democratic
        Labour Party
hunger strikes (1981), 76, 98

INCORE, 2
Inkatha/Inkatha Freedom Party, 59,
    136, 138; *see also* Buthelezi,
    Chief
internationalisation, 36–7, 65, 66–7,
    111, 113, 123, 124–5, 132, 144,
    146–9, 153, 156, 162, 173
    and ending of Cold War, 147–8,
        150, 152, 153, 163
    and European Union, 133, 144,
        146, 162
    and globalisation, 124, 144,
        146, 150, 163; *see also*
        glocalisation
    in Mills, 36–7, 43, 111–12, 154
Irish Boundary Commission, 10
Irish Council for Voluntary Action,
    133–4
Irish famine, 54
Irish Republic, xi, 7, 54, 125
    anti-apartheid movement in, 7
Irish Republican Army, Provisional
    (IRA), 8, 54, 64, 65, 67, 80, 81,
    82, 83, 88, 92, 98, 99, 103, 105,
    120, 121, 129, 143, 145, 146,
    148, 176
    and symbolic links with ANC, 8
    early Republican strategy
        towards armed struggle,
        67, 81–2
    revisions in Republican strategy
        towards armed struggle, 98–9,
        100, 101–2, 103–6, 118, 120–1,
        145–6, 148, 161–2, 174
    see also Sinn Féin
Israel–Palestine conflict, 2, 7, 9

Jenks, Chris, 28, 175
Johannesburg, 51, 101
Johnston, Alexander (Sandy), xi, 80, 84, 85

King, Martin Luther, 39
Knox, Colin, 131, 136, 137, 143
Kornhauser, William, 176

Lazarsfeld, Paul, 28, 29, 30, 167
Lederach, John Paul, 7, 87, 105, 160
Loyalist Volunteer Force, 94

MacBride principles, 8, 124
MacGinty, Roger, 2
Mandela, Nelson, 8, 13, 45, 90, 96, 98, 99, 100, 152, 162; *see also* African National Congress
Mandeville, Bernard, 165
Marx, Anthony, xi
Marx, Karl, 5, 20, 25, 26, 35, 50, 166, 167, 168, 169
McAllister, Ian, 2, 55, 83
McCausland, Nelson, 119
McClinton, Pastor Kenny, 127
McCrone, David, xi
McGarry, John, 8, 134, 135
McGuinness, Martin, 67, 97, 99; *see also* Sinn Féin
McMichael, Gary, 128, 129; *see also* new Loyalism
Merton, Robert K., 25, 33
methodological individualism, 72, 73
Miliband, Ralph, 20, 21, 22, 26, 27, 29
Mills, Charles Wright
  biographical details of, 21–8
  in the Bureau of Applied Social Research, 28–9
  and classical sociology, 6, 20, 21, 26, 167
  at Columbia University, 22, 24, 28–9
  critique of sociology, 6, 21, 24, 28–32, 73
  and Cuban revolution, 24, 26, 27
  and his family, 22–3
  and globalisation, 5
  on internationalisation, 36–7, 43, 111–12, 154
  personal ethics of, 42, 155
  on power, 31–2, 36
  and *The Power Elite*, 26, 27, 40, 76
  and private troubles–public issues, 15, 34, 38, 40, 74–107, 109, 156
  reputation since death, 3, 5, 27
  and sociological imagination, ix, x, 3, 4, 15, 17–44, 151–78
  and sociology's ethical duty, 38–9, 40–1, 176–8
  and *The Sociological Imagination*, ix, 19, 20, 25, 26, 27, 29, 32, 36, 39, 40, 73, 156, 163, 175, 176
Mitchell, George, 9, 90, 152
Moen, Declan, 94, 99, 120
Motlana, Nthato, 97

National Party (in South Africa), 9, 93, 95, 114, 140, 141, 152; *see also* de Klerk, F.W.
Naude, Dr Beyers, 137
new Loyalism, 127–9; *see also* Ervine, David; McMichael, Gary; Spence, Gusty
Northern Ireland
  contested history of, 47
  continued violence in, 1–2, 103, 120, 152
  crime in, 18, 121, 127, 131
  economy, 53, 115, 123–7
  and impact on sectarianism, 123–4
  ethnic boundaries in, 11–12
  history of conflict and violence, 10–11, 55, 69, 83–5
  integrated education in, 143–4
  mixed marriages in, 142–3, 145
  new Loyalism in, 127–9
  non-governmental organisations in, 142
  and partition, 53, 54, 61, 62

Index

peace process in
  early attempts at reform, 62–8, 149, 157, 170
  types of explanation of, x, 45, 111, 151–2
  see also peace process
social exclusion in, 11, 54, 62, 83, 101–2, 115, 116, 118, 125
sociological approaches on, 111
Northern Irish–South African links, 5, 6–10
and minority group comparisons, 8, 67

O'Bradaigh, Ruari, 91
O'Duffy, Brendan, 84
O'Hearn, Denis, 125
O'Leary, Brendan, 84, 96, 97, 118
O'Malley, Padraig, ix, 8, 9, 81, 99
O'Neill, Terrence, Capt., 62, 63–5; see also Ulster Unionism
Orange Order, 64, 88, 96, 101, 105, 134, 144
Orange Volunteers, 88, 92, 94

Paisley, Rev. Ian, 65, 91, 95, 103, 127
  see also Democratic Unionist Party; Free Presbyterian Church
Parsons, Talcott, 3, 25, 26, 30, 31, 33, 73, 167
Patton, Joel, 144
peace
  common-sense definitions of, 1, 13, 79, 158–9
  defined, 13–14
  active versus passive definitions, 14
  ontological price of, 75, 86–9, 106, 110, 163
peace process
  and civil society, 129–39
  and counterfactualism, 154–5
  and democratic deficit, 129–39
  and demography, 112–21, 150, 162
  early attempts at, 62–8, 114, 135, 149, 157, 170
  and gender, 132
  and grassroots peacemaking, 14–15, 81–2, 87–8, 131–2, 134–5, 142
  grassroots versus elite peacemaking, 15, 138, 146
  impact of prison experiences on, 94, 99–100
  internationalisation of, 36–7, 65, 66–7, 111, 113, 123, 124–5, 132, 144, 146–9, 153, 156, 162, 173; see also internationalisation
  Millsian model of, 42–3, 153–4
  and new lines of differentiation, 134–5, 139–46
  ontological costs of, 75, 86–9, 106, 110, 163
  and private troubles–public issues, 74–107, 156, 159–63, 172
  and religion/religious conversions, 94, 105–6, 127–8, 136, 137, 138
  role of key individuals in, 36, 38–9, 45, 75, 89–107, 159–63
  types of key individual, 90–100, 110, 160, 172
  types of explanation of, x, 45, 111, 151–2
Plantation, in Ulster; see under colonialism in Northern Ireland
Popper, Karl, 3
post-violence, transition to 2, 6, 14; see also peace process
postmodernism, 33, 37
Protestantism, 49, 52, 61, 65, 66, 81, 82, 88, 91, 92, 94, 105, 139–40, 144

Quirk, Padraic, 131, 136, 137, 143

racism, 48, 49, 120, 158
Ramaphosa, Cyril, 8, 100
Rawls, John, 113
Republicanism, see under Irish Republican Army; Provisional Sinn Féin
reform process, see under peace process

religion, role in peace process, 94, 105–6, 127–8, 136, 137, 138
Retief, Piet, 57
Rhodes, Cecil, 57
Royal Ulster Constabulary (RUC), 64, 66, 76, 83–4, 101, 121
   reform of, 101
Runciman, W.G., 1, 2, 3, 4, 18, 20, 31, 90, 152, 165

Sampson, Anthony, 99
Schutz, Alfred 71, 72, 76
Scottish Enlightenment, x, 5, 18, 133, 166
sectarianism, 48, 86
secularisation, 48, 139–40, 144, 150, 163, 174
Seidman, Steven, 20, 26, 177
Shankill, 118, 128
Sharpeville, 58, 65
Shils, Edward, 25
Sinn Féin, 8, 67, 78, 82, 83, 98, 101, 102, 104, 105, 118, 120, 126, 128, 138, 143, 145, 146, 148, 149, 172, 174
   see also Adams, Gerry; Irish Republican Army, Provisional; McGuinness, Martin
Sinnott, Richard, 104
Sisulu, Walter, 99
Slovo, Joe, 100
Smith, Adam, x, 166
Smooha, Sammy, 96
Smuts, Jan, 10, 57
Social Democratic and Labour Party, 98, 144, 145, 146; *see also* Hume, John
social differentiation
   new lines of in Northern Ireland, 116, 117–18, 119, 125, 134–5, 139–46, 162, 163, 171–2
   new lines of in South Africa, 114, 134–5, 139–46, 162, 163, 171–2
social exclusion
   in Northern Ireland, 11, 54, 62, 83, 101–2, 115, 116, 118, 125

   in South Africa, 11, 58, 63, 100–1, 107, 113–15, 123
sociology
   agency–structure debate in, x, 4, 19, 32, 33, 34, 37, 71–2, 73, 74, 156, 168, 170, 173–6
   and common sense, 17–18, 71–2, 75–6
   in eighteenth century, 18, 33, 165, 166
   and engagement with public issues, ix, 4, 5, 26, 32, 74, 176–7
   and history, x, 19, 33, 34–6, 156–9, 168–70, 173
   in nineteenth century, 5, 18, 19, 25, 33, 166, 167
   and politics, ix, 19, 33, 36–7, 111–49, 156, 173–5
   and prediction, 2–3, 12, 17
   and theory, 3
   and views of Northern Ireland, 111
   in the United States, 20, 21, 28–32, 73, 165, 167
South Africa
   apartheid in, 9, 57, 80, 85–6, 100, 103, 114, 135, 136, 153
   Bantustan policy in, 62–3, 98
   contested history of, 47
   continued violence in, 1–2, 59, 103, 136–7, 138–9
   crime in, 58, 59, 92, 101
   economy of, 113, 121–3, 147–8
   ethnic boundaries in, 11–12
   history of conflict and violence in, 10–11, 58–9, 69, 79–81
   non-governmental organisations in, 136–9
   peace process in
      early attempts at reform, 62–8, 114, 135, 157, 170
      types of explanation of, x, 45, 111, 151–2
      see also peace process
   social exclusion in, 11, 58, 63, 100–1, 107, 113–15, 123

South African Institute of Race
    Relations, 85
South African National Peace
    Accord, 139
South African Police, 57, 84, 85,
    114, 115, 137
Soweto uprising (1976), 58, 65, 67,
    114, 137
Spence, Gusty, 65, 93, 94, 100
    see also new Loyalism
Spence, Jack, xi, 101
Spencer, Herbert, 5, 19, 26, 166
Swift, Jonathan, 48

Taylor, Rupert, 131, 132, 133, 135, 142
terrorism, see under armed struggle
Tomlinson, Mike, 115
Treurnicht, Andries, 104
Trimble, David, 45, 93, 95, 96, 97,
    103, 104, 162, 172
    and peace strategy 96–7, 104,
    119–20, 161–2
    see also Ulster Unionism
Truth and Reconciliation
    Commission, South African,
    77, 83, 139
Tutu, Archbishop Desmond, 97, 137

Ulster Defence Association, 88,
    121, 128
Ulster Unionism, 8, 53, 64, 66, 67,
    68, 83, 93, 96, 120, 129, 143,
    149, 164, 172
    and Good Friday Agreement, 78,
    83, 97, 101, 102, 110, 125,
    126, 145, 161
    and new Loyalism, 127–9
    types of, 92–3, 172
    see also Democratic Unionist Party;
    Paisley, Rev. Ian; Trimble,
    David
Ulster Volunteer Force, 64, 93,
    95, 127
Umkhonto we Sizwe, 59, 80, 81, 85,
    100; see also African National
    Congress

United Democratic Front (UDF), 137
    and alliance with ANC, 138

van Riebeeck, Jan, 55
Viljoen, Constand, 91, 93, 104
violence
    continuance in Northern
    Ireland, 1–2, 103, 120, 152
    continuance in South Africa, 1–2,
    59, 103, 136–7, 138–9
    history of in Northern Ireland,
    10–11, 55, 69, 83–5
    history of in South Africa, 10–11,
    58–9, 69, 79–81
    private troubles–public issues
    caused by, 75–107, 109
    translation into a public
    issue, 77–8, 79, 82–6, 110
    and victimhood, 83–6, 87, 110,
    158, 160, 161, 171
    see also armed struggle;
    conflict, zero sum;
    peace process

Wallis, Jim, and Sojourner
    movement, 83
Weber, Max, 5, 19, 20, 25, 26, 27,
    31, 40, 71, 166, 167, 170
    and *Economy and Society* 19, 27
Welfare state, narrowing of, 126–9,
    130, 146, 150
White, John, 121; see also Ulster
    Defence Association
Whyte, John, 152
Whyte, William, 25–6
Wilford, Rick, 2, 67
World Bank, 112, 113
Wright, Frank, 12
Wrong, Denis, 31

Xhosa, 152

Yeats, W.B., 48

Zulu, 9